## Transformations of the State

Series Editors: **Achim Hurrelmann**, Carleton University, Canada; **Stephan Leibfried**, University of Bremen, Germany; **Kerstin Martens**, University of Bremen, Germany; **Peter Mayer**, University of Bremen, Germany.

*Titles include*:

Joan DeBardeleben and Achim Hurrelmann (*editors*)
DEMOCRATIC DILEMMAS OF MULTILEVEL GOVERNANCE
Legitimacy, Representation and Accountability in the European Union

Klaus Dingwerth
THE NEW TRANSNATIONALISM
Transnational Governance and Democratic Legitimacy

Achim Hurrelmann, Steffen Schneider and Jens Steffek (*editors*)
LEGITIMACY IN AN AGE OF GLOBAL POLITICS

Achim Hurrelmann, Stephan Leibfried, Kerstin Martens and Peter Mayer (*editors*)
TRANSFORMING THE GOLDEN-AGE NATION STATE

Kerstin Martens, Alessandra Rusconi and Kathrin Leuze (*editors*)
NEW ARENAS OF EDUCATION GOVERNANCE
The Impact of International Organizations and Markets on Educational Policy Making

Peter Starke
RADICAL WELFARE STATE RETRENCHMENT
A Comparative Analysis

Jens Steffek, Claudia Kissling and Patrizia Nanz (*editors*)
CIVIL SOCIETY PARTICIPATION IN EUROPEAN AND GLOBAL GOVERNANCE
A Cure for the Democratic Deficit?

Hartmut Weßler, Bernhard Peters, Michael Brüggemann, Katharina Kleinen-v.Kőnigslőw and Strafnie Sifft (*editors*)
TRANSNATIONALIZATION OF PUBLIC SPHERES

Hartmut Weßler (*editor*)
PUBLIC DELIBERATION AND PUBLIC CULTURE
The Writings of Bernhard Peters, 1993–2005

Jochen Zimmerman, Jörg R. Werner and Philipp B. Volmer
GLOBAL GOVERNANCE IN ACCOUNTING
Rebalancing Public Power and Private Commitment

---

**Transformations of the State**
**Series Standing Order ISBN 978–1–4039–8544–6 (hardback)**
**978–1–4039–8545–3 (paperback)**

You can receive future titles in this series as they are published by placing a standing order. Please contact your bookseller or, in case of difficulty, write to us at the address below with your name and address, the title of the series and the ISBN quoted above.

Customer Services Department, Macmillan Distribution Ltd, Houndmills, Basingstoke, Hampshire RG21 6XS, England

---

This illustration is taken from the original etching in Thomas Hobbes' *Leviathan* (1651). Palgrave Macmillan and the editors are grateful to Lucila Muñoz-Sanchez and Monika Sniegs for their help in redesigning the original to illustrate what 'transformations of the state' might mean. The inscription at the top of the original frontispiece reads '*non est potestas Super Terram quae Comparetur ei*' (Job 41.33): 'there is no power on earth which can be compared to him'. In the Bible, this refers to the seamonster Leviathan. (Original Leviathan image reprinted courtesy of the British Library.)

# Global Governance in Accounting

## Rebalancing Public Power and Private Commitment

Jochen Zimmermann, Jörg R. Werner and
Philipp B. Volmer
*Department of Accounting, Bremen University, Germany*

Transformations
of the State

CRC 597

First published 2008 by
PALGRAVE MACMILLAN
Houndmills, Basingstoke, Hampshire RG21 6XS and
175 Fifth Avenue, New York, N.Y. 10010
Companies and representatives throughout the world

PALGRAVE MACMILLAN is the global academic imprint of the Palgrave
Macmillan division of St. Martin's Press, LLC and of Palgrave Macmillan Ltd.
Macmillan® is a registered trademark in the United States, United Kingdom
and other countries. Palgrave is a registered trademark in the European
Union and other countries.

ISBN-13: 978–0–230–51814–8 hardback
ISBN-10: 0–230–51814–1 hardback

This book is printed on paper suitable for recycling and made from fully
managed and sustained forest sources. Logging, pulping and manufacturing
processes are expected to conform to the environmental regulations of the
country of origin.

A catalogue record for this book is available from the British Library.

A catalog record for this book is available from the Library of Congress.

10   9   8   7   6   5   4   3   2
17   16   15   14   13   12   11   10   09   08

Printed and bound in Great Britain by
CPI Antony Rowe, Chippenham and Eastbourne

# Contents

# List of Exhibits

# List of Abbreviations

| | |
|---|---|
| AAA | American Accounting Association |
| AADB (UK) | Accountancy & Actuarial Discipline Board |
| ACCA (UK) | Association of Chartered Certified Accountants |
| AcSEC (US) | Accounting Standards Executive Committee |
| ADRs | American Depository Receipts |
| AF (UK) | Accountancy Foundation |
| AG (DE) | Stock Corporation (*Aktiengesellschaft*) |
| AIA | American Institute of Accountants |
| AICPA | American Institute of Certified Public Accountants |
| AIM (UK) | Alternative Investment Market |
| AIU (UK) | Audit Inspection Unit |
| AktG (DE) | Stock Corporation Act (*Aktiengesetz*) BGBl. I 2007, p. 1089 |
| AMEX | American Stock Exchange |
| AnSVG (DE) | Investor Protection Improvement Act (*Anlegerschutzverbesserungsgesetz*) BGBl. I 2004, p. 2630 |
| APAG (DE) | Auditor Oversight Act (*Abschlussprüferaufsichtsgesetz*) BGBl. I 2004, p. 3846 |
| APAK (DE) | Auditor Oversight Commission (*Abschlussprüferaufsichtskommission*) |
| APB (UK) | Auditing Practices Board |
| APB (US) | Accounting Principles Board |
| ARB (US) | Accounting Research Bulletins |
| ARC (EU) | Accounting Regulatory Committee |
| ASB (UK) | Accounting Standards Board |
| ASB (US) | Auditing Standards Board |
| ASC (UK) | Accounting Standards Committee |
| ASR (US) | Accounting Series Release |
| ASSC (UK) | Accounting Standards Steering Committee |
| AuRC (EU) | Audit Regulatory Committee |
| BaFin (DE) | Federal Financial Supervisory Authority (*Bundesanstalt für Finanzdienstleistungsaufsicht*) |

| | |
|---|---|
| BAWe (DE) | Federal Securities Supervisory Office (*Bundesaufsichtsamt für Wertpapierhandel*) |
| BGBl. (DE) | Federal Gazette (*Bundesgesetzblatt*) |
| BilKoG (DE) | Financial Reporting Control Act (*Bilanzkontrollgesetz*) BGBl. I 2004, p. 3408 |
| BilReG (DE) | Accounting Law Reform Act (*Bilanzrechtsreformgesetz*) BGBl. I 2004, p. 3166 |
| BoE | Bank of England |
| CA (UK) | Companies Act |
| CAICE (UK) | Companies (Audit, Investigations and Community Enterprise) Act |
| CalPers | California Public Employees' Retirement System |
| CAP (US) | Committee on Accounting Procedure |
| CCAB (UK) | Consultative Committee of Accountancy Bodies |
| CCABI | Consultative Committee of Accounting Bodies in Ireland |
| CDAX | German index composed of all stocks traded under both the Prime Standard as well as General Standard |
| CEO | Chief Executive Officer |
| CESR | Committee of European Securities Regulators |
| CFO | Chief Financial Officer |
| CFR (US) | Code of Federal Regulations |
| CGAA (UK) | Co-ordinating Group on Audit and Accounting Issues |
| CIMA (UK) | Chartered Institute of Management Accountants |
| CIPFA (UK) | Chartered Institute of Public Finance and Accountancy |
| COM | European Commission |
| CPA (US) | Certified Public Accountant |
| DAX (DE) | leading index of the Frankfurt Stock Exchange |
| DE | Germany (*Deutschland*) |
| DPR (DE) | Financial Reporting Enforcement Panel (*Deutsche Prüfstelle für Rechnungslegung*) |
| DRS | German Financial Reporting Standards (*Deutsche Rechnungslegungs Standards*) |
| DSOP (UK) | Draft Statement of Principles |
| DTI (UK) | Department of Trade and Industry |
| EC | European Commission (depending on context also European Council or European Community) |
| ED | Exposure Draft |
| EEC | European Economic Community |
| EFRAG | European Financial Reporting Advisory Group |
| EGAOB | European Group of Auditors' Oversight Bodies |
| EITF (US) | Emerging Issues Task Force |

| | |
|---|---|
| EP | European Parliament |
| EU | European Union |
| e.V. (DE) | registered association (*eingetragener Verein*) |
| FAF (US) | Financial Accounting Foundation |
| FaSAC (US) | Financial Accounting Standards Advisory Council |
| FASB (US) | Financial Accounting Standards Board |
| FDI | Foreign Direct Investment |
| FEE | European Federation of Accountants |
| FEI (US) | Financial Executives International |
| FFG (DE) | Financial Market Promotion Act (*Finanzmarktförderungsgesetz*) BGBl. I 2002, p. 2010 |
| FIN (US) | FASB Interpretations |
| FinDAG (DE) | Federal Financial Supervisory Authority Act (*Gesetz über die Bundesanstalt für Finanzdienstleistungsaufsicht*) BGBl. I 2002, p. 1310 |
| FPIs | Foreign Private Issuers |
| FRC (UK) | Financial Reporting Council |
| FREP (DE) | Financial Reporting Enforcement Panel (see DPR) |
| FRRP (UK) | Financial Reporting Review Panel |
| FRS (UK) | Financial Reporting Standards |
| FSA (UK) | Financial Services Authority |
| FSAP (EU) | Financial Services Action Plan |
| FSE | Frankfurt Stock Exchange |
| FSF | Financial Stability Forum |
| FSMA (UK) | Financial Services and Markets Act (Act of the UK Parliament and Explanatory Notes, Public Act 2000, Chapter 8) |
| GAAP | Generally Accepted Accounting Principles |
| GASB | German Accounting Standards Board |
| GASC | German Accounting Standards Committee |
| GCGC (DE) | German Corporate Governance Code |
| GDP | Gross Domestic Product |
| GoA (DE) | Principles of Proper Auditing (*Grundsätze ordnungsmäßiger Abschlussprüfung*) |
| GoB (DE) | Principles of Orderly Bookkeeping (*Grundsätze ordnungsmäßiger Buchführung*) |
| HGB (DE) | Commercial Code (*Handelsgesetzbuch*) RGBl. 1897, p. 219 most recent: BGBl. I 2007, p. 1330 |
| HR | House of Representatives |
| IAASB | International Auditing and Assurance Standards Board |

| | |
|---|---|
| IAS/IFRS | International Accounting Standards/International Financial Reporting Standards |
| IASB | International Accounting Standards Board |
| IASC | International Accounting Standards Committee |
| IASCF | International Accounting Standards Committee Foundation |
| ICAEW | Institute of Chartered Accountants in England and Wales |
| ICAI | Institute of Chartered Accountants in Ireland |
| ICAS | Institute of Chartered Accountants of Scotland |
| IDW (DE) | Institute of Auditors (*Institut der Wirtschaftsprüfer*) |
| IFAC | International Federation of Accountants |
| IFRIC | International Financial Interpretations Committee |
| IFRS | International Financial Reporting Standard |
| IMF | International Monetary Fund |
| IOSCO | International Organization of Securities Commissions |
| IP | European Commission Press Release |
| ISA | International Standards on Auditing |
| IT | Information Technology |
| KAGG (DE) | Capital Investment Companies Act (*Gesetz über Kapitalanlagegesellschaften*) BGBl. I 1957, p. 378 |
| KapAEG (DE) | Capital Raising Facilitation Act (*Kapitalaufnahmeerleichterungsgesetz*) BGBl. I 1998, p. 707 |
| KapMuG (DE) | Capital Investors Model Proceedings Act (*Kapitalanleger-Musterverfahrensgesetz*) BGBl. I 2005, p. 2437 |
| KonTraG (DE) | Corporate Sector Supervision and Transparency Act (*Gesetz zur Kontrolle und Transparenz im Unternehmensbereich*) BGBl. I 1998, p. 786 |
| LSE | London Stock Exchange |
| MDAX (DE) | index comprised of 50 Prime Standard shares from classic sectors ranking immediately below the companies included in the DAX |
| NAA | National Association of Accountants |
| NASBA | National Association of State Boards of Accountancy |
| NASD (DE) | National Association of Securities Dealers |
| NASDAQ (US) | National Association of Securities Dealers Automated Quotation |
| NOMAD (UK) | Nominated Advisor |
| NYSE | New York Stock Exchange |

| NYS&EB | New York Stock & Exchange Board |
|---|---|
| OECD | Organisation for Economic Cooperation and Development |
| OTC | Over The Counter |
| OTCBB (US) | Over-The-Counter Bulletin Board |
| PCAOB (US) | Public Company Accounting Oversight Board |
| PFI (UK) | Prevention of Fraud Investments Act |
| PH (DE) | Audit Guidelines (*Prüfungshinweise*) |
| PIOB | Public Interest Oversight Board |
| POB (UK) | Professional Oversight Board |
| POB (US) | Public Oversight Board |
| POBA (UK) | Professional Oversight Board for Accountancy |
| PS (DE) | Auditing Standards (*Prüfungsstandards*) |
| Pub.L. | Public Law |
| QIB | Qualified Institutional Buyers |
| QMV | Qualified Majority Vote |
| R&D | Research and Development |
| RGBl (DE) | Federal Gazette (*Reichsgesetzblatt*) |
| RIC (DE) | Financial Reporting Interpretations Committee (*Rechnungslegung Interpretation Committee*) |
| SA (US) | Securities Act (Pub.L. 73-22, 48 Stat. 74) |
| SAC | Standards Advisory Council |
| SASs (UK) | Statements of Auditing Standards |
| SDAX (DE) | Small-Cap-DAX index for 50 smaller companies |
| SE | Stock Exchange |
| SEA (US) | Securities and Exchange Act (Pub.L. 73–291, 48 Stat. 881) |
| SEC (US) | Securities and Exchange Commission |
| SFA (UK) | Securities and Futures Authority |
| SFAC (US) | Statement of Financial Accounting Concepts |
| SFAS (US) | Statement of Financial Accounting Standards |
| SIB (UK) | Securities and Investment Board |
| SOA (US) | Sarbanes–Oxley Act (Pub.L. 107–204, 116 Stat. 745) |
| SORP (UK) | Statements of Recommended Practice |
| SROs (UK; US) | Self-Regulatory Organizations |
| SSAP (UK) | Statements of Standard Accounting Practice |
| Stat. | United States Statutes at Large |
| SWX | Swiss Exchange |
| TecDAX (DE) | index tracking the performance of 30 largest German companies from the technology sector |

| | |
|---|---|
| TEG | Technical Expert Group |
| TransPuG (DE) | Transparency and Disclosure Act (*Transparenz- und Publizitätsgesetz*) BGBl. I 2002, p. 2681 |
| UITF | Urgent Issues Task Force |
| UK | United Kingdom |
| UKLA | United Kingdom Listing Authority |
| UMAG (DE) | Business Integrity and Modernization of Shareholder Actions Act (*Gesetz zur Unternehmensintegrität und Modernisierung des Anfechtungsrechts*) BGBl. I 2005, p. 2802 |
| US/USA | United States of America |
| US GAAP | United States Generally Accepted Accounting Principles |
| USM (UK) | Unlisted Securities Market |
| VorstOG (DE) | Director Remuneration Disclosure Act (*Vorstandsvergütungs-Offenlegungsgesetz*) BGBl. I 2005, p. 2267 |
| WpHG (DE) | Securities Trading Act (*Wertpapierhandelsgesetz*) BGBl. I 1998, p. 2708 |
| WPK (DE) | Chamber of Public Accountants (*Wirtschaftsprüferkammer*) |
| WPO (DE) | Public Acountant Act (*Wirtschaftsprüferordnung*) |
| WpPG (DE) | Securities Prospectus Act (*Wertpapierprospektgesetz*) BGBl. I 2005, p. 1698 |
| WpÜG (DE) | Securities Acquisition and Takeover Act (*Wertpapiererwerbs- und Übernahmegesetz*) BGBl. I 2001, p. 3822 |

# Acknowledgements

The authors owe thanks to a number of individuals and institutions.

First and foremost, we gratefully acknowledge the financial support from the Volkswagen Foundation. The Volkswagen Foundation generously supported our research efforts for more than two years and made the writing of this book possible. Second, our appreciation goes to the *Deutsche Forschungsgemeinschaft* and the Collaborative Research Unit *Sonderforschungsbereich* (Statehood in Transition) in particular. Being an associated project of the *Sonderforschungsbereich* in its first phase from 2003 to 2006, and being a regular since 2007, we have benefited hugely from a stimulating research environment.

Third, we owe gratitude to the person whose support made this book possible in the first place: Stephan Leibfried, the Speaker of the *Sonderforschungsbereich*. His constant encouragement helped broadening and sharpening our thinking, and he gave us confidence to stretch the limits of what is – at least in Germany – seen as 'proper' accounting research.

Fourth, valuable assistance was provided by a number of individuals. Resisting convergence pressures, we extend our thanks following a quaint German tradition and also list the individuals' academic degrees. We were able to draw from postgraduate research work undertaken at the University of Bremen's Accounting Department: Dipl.-Kffr. Kersten Pohlmann's thesis contributed to our understanding of the Sarbanes–Oxley Act, and Dipl.-Kfm. Marc Sauerbier's thesis on developments in auditing regulation was most helpful for our comparative analysis. Dipl.-Kfm. Ulf Luthardt's thesis supported us in the discussion of legitimizing standard-setting in the EU. We could also count on the assistance of the Accounting Department's research staff: Dipl.-Kfm. Stephan Abée provided important insights into the stock markets and their regulation. Dipl.-Ök. Stefan Veith contributed to the analysis of enforcement agencies and also helped us with the graphs. We could rely on the technical assistance of Dipl.-Ök. Jan-Philipp Kilian, Michal Lehuta, B.A. and cand. rer. pol. Johannes Schymczyk. We very much appreciate their hard work for the sake of our project.

# Series Editor's Preface

When we think about the future of the modern state, we encounter a puzzling variety of scholarly diagnoses and prophecies. Some authors predict nothing less than the total demise of the state as a useful model for organizing society – its powers eroded by a dynamic global economy and by an increasing transference of political decision-making powers to supranational bodies. Others disagree profoundly. They point to the remarkable resilience of the state and its core institutions. For them, even in the age of global markets and politics, the state remains the ultimate guarantor of security, democracy, welfare and the rule of law. These debates raise complex questions for the social sciences: what is happening to the modern liberal nation state of the OECD bloc? Is it an outdated model? Is it still useful? Is it in need of modest reform or far-reaching changes?

The state is a complex entity, providing many different services and regulating many areas of everyday life. There can be no simple answer to these questions. The 'Transformations of the State' series will try to disaggregate the tasks and functions of the state into four key, but manageable dimensions:

1. the monopolization of the means of force
2. the rule of law as prescribed and safeguarded by the constitution
3. the guarantee of democratic self-governance
4. the provision of welfare and the assurance of social cohesion.

In the OECD world of the 1960s and 1970s these four institutional aspects merged as the central characteristics of the modern state, forming a synergetic whole. This series is devoted to empirical and theoretical studies exploring the transformations of this historical model and the promise it still holds today and for the future. Books in the series address research on one or several of these dimensions, in all of which crucial change is taking place. Although political science is the main disciplinary approach, many books will be interdisciplinary in nature and may also draw upon law, economics, history and sociology. We hope that taken together these books will provide their readers with the 'state of the art' on the 'state of the state'.

This book contributes to the work of the Collaborative Research Center *Transformations of the State* at the University of Bremen (Germany), and is funded by the German Research Foundation (DFG). The state analyses pursued by the Center are readily accessible through two overview volumes: Stephan Leibfried and Michael Zürn (eds), *Transformations of the State?* (2005); and Achim Hurrelmann, Stephan Leibfried, Kerstin Martens and Peter Mayer (eds), *Transforming the Golden-Age Nation State* (2007), published in the 'Transformations of the State' series. Further information on the Center can be found at www.state.uni-bremen.de.

Achim Hurrelmann
*Carleton University*

Stephan Leibfried, Kerstin Martens and Peter Mayer
*University of Bremen*

# Part I

# Transformations of Statehood in Accounting: The Framework

It is a truth universally acknowledged that the increasing integration of the world economy leads to the demise of the nation state. No matter how little known a policy area may be, this truth is so well fixed in people's minds that convergence of business systems must be the right conclusion for the matter in hand.

There are relatively few studies that systematically enquire whether institutional settings of nation states do indeed converge and whether new governance modes emerge, possibly on a global scale, that supersede national regulations, or curtail the traditional role and discretion of nation states. This book aims at contributing to the evolving research on the role of the nation state and addresses the field of accountancy, in particular the field of financial reporting. We will analyse if new, possibly global structures emerge that cope better with the effects from globalization than national solutions and whether these structures complement or supplant the nation states' regulation. We provide three detailed country studies for prominent capitalist economies, which are organized along the inner logic of the financial reporting process. For our analysis, we consider the following countries: Germany, the United Kingdom (UK) and the United States (US). We chose these countries as they allow a rich contrast due to their institutional set-up.

Relevance and quality of financial reporting are closely related to domestic corporate governance systems, which appear in two types: outsider systems and insider systems. When there is a separation of decision-making between the suppliers of money to the firm and users of money in the firm, that is when financiers are not involved in managerial decision-making, one speaks of an outsider system. Insider systems are those in which financiers of a company have a say in managerial decision-making. This is particularly pronounced when the function of the financier and the function of the manager coincide – a case that often happens in family-owned, medium-sized firms. These insider and outsider governance systems normally correspond to a particular legal system: insider systems are based on code law; outsider systems typically have a common law tradition. Insider systems can mostly be found in Continental European countries, and Germany is a prominent example. Anglo-Saxon countries tend to have outsider systems. For such systems and countries, the US is an exemplar. Including the US and Germany in a study on the transformation of accounting systems is thus an obvious choice. However, changes in both systems might not only be due to different economic needs of adaptation. The regulatory environment also needs to be taken into account. To control for the effect of EU membership, we consider a further Anglo-Saxon common law country that is exposed to Europeanization in the same way as Germany: the UK. When the UK's accounting regulation displays tendencies similar to Germany then Europeanization, and not corporate governance, is the likely cause for change. When Germany transforms and the UK remains stable then the underlying corporate governance systems can be identified as the reason for re-configurations.

For the three countries, our study contrasts the national regulatory models of accounting that were present in the golden-age nation state with today's situation. In this context, we define the golden age as the heyday of the nation state, first observable in the OECD world of the 1960s and early 1970s, which lasted until around the 1980s (Hobsbawm 1995; Leibfried and Zürn 2005). In this period, nation states were indisputably responsible for the four key functions of statehood: they set law, provided legitimacy, intervened into the private spheres of their citizens and economic actors to provide welfare and supplied key resources like security (Hurrelmann *et al.* 2007; Leibfried and Zürn 2005). This does not imply that statehood followed an identical model in the OECD world during that period, but such a distinction sets the OECD countries apart from the non-OECD world, where the nation state did not necessarily bundle these four dimensions. Since the 1980s, statehood is, however, changing, making the golden age an obvious starting point for an analysis of transformation processes.

In our analysis, we restrict ourselves to organizational changes in the national accounting regimes and in particular its financial reporting regimes. We are thus mainly interested in *how* accounting was and is actually governed. We do not look at *what* information the accounting systems produce but *who* forces companies to do so. Additionally, we consider only accounting mechanisms for listed firms because major changes took place only for these entities. In the long run, however, it is likely that these changes will affect the unlisted, mainly small and medium-sized companies as well.[1]

Throughout the study, we focus on financial reporting as the most dynamic part of accounting, which we separate into its two constituent parts 'disclosure' and 'enforcement'. In the area of disclosure regulation, our focus is on the function of setting rules, and particularly on the actors in the development of Generally Accepted Accounting Principles (GAAP) that have to be followed by listed companies. When we refer to accounting rules within this book, we usually imply the specific rules on recognition and measurement, as these rules determine the content of the key financial reporting instruments, namely 'balance sheet' and 'income statement'. Accounting rules are usually developed by more than one organization, and standard-setting describes how most of these rules evolve. Designated standard-setters such as the International Accounting Standards Board (IASB) now play the most prominent role here, but further interventions of either governmental or non-governmental organizations are often present in the process of developing accounting rules. These other actors, of whom public accountants and stock exchanges are an important subgroup, will therefore also be considered in some detail. For the area of enforcement we apply the same logic. Again, we are interested in *how* enforcement is organized, for instance which mechanisms are applied and which actors are responsible for the verification of accounting information. This also implies that we are not interested in the actual contents of enforcement rules, but in the way in which they emerge.

The remainder of the book is organized as follows: In Part I, Chapter 1 embeds the analysis of accountancy in the wider corporate governance debate and presents the analytical tools that we are going to apply in the descriptive parts of our study. Chapter 2 introduces the three national accounting models and reviews the most important changes in the two core areas of accounting regulation, namely disclosure and enforcement.

The following two parts cover these areas of accounting in closer detail. Part II of the book deals with disclosure regulation. Chapter 3 looks at early changes in accounting standard-setting that have weakened the traditional model of the golden-age nation state. In Chapter 4, we consider the new role of transnational arrangements in disclosure regulation, namely the supply of International Financial Reporting Standards (IFRS) and how the European Union (EU) legitimizes their application. The informational needs of stock markets and the balance between private and public approaches to satisfy them are considered in Chapter 5.

Here, it will be of particular interest how the nation state deals with the transformation of the business model of stock exchanges.

Enforcement is studied in Part III of the book. Chapter 6 begins with a discussion of auditing as the traditional enforcement device, and analyses why nation state arrangements seem sandwiched between societal and transnational arrangements. The nation state's strongholds are enforcement agencies that are increasingly mandated to ensure credibility of financial reporting. Their role will be covered in Chapter 7.

It is still an open question whether the power of the nation state has increased or decreased in the process of globalization. Part IV of the book studies this question by presenting two findings that seem to be contradictory at first glance. Financial globalization and cross-listings seem to curtail the power of the nation state, and they increase the leverage of businesses lobbying for 'global' solutions. We discuss this in Chapter 8. In Chapter 9, we look at an example that signals the exercise of seemingly increased regulatory powers: the Sarbanes–Oxley Act (SOA), which was passed by US Congress in 2002 but also applies outside US jurisdictions. This chapter provides evidence that such regulatory action is likely to affect regulations in other countries. This seems to signal that at least some nation states gain in power when the economic world globalizes. Both cases will also allow us to take a closer look at whether regulatory races go 'to the bottom' or 'to the top'.

The final part, Part V, of the book relies on a quantitative concept to pull together the identified changes in disclosure and enforcement regulation. This allows us to measure to which extent convergence in the systems in regard to 'privatization' and 'internationalization' took place and whether the corridor of nation state solutions has actually narrowed.

# 1
# Accounting: A Socio-economic View

## 1.1 The localization of accounting: Business and regulatory contexts

To those uninitiated to the world of accounting, the use of different accounting information sets, the choice of which depends on the respective business contexts, may be perplexing. Many expect one single truthful report about a firm or a project and not a possible diverse set of numbers with the comment 'it depends'. For the accountant, it is sometimes perplexing to find out in how many ways and with which motives the state can get involved to regulate aspects of accounting, and that many institutions thought of as 'genuine' to the accounting world operate in the long shadow of the state. The following brief sketch may thus serve as an introduction for both the accountant and the non-accountant.

Accounting is typically subdivided into three clusters or systems: tax, financial and managerial accounting. While one could think that the three coincide if not for the sake of truthful reporting then at least for the sake of efficiency, this is not the case. Each accounting system serves a different purpose and therefore determines a different pattern of timing the inflows and outflows of cash into a profit and loss account. Thus, the same real-world situation can be 'transposed' into accounting reports that differ from one another. A managerial accounting system, for instance, can be optimistic about future cash flows and report them as profits before the cash has actually been received. When judging the performance of managers, a likely future cash inflow is a good measure of their actions. However, if tax accounting systems apply the same logic and determine taxable income and the tax due on cash flows not yet received, then the taxpayer may in certain instances have to take out credit as the actual funds for the tax payments have not yet materialized. Therefore tax accounting systems are likely to be structured around the actual cash flows, which coincide with the ability to pay. From this argument it is obvious that accounting cannot be the same for all purposes – tax, financial or managerial – rather to the contrary, the accounting rules change with the purpose. Of course, there will not be a wholesale change of all rules; many of them will look similar and some of them will even have influenced one another. The important idea is that different principles guide the formulation of accounting rules.

Of all three systems, the tax accounting system is the least interesting in the context of this book, even though we concern ourselves with changes in statehood. This is surprising only at first glance. While it is true that the state is keenly interested in receiving tax income from businesses, the governance of the tax accounting system has been relatively stable for a very straightforward reason: the state by and large determines the rules for the recognition of taxable income by means of tax law and minor regulations. While the contents of these rules are often subject to change, their organizational mode tends to be stable. And while there may have been some internationalization for some sources of revenue, the mix between the roles of public and private actors did hardly change from the golden age until today. One could even argue that tax accounting does not lie at the heart of what accounting stands for as its sole purpose is driven by the state's revenue motive and the state is the only addressee of the reports, and typical accounting deals with multiple audiences and a trade-off of their informational demands. This will become evident in examining the remaining two clusters, the managerial and the financial accounting systems.

Managerial accounting operates at the entity level, and its results are not distributed to an outside audience. Its purpose is to determine the cost and profit contributions of single products, product lines or managers. Its addressees are the decision-makers in all their capacities: not only as superiors when they use this data for evaluation, but also as subordinates when they use it as a guide to determine which decisions are (seen to be) in the company's interest. Financial accounting, in turn, reaches from the entity level to the outside. It is often described to report 'financial performance' to a wider audience of stakeholders such as owners, creditors, suppliers, employees and the general public. This wide array of stakeholders often found in the textbooks is rather unhelpful as it excludes nobody (maybe with the exception of the tax authorities), mixes their respective interests and clouds the understanding of the accounting issues at hand.

While financial accounting builds the bridge from the entity – the firm – to the outside, it is a matter of debate to which outside group financial accounting is primarily addressed.

One possible set could be the financiers of the firm. The rather old-fashioned term 'financier' is used to describe those that hold a longer-term financial interest in the firm. This interest may arise by supplying equity capital or by granting (longer-term) credit, and financiers typically provide resources directly to the entity. Investors make up the second possible group to which financial accounting may be addressed. They consist of shareholders and, inasmuch as their primary interest is in trading these financial instruments, the holders of corporate bonds. The key difference between 'financiers' and 'investors' is the motive and the time horizon for their investments. Investors buy property rights from other shareholders, do not contribute a significant amount of resources directly to the entity, and release their invested capital not with the cash flows generated at the entity level but by selling their shares. Cash dividends, the investor's share of the entity-level cash flows, make up only a small fraction of the overall takings. The majority comes from the appreciation of the stocks, which are cash flows expected in the future. While standard financial economics cannot recognize this difference – with perfect markets and profit-maximizing investors these differences are simply assumed away – institutional set-ups reflect it: the organization of financial accounting and also the state's involvement in regulation differ with respect to these groups.

Financiers with a long-term interest in a firm build an economic entity that is more than just a 'nexus of contracts'. Within this institution, conflicts arise over the use and distribution of the cash flows; and these conflicts need to be resolved between the financiers. This can be done by statute, but the state often gets involved using company law – by prescribing rules for incorporation, by assigning voting rights, by determining rules for sharing cash flows between equity financiers themselves on the one hand and between them and creditors on the other – and the state sets rules for the wind-up of the firm. The state has an interest in financial accounting as soon as the company law makes use of accounting rules, for instance in determining what is profit and how to distribute it.

Shareholders who invest in the short term only have a perfunctory interest in the entity as such: they are interested in the returns that they can generate with their investment, and most of their returns will be derived from cashing in on stock price appreciation, and this is trading in future expected cash flows. For them, the investment is also more part of a portfolio to which a particular share contributes a risk-and-return profile. This means that the shareholders are keenly interested in being well informed about firm characteristics in regard to future cash flows as they enable them to trade shares in an informed manner. Trading shares requires a different set of information than resolving conflict between financiers. Agents, for instance institutions where shares are traded, may be requiring rules for disclosure. The state, if it gets involved at all, tends to use securities law to assist these types of investors. When reliable information about financial performance of a firm is necessary for informed trading, the state is likely to regulate accounting.

Surprisingly, even management accounting is no stranger to state intervention. As managerial accounting determines what are 'good decisions' within a firm it is not immediately obvious why the state should intervene to provide a higher level of welfare. Here, state intervention has often taken the route of soft law, formulating rules of sound management practice. Exemplars are corporate governance codices, which often refer to how information should be used and presented. If these codices address concerns of outside stakeholders they also have a possible impact on financial reporting and need to be considered in this context. By and large, though, the state abstains from regulating management accounts, and this is the reason why management accounting will be of subordinate concern in our study.

As Exhibit 1.1 shows, not only does accounting serve a number of purposes, the state can also get involved in accounting using different entry routes and pursuing different purposes. The long shadow of the state falls on all systems of accounting, but changes in statehood will become most manifest in one area: financial accounting. In tax accounting the role of the state is too fixed; and in managerial accounting the role of the state is only peripheral. We therefore choose financial accounting as the object of our analysis.

Unfortunately, state intervention, being the result of a political process, never falls neatly into one of the categories of company law, securities law or governance regulation. It may use company law to order dissemination of information to shareholders; it may use corporate governance rules to influence financial reporting; it may use securities regulation to provide mechanisms of good corporate governance. Sometimes the state intervention will rely on some positive correlation of instruments, improving, say, conflict resolution in firms (a company

*Exhibit 1.1*   Localization of accounting

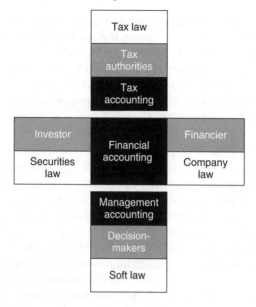

law issue) and at the same time improving as a side effect the quality of financial reporting on capital markets.

At the same time, securities law will not only extend to accounting, but also regulate other matters of investor protection such as insider trading, and company law may be relying less on accounting to distribute claims to property but more on providing voting rights or representation in decision-making bodies. In the extreme case, company or securities law may be silent about accounting altogether. There are reasons why the law may be silent: the state does not care for the well-being of investors or financiers or the state is satisfied with the arrangements privately found in the markets. If this is not the case, some regulation will be likely to be in the statute books. We will formalize this argument later as outcome, supervision or operating responsibility of the state.

## 1.2   The policy fields of financial reporting

From a functional perspective, financial reporting can be separated into its functional components. This is the production and dissemination of information, which we refer to as disclosure, and its enforcement. Enforcement encompasses all mechanisms to ensure that the disseminated information is materially correct. Both policy fields require decisions as to which role the state, societal and private actors should play to provide public welfare.

### The disclosure regime

All information disseminated by a company could be understood as disclosure. Disclosure would then comprise quantitative and qualitative reports, for instance on human relations or sustainability, and it would encompass matters as diverse as marketing or investor relation communications. Such an all-embracing concept of disclosure does not allow for much precision. We will therefore use the term 'disclosure' in a narrower sense: disclosures are communications intended to disseminate information on the financial state of a firm to a wider and non-specified audience (Merkt 2001). We do not only narrow down our analysis to quantitative, namely financial, aspects. Our definition also implies that disclosure and information are distinct categories. Once a disclosure is made, nobody can be excluded from its access. While information can also be provided through private channels, all disclosures are available for the general public. Disclosures thus aim at enhancing information available for an anonymous and general public.

Making corporate information available for the public helps alleviating information asymmetries and is thus an important mechanism to reduce agency problems, which occur for instance between managers and shareholders or between creditors and lenders. Due to the lack of other contractual solutions capital markets in particular need disclosures. Hence, companies which strongly rely on such markets get incentives to provide disclosures and to supply actual or potential investors with information relevant for making their decisions. For them, disclosures are necessary to participate successfully in capital markets. The state shares an interest in disclosures as soon as the efficiency of capital market becomes a political concern.

The 'interest' of the state does not imply immediate action by setting legal disclosure standards or by intervening in some other way. Private incentives for the demand and supply of information may suffice to initiate disclosures because incentives to divulge information increase when a company becomes more dependent on equity or debt financing via capital markets. However, this has not been put to the test recently: even though private incentives for providing information exist, one finds legal minimum disclosure requirements in practically every country since the early 20th century. This may be because the private incentives are deemed to be weak. However, disclosures mandated by legal regulation do not fully crowd out voluntary disclosures. Both exist side by side. While voluntary disclosures have supplementary character and can be defined as all information disclosed additionally to mandatory requirements, mandatory disclosures ensure that there is a minimum amount of publicly available information (Healy and Palepu 2001). The latter protects individual investors from concealment of material, for example substantially price-sensitive information, by the firm (Wüstemann 2003). Such regulation increases the overall welfare that capital markets bring about: assuming semi-strong information efficiency of capital markets, prices include all publicly available information. Hence, even relatively uninformed investors are price-protected when there is a sufficient amount of information embedded in the prices of the securities traded (Scott 2006).

Information is disclosed through different channels. Financial reports, an end product of the accounting process, are the most important source of such disclosures. Once published, accounting information in these reports is used for different purposes by various groups of stakeholders, particularly investors, creditors and employees. Supporting decision-making is now seen as the most prominent use, and examples for decisions based on accounting information are decisions to invest or disinvest equity capital or to lend money.

This functional view is the most common but not the only one on accounting. To provide an insight into the scope of possible roles of accounting, we mention but two. These views are not typically acknowledged in mainstream accounting research, but may be illuminating from a social science perspective. Here, some authors assert that the role of corporate disclosures is not only to report on economic entities but also to contribute to 'constructing' them (Borger 1999; Hines 1988). Obvious examples are economic entities that get visible only through accounting, namely groups. Property rights, in the strict legal sense, arise from ownership of company shares. However, a company's ownership of subsidiaries gives shareholders a further, but only indirect claim to those economic assets that the company owns in turn. Economic ownership is therefore broader than ownership in the legal sense as it encompasses the property rights to the subsidiary firms owned by the mother firm. This concept

underlies consolidated accounts, in which all assets and claims are reported in the context of economic ownership. As a legal entity, groups do
not exist, but the accounts see through the legal arrangements and make
all the claims, including the indirect ones, visible. In this sense, accounts
create the economic entity. The second role has to do with the part
that financial accounting plays in internal (self-)regulation. The oblig-
ation to render accounts requires a somewhat effective management.
The emergence of accounting, at least in code law countries, can partly
be explained by the paternalistic aim of the state to force merchants
to inform themselves about the economic situation of their businesses
(Leffson 1975).

### The enforcement regime

Disclosure regulation cannot be considered in isolation from its enforcement regime (Ball 2001): the information and control rights provided
by the disclosure system can be put to work only if they can be effectively enforced. In the context of financial reporting, enforcement serves
the purpose of safeguarding the faithful representation of disclosures. Its
economic function is to add credibility to disclosed statements. As a full
verification of accounting information would be too costly, enforcement
is in fact a system of sanctions and partial checks.

The most common form of enforcement in accountancy is auditing,
where private auditing firms verify the correctness of a company's financial statements on a contractual basis. Sanctions are incentives to abstain
from disclosing fraudulent information. These are set by imposing fines,
increasing litigation risk and establishing personal liability, for instance
by making false disclosures a punishable offence. These sanctions are
often accompanied by institutionalized policing arrangements including the operation of enforcement agencies that either examine random
samples of financial reports or investigate them in cases of suspicion.
Societal actors may also pursue enforcement strategies, for instance by
applying ethical rules and conferring or withdrawing membership status.

## 1.3  The function of accounting within the varieties of capitalism

Recent research on the varieties of capitalism stresses the system-
dependent importance of financial reporting and disclosure systems
for economic decision-making (Werner 2008). The different accounting
practices are based on the way in which an economic system is organized and how business operations are financed and controlled. We first

present the overarching argument, and then consider how this argument applies to Germany as an 'insider' economy on the one hand and the UK and the US as the 'outsider' economies on the other. The future of these systems are considered at the end of this section.

## The argument for different functionalities: Some theory

The style of the national corporate governance system furnishes contracting parties with system-specific information claims that are transmitted by the disclosure system (Wüstemann 2003). As the corporate governance system itself depends on the type of the national business system, the disclosure regime is complementary to the 'variety of capitalism' existent in a particular nation state (Ball 2001). The relationship between corporate governance and disclosures is, for instance, described in Sloan (2001), who argues that 'financial accounting provides financiers with the primary source of independently verified information about the performance of managers. Thus, it is clear that corporate governance and financial accounting are inexorably linked. Indeed, many of the central features of financial accounting, such as the use of historical costs, the reliability criterion, the realization principle and the conservatism principle are difficult to understand unless one adopts a corporate governance perspective.'

The formation of meaningful prices on capital markets rests on disclosures. They are thus necessary preconditions for the existence of well-functioning capital markets. Disclosures also play a role in corporate governance by providing economic actors with reliable measures for contracting. Such measures are, for instance, used for equity and debt contracting and, equally important, for contracts with managers (Bushman and Smith 2001; Lambert 2001; Sloan 2001). Lastly, disclosures enable stakeholders to enforce their claims in better ways, for instance in lawsuits (Hay and Shleifer 1998; La Porta *et al.* 1998). The particular 'variety of capitalism' now defines the role that disclosures and, in particular, financial reports play in the coordination efforts of the economic actors. This explains why countries with insider economies have a financial reporting system different from those with outsider economies. The concepts of code law and common law countries are often used somewhat interchangeably with the concepts of insider and outsider economies. While one cannot deny a correlation between these two organizational forms, conclusions must be drawn from the underlying economics, which are not captured in the procedural notion of 'code' and 'common' law. We therefore prefer the concept

of insider and outsider economies to the differentiation between code
and common law countries and use this typology wherever appropriate.

The implications of corporate governance on financial reporting will
be discussed in the following subsections. Here, we refer to Germany as a
typical example of a country with an insider-style corporate governance
system and to the UK and the US as typical outsider systems.

### The functions of accounting in insider economies: The case of Germany

Germany has an insider-style corporate governance system. In the terminology of Hall and Soskice (2001), Germany follows the model of
a coordinated market economy. This type of capitalism is characterized by a broad range of non-market-based forms of coordination. The
authors note that 'non-market modes of coordination generally entail
more extensive relational or incomplete contracting, network monitoring based on the exchange of private information inside networks,
and more reliance on collaborative, as opposed to competitive, relationships to build the competencies of the firm' (Hall and Soskice
2001). Accordingly, external equity financing through capital markets
was comparatively less developed in Germany, especially for small and
medium-sized companies. German firms traditionally relied to a large
extent on internal and debt (bank) financing. Evidently, these financing patterns go hand in hand with relatively weak capital markets. As
the German social security system is by tradition of the pay-as-you-go
kind, this arrangement slowed down the development of capital markets
further.

The absence of an active market for corporate control can be regarded
as one of the preconditions for the emergence of the particular German corporate governance system. Its near-non-existence, which lasted
over decades (Hackethal *et al.* 2005; Schmidt 2003), fostered network-
like relationships and a long-term rather than a short-term cooperative
orientation (see, for example, Hall and Soskice 2001). Ownership concentration in German companies is traditionally high, and this appears
to be the typical solution when investor protection is poor (La Porta *et al.*
2000; La Porta *et al.* 1997). With low investor protection, the demand for
holding only small stakes in a firm is also typically low. This depresses
market prices for shares and makes external equity financing relatively
unattractive, reinforcing the traditional financing pattern. Holding large
proportions of shares ('blockholdings') also enables investors to realize
control benefits, which can be explained by obtaining information and

control rights, for example through representation in the supervisory boards (La Porta *et al.* 1998).

Germany's typical corporate governance institutions translate into its accounting system. Generally, the demand for high-quality accounting information is lower because blockholders or banks, which are important providers of finance, already have timely access to information through other channels than financial reporting (García Lara *et al.* 2005). The most important stakeholders in insider-oriented corporate governance regimes are thus less dependent on the availability of public disclosures. Instead of relying on public disclosures and financial reporting, insider systems feature a 'system of legally mandated and explicit reporting and disclosure duties within the firm, which disseminates decision relevant information to key contracting parties (but not to the public)' (Wüstemann 2003). Insider economies are often found in code law countries. Ball *et al.* (2000) argue that in these countries 'the demand for accounting income ( . . . ) is influenced more by the payout preferences of the agents for labor, capital and government, and less by the demand of public disclosure'.

## The functions of accounting in outsider economies: The UK and the US

The corporate governance systems in the US and the UK are typical outsider control systems. Both countries have, originating from the UK, an Anglo-Saxon common law tradition. In regard to the national business systems and again following the terminology of Hall and Soskice (2001), both countries can be described as liberal market economies. In such economies, markets play a greater role in the coordination of economic actors. This also translates into typical financing patterns of firms domiciled in such countries. (Anonymous) investors have to be supplied with high-quality information that enables them to meet their economic decisions such as buying, holding or selling shares. Such information can be found in financial reports. As outside investors cannot rely on internal levers of control, their protection is of particular concern for the efficiency of liberal market economies. These business systems thus feature a high degree of institutionalized investor protection. The latter is *inter alia* ensured by a developed disclosure system, which is typically accompanied by a strong enforcement regime.

Through this sort of regulation, benefits from controlling large proportions of shares decrease. Stocks thus are typically held more widely in liberal market economies. A higher degree of institutionalized investor protection hence contributes to the development of larger equity markets compared to insider economies (La Porta *et al.* 1997). This also coincides with the existence of an active market for corporate control, sometimes also denoted as takeover market. The control mechanism works in the following way: if performance is poor, market values of the firm will fall, and this makes the poorly performing firm a takeover target. After the takeover, the new owners are likely to replace the top managers or to change business strategies to increase share prices. This constant threat is likely to make managers focus on achieving good returns on their strategies. The existence of active takeover markets thus also contributes to a higher degree of investor protection.

Evidently, the role of financial reporting for economic decision-making must be more pronounced in outsider corporate governance systems. Anglo-Saxon accounting was thus described as being 'micro-orientated and judgmental, reflecting business practice and professional rules' (Alexander and Archer 2003). However, whether the differences between Anglo-Saxon and Continental European countries are that clear-cut has recently been an issue of debate (see for example Alexander and Archer 2003; Nobes 2003) and will also be analytically addressed in Part V of this book.

## Similar challenges and different pressures

Generally, both outsider and insider models have their merits and short-comings. While it is currently fashionable to believe in the superiority of outsider models, it is noteworthy that even in the 1990s some authors saw comparative advantages of insider systems in the German or Japanese style (Porter 1992). For instance, Wever and Allen (1992) argued that 'Germany's ability to design a cohesive economic and social system that adapts continuously to changing requirements goes a long way toward explaining the country's competitive success.'

An important empirical observation is that both insider and outsider models displayed a stable existence over a long time. Both were successful solutions to the respective requirements that they had to meet. From this perspective, both systems were functionally equivalent to each other, at least to a large extent. The occurrence and retention of both systems can be explained by their optimal adaptation to the respective infrastructural environments, particularly typical financing patterns and the respective corporate governance systems, and by path dependency (Wüstemann 2003).

It is now often opined that the process of economic globalization in particular necessitates a shift towards an arm's length financing system (Hall and Soskice 2001; Leuz and Wüstemann 2004). When there is, due to globalization, strong reliance on (equity) markets and a need for lower capital costs, liberal market economies have comparative advantages. This may lead to a convergence in the varieties of capitalism, which means that different political and economic systems adjust to imitate the one 'best-suited' model (Strange 1996). Even though we do not explicitly address the question as to whether there is a worldwide convergence of corporate governance and business systems, it is likely that changes in the respective disclosure and enforcement systems provide evidence for such an underlying process: a stronger reliance on equity financing requires the externalization of information, thus strengthening disclosure and enforcement.

In that vein, Hansmann and Kraakman (2001) predict the 'end of history of corporate law' as Continental European company law will converge to the US model. The presumed convergence is to occur because insider models are not able to cope with needs emerging through globalization: worldwide integration led to massive demands for new capital even from companies in insider economies (Kübler and Assmann 2006). Particularly, large and internationally acting corporations were facing increasing transparency demands of global investors when they wanted to raise fresh capital. These demands could only be met with difficulty due to poor disclosure regulation in the home market. The ensuing transparency, induced by outside capital, led to increasing market pressures, which also necessitated to reconsider traditional business practices founded on networking and long-lasting (but not necessarily efficient) relationships. Changes also affected banks, which played an important role in the governing coalition of insider economies (see, for example, Hackethal *et al.* 2006). Their strategic reorientation towards investment banking rather than credit provision made them leave the governing coalition, again reinforcing the need for big industrial companies to increasingly collect funds from equity markets.

## 1.4 Governance modes and the role of the state

To analyse whether actors within the accounting regimes have taken on new roles or discarded their old ones, we refer to the categories put forward in Streeck and Schmitter (1985). In their seminal work on the analysis of governance in different policy fields, they distinguish between three major bases of social order: market, with its guiding principle of dispersed competition; the state with hierarchical control; and community with 'spontaneous' solidarity.[i] In the ideal market solution, entrepreneurs seek to maximize their profit in exchange for a good or service provided to their customers on a transactional basis. The ideal state mode of organization is bureaucratic in principle – allocation decisions are made hierarchically. In the community ideal, finally, leaders of societal groups seek esteem, while their followers cherish the sense of belonging to the group as such (Streeck and Schmitter 1985). Although each of the three principles is said to have its own integrity and tendency towards reproduction, contemporary social order is in fact a continuous struggle of the three for 'the allegiance of specific groups, for the control of scarce resources, for the incorporation of new issues, for the definition or rules regulating [behaviour], and so forth' (Cummins *et al.* 1994).

As Puxty *et al.* (1987) note in their early application of this governance framework to accounting, the identified modes do not appear in their pure forms but rather in differently balanced combinations. Schuppert (1990) acknowledges that the variety of different governance modes is much broader than the 'state', 'community' and 'market' archetypes suggest. Adopting an actor-centred view, this finding is also true for the type of governance observable in disclosure and enforcement regulation. First, disclosures are in all jurisdictions based on legal stipulations, mostly in the form of company and securities law. However, these legal stipulations are not sufficient for providing detailed technical rules on how to prepare financial disclosures. Such guidance has to be provided by further actors, who traditionally varied across countries. These actors are, respectively, associated with (or rooted in) the three governance modes described.

In the state sector, agencies, courts and to a smaller extent bodies under public law, for instance mutual stock exchanges, may play an additional role in setting disclosure rules. Enforcement can also be enacted by state agencies, courts and bodies under public law, with courts being important for the evolvement of litigation risk. Communitarian involvement in accounting governance includes responsibilities of actors like official (private) standard-setters, unofficial/factual standard-setters or influential academics and practitioners. In regard to enforcement, communitarian governance can be exercised by institutions that are necessitated by company law, such as (supervisory) boards and their committees, as well as the statutory audit. While these institutions are stipulated by law, they do not fully belong to the state sector as only private actors are involved. Finally, markets also play a role in governance when there is a strong reliance on private contracts and arrangements. A real-life configuration will be made up of a combination of these components and actors, both in disclosure and in enforcement.

The traditional analysis of governance modes keeps silent on the territoriality of the respective actors. It has, however, to be kept in mind that both private and state governance can be exercised from a national or an international base. In the golden age, governance was generally localized at the national level, and this was also true for the localization of disclosure and enforcement. Two patterns of change show up in this context (Zürn and Leibfried 2005). The first may be denoted as 'transnationalization', referring to a combination of privatization and internationalization. The second can be called 'supranationalization', which can be characterized by a combination of internalization and involvement of actors rooted in the state sector. Obviously, Europeanization must be regarded as a special case of supranationalization.

The specific constellation of a governance mode cannot be construed without reference to the state. It is the state that decides which options are admissible in the first place. As soon as the state rules out an option, it is unattainable for the governance configuration. The state may, for instance, decide to crowd out all communitarian (societal) regulation by setting its own detailed rules or it may decide not to allow an internationalization of competencies. In this context, the decisive question is, whether the state takes on responsibility for the regulation of a particular policy field and, if so, of which kind this responsibility is?

State responsibilities can be classified into three different levels (Schuppert and Bumke 2000): operation responsibility, supervision responsibility and outcome responsibility. When taking on operation responsibility, the state performs relevant services for the provision of a normative good[1] such as welfare or security through its own administrative agencies. Supervision responsibility means that the state takes legislative decisions on the provision of a normative good. Supervision responsibility necessitates cooperation with societal or private actors in a particular policy field (Grimm 1990; Schuppert 1990). This can be interpreted as an incorporation of the addressees of law into the sphere of the state, which has become increasingly noticeable. Observations include that law becomes less hierarchical, that law-makers increasingly try to convince or persuade constituents instead of forcing them to follow specific rules and that there is an increasing amount of soft law, that is non-binding regulation (Ritter 1990). Supervision responsibility does not imply a state's own operational activities but delegating the regulation to third (mostly self-regulating) parties who guarantee a certain level of provision in respect of normative goods. The state might not intervene at all as long as self-regulation leads to satisfactory outcomes.

When taking on outcome responsibility, the state is expected to intervene if a normative good is put in jeopardy. Taking on outcome responsibility only leads to a very low level of intervention in general. It should be noted that the state can, in fact, rarely completely discard this sort of responsibility. The outlined concepts are summarized in Exhibit 1.2. It offers a comprehensive analytical framework for enquiries into accounting governance and shows possibilities of change. It will be used here to contrast the different governance modes and hence to capture the effect of the recent transformations of the British, the German and the US disclosure and enforcement systems.

In regard to the policy fields of disclosure and enforcement regulation, we expect to find opposite trends in insider and outsider economies. In insider systems such as Germany, we suppose that due to globalization a retreat of the state from bearing operation responsibility will be observable. This also implies that we expect an increasing participation of private-sector actors in the governance of the respective policy fields. However, applying the term 'privatization' to this phenomenon may be too simple as private involvement can also occur in addition to existing regulation. It is the total amount of regulation and the sharing pattern of responsibilities for the policy fields between public and private actors that is decisive in this issue. Only if the state sector's traditional responsibilities are simply transferred to the private sector talking about privatization is justifiable.

*Exhibit 1.2*   Framework for analysing possible shifts in accounting governance

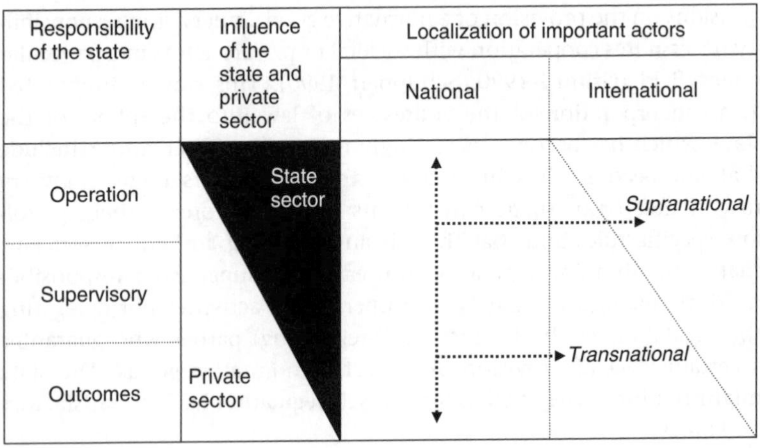

In outsider systems, we expect that state responsibilities increase in such a way that a *laissez-faire* approach of the golden age – inasmuch it existed in the first place – is abandoned in favour of the state taking on the supervision responsibility for the provision of normative goods. This implies that the state sector plays an increasing role in the governance of disclosure and enforcement, at least by mandating private actors that previously regulated without a nation state's remit.

The expectation that outsider economies will witness more state involvement seems counter-intuitive only at the first glance. Two reasons make state involvement more likely. First, capital markets have become important for societal arrangements beyond the provision of finance, for instance in providing funds for retirement. A malfunction or even a collapse of the markets would have severe repercussions for the nation state, which bears the responsibility for its citizen's economic welfare. The second reason is the increasing cross-fertilization of regulatory regimes. Regulation has become somewhat contagious: if it exists in one state, it is likely to appear eventually in the other. The crisis theory of regulation provides a pertinent explanation: politicians have to demonstrate to their electorate, who is increasingly aware of other existing arrangements, that 'everything' has been done to avert the crises and 'all' safeguards have been applied for the future.

Taken together, these developments make convergence of regimes very likely. Convergence then may take the form of shared transnational and supranational solutions.

# 2
# Transformation of Role Models: Germany, the UK and the US

This chapter sketches developments in the financial reporting systems of Germany, the UK and the US, all of which will be discussed in greater detail in Part II. These three national configurations have been selected for different reasons. All three systems traditionally display diverging goals, functions and institutional set-ups in financial reporting, which are contrasted throughout the following chapters. The US regulation focuses exclusively on listed companies, is founded on strict enforcement and provides detailed rules. The UK system has a long-standing tradition of mainly societal (community) accounting governance by the accounting profession. It focuses on capital markets, which is similar to the US system, but has a broader scope and emphasizes professional judgement instead of detailed rules. Finally, traditional German accounting concentrated more on creditor protection and on using accounting for problem-solving within firms while capital markets played a subordinate role; the system is also highly influenced by jurisdiction. The British and German systems stand for two extremes in the European spectrum of accounting systems that spans between the so-called Continental European (Germany) and Anglo-Saxon approach to accounting. This necessarily rough distinction differentiates mainly between a predominant role of equity financing (Anglo-Saxon) and of bank financing (Continental) in funding companies and has remained dominant for almost three decades in comparative accounting research (Flower 2004; Nobes 1983; 2003; Nobes and Parker 2004).

In fact, the three national configurations represent three different paths of accountancy with diverse formative institutional developments. In particular, the institutionalized role of the state in accounting differs, and there is substantial variation in the importance and function of enforcement in the respective nation states.

## 2.1 UK accounting: Diversity, professions and 'fair presentation'

Financial reporting looks back on a long-standing tradition in the UK. Between the 16th and the 19th century, Britain was leading the evolution of accounting. British literature rightly claims the emergence of the 'accounting profession' as one of their nation's contribution to accountancy (Flower 2004). The tradition of a strong profession, which regulates many accounting and financial reporting issues out of its own initiative, has spread not only into many parts of the Commonwealth but, for example, also to the Netherlands and the US. At the same time, this initiative from the societal actors sets Britain apart from the Continental European model.

Privately organized societies and institutes of accountants shaped the British accounting system from the 1850s by admitting and educating their members. The state applied a *laissez-faire* approach until the beginning of the 20th century and rarely interfered in the financial reporting of most commercial and industrial companies (Parker 1990).[1] Not the state but societal arrangements – mainly the accounting profession – provided the rules for preparing financial reports: in the absence of legal stipulations, the professional bodies of the accounting profession issued guiding principles for their members to promote a 'true and fair view' in their professional judgement. These could vary from one professional body to another (Walton 1993).

Companies Acts passed successively from 1844 did not contain any rules concerning the format or content of financial statements (Roberts *et al.* 2005). The first notable involvement of the state occurred in 1907, when company law introduced mandatory disclosures of audited balance sheets. Before, disclosure was minimal, legal rules for recognition and measurement did not exist, and auditing as an enforcement mechanism was mandatory only for a small number of companies. Generally, ' ... the company was seen as a private arrangement involving shareholders and directors, and secrecy in business matters was regarded as a virtue' (Roberts *et al.* 2005).

State interference was augmented when the important Companies Act 1948 outlined more specific rules on disclosure. Next to the balance sheet, profit and loss accounts were to be disclosed and consolidated accounts had to be published. The Act demanded from firms a true and fair view (fair presentation) according to the demands of skilled addressees, especially investors (Flower 2004; Walton 1993). It also introduced some concrete yet basic accounting rules, such as the distinction between reserves and provisions in order to make the creation of hidden reserves more difficult (Nobes and Parker 2004). But laws remained of rather little importance, and jurisdiction also traditionally avoided interfering with questions of recognition and measurement (Flower 2004).

This 'golden age of *laissez-faire*' lasted about until the British accession to the European Economic Community (EEC). It is an exemplar of how markets and societal actors provided welfare without operational or supervision responsibility of the nation state. Edwards *et al.* (1997) show that the market produced efficient outcomes in auditing regarding the 'coverage' of firms with professional accountants despite the lack of state regulation. After evaluating auditor–client relationships from historical documents, the authors document that a vast majority of firms engaged professional accountants already in the 19th century even though it was not mandated by the state, and these results are by no means limited to big companies. Furthermore, the authors demonstrate that, contrary to conventional wisdom, professional accountants did not generate their biggest stake of returns through bankruptcy audits but rather via regular audits.

The impending EEC membership made the diversity of accounting rules within the UK seem arcane. It would be difficult for an outsider to understand why the different professional organizations would not apply one set of rules in one member state. Therefore, the professional bodies started to harmonize rules among the institutes/societies by founding the Accounting Standards Committee (ASC) as their common standard-setter in the 1970s. This was a first step towards one set of standards and eventually to GAAP and decreased the variety in recognition and measurement methods significantly. Nevertheless, the procedures to promulgate standard practice were comparatively slow. Often the final standards were based on compromises (Choi and Meek 2005). The competitive societal mechanism that had relied on a variety of professional bodies started to collapse, and it was further diminished when the national legislator transformed European regulations into successive Companies Acts after 1981. A greater degree of centralization and an increased role of the nation state ensued. Still, the UK held on to private arrangements wherever possible.

Today's financial reporting regulation is shaped by a network of privately incorporated actors that cooperate closely with the state (Fearnley and Hines 2003). The regulatory and supervisory competencies in financial reporting and auditing are bundled in a not-for-profit organization that is financed by the state, the profession and the companies to which its standards apply. It operates under the name of the Financial Reporting Council (FRC), a limited liability company with state guarantee, whose directors are drawn from the business world but are appointed by the state. The FRC's probably best-known subsidiary, the Accounting Standards Board (ASB), promulgates the pertinent accounting standards. The Financial Reporting Review Panel (FRRP) enquires into violations of accounting rules. Auditing is regulated by the Professional Oversight Board (POB) supervising the auditing profession, especially in terms of admission and qualification. The Auditing Practices Board (APB) pronounces rules on auditing, and the Accountancy Investigation and Disciplinary Board (AIDB) conducts active oversight. All these bodies are staffed by the FRC.

As a consequence of the reforms, the role of the respective professional bodies is much reduced. In acknowledging that there is a wide array of interests in financial reporting, the ASB now also draws its membership from the corporate and investment world. The other bodies ensure that violations of disclosure and enforcement rules are quickly and transparently dealt with, which also means that the disciplinary proceedings of the professions have partly lost their importance. The increased supervisory role bundled in the Reporting Council can also be seen as a consequence of the centralized structure of accounting regulation, which has made competition between the professions impossible. Overall, the state has taken on only a coordinating role: a closer look at the membership of the Council bodies reveals some distance to the state and political decision-making. Members are still drawn from the major representatives of the corporate world at large and not from the government executive or politics.

The collapse of the competitive societal system has not been confined to financial reporting and auditing. Today's regulation has further changed for listed firms. They are no longer supervised by the stock exchanges where their shares are traded. The Financial Services Authority (FSA) emerged as another relevant regulator for listed firms, pronouncing listing requirements and enforcing disclosure rules. Although often being regarded as a governmental agency (Fearnley and Hines 2003), the FSA is a private-sector organization, registered as a limited company. However, it reports to the Treasury and is equipped with wide-ranging quasi-governmental competencies, such as imposing penalties on firms that fail to meet particular disclosure requirements.

The British financial reporting system has undergone substantial changes since the golden age of the nation state. Starting off with only very little state intervention in the form of rudimentary legal stipulations and vast self-regulation, the public sector has increased its influence over time. Especially in the field of disclosure regulation, changes were triggered to a large extent by EU harmonization leading to more detailed stipulations in the Companies Acts. Today's system relies, both in disclosure and in enforcement regulation, on a number of bodies under private law and a quasi-governmental agency in securities regulation. In contrast to the settings in the golden age, all of these institutions are officially acknowledged and at least indirectly monitored by the government. In sum, the public sector gained in importance, significantly abstaining, however, from operational responsibilities wherever possible.

## 2.2   German accounting: Commercial Code, jurisprudence and taxation

German accounting traditionally relied less on the forces of professional self-organization. Nevertheless, it would be a rather simplifying assumption that accounting stipulations can mostly be found in the form of law. Instead, one may describe traditional German accounting as an outcome of different institutions' interference with corporate disclosures under the clear leadership of the government. German accounting regulations differed fundamentally not only from the converging international accounting rules (IFRS, US GAAP) in their contents but also in their institutional set-up. This necessitated more radical steps towards harmonized financial reporting: instead of subsequent adjustments some rather sweeping reforms were undertaken. For this reason, we speak about 'traditional' German accounting when referring to the settings during the golden age of the nation state around the 1970s.

First introduced in 1897, the German Commercial Code (HGB) at least technically constitutes the primary source of accounting regulation. However, this law did not contain many detailed rules on financial reporting until EU regulation was transposed into German law, amending the HGB.[2] What is important in understanding the role of the state *vis-à-vis* societal and private actors is the concept of German GAAP to which the Commercial Code refers as it specifies that accounts have to be rendered in accordance with GAAP. German GAAP consist of different inputs: they comprise regular practice, academic inputs, jurisprudence and professional opinions. Here, jurisprudence is of outstanding importance, as court decisions represent final decisions on what is acceptable as GAAP. Tax jurisdiction and the courts had a high degree of influence on accounting practice. But the auditing standards of the private Institute of Auditors (IDW) are also of importance, especially due to their binding character for auditors (see Marten *et al.* 2003).

The importance of courts in advancing German GAAP can at least partly be explained by the interconnection of financial reporting with taxation: financial reports technically represent the basis for determining taxable income. Although initially the causation went from company to tax accounts, the high practical relevance of taxation inverted this relation and verdicts of courts dealing with taxation were often considered as the major source of accounting rules (Born 2002). The legal interconnection applies only to company, not consolidated accounts. As company and group accounts tended not to differ in practical terms in the golden age, many outside Germany believed that the applicable regulations for company and group accounts were the same, and thus believed that tax legislation had a pervasive influence on German financial reporting. This prejudice about German group accounting exists until today (see, for example, Choi and Meek 2005).

The German Accounting Standards Board (GASB) was set up in the late 1990s as a last-minute attempt to retain state control over group accounting when large international firms started turning to international or US accounting standards. The GASB membership is determined fully by the private sector, but the regulations of the GASB must be approved by the state. The International Accounting Standards (IAS) regulation at the European level rendered this attempt meaningless. As all national bodies in Europe, the Board lost its competencies in setting accounting rules for listed groups and gave way for the EU-wide solution of uniform IFRS application. Today, the GASB focuses on developing group accounting for non-listed companies and on participating in the International Accounting Standards Board (IASB's) deliberations.

The profession has been notably absent in disclosure regulation. This is partly due to its size, and partly due to regulation. In Germany, the accounting profession is understood in a much more narrow sense, and only auditors qualify for membership. The first professional body of auditors was founded in Berlin in 1900. A national institute, the IDW, was established in 1930. Unlike with its British counterparts, membership was voluntary and carried neither weight nor responsibility. This changed in 1934 when all auditors had to become members to practise – an arrangement corresponding to other 'purification' attempts of the time. After a short wartime interlude of another body under public law, the IDW resumed its role as an oversight body. In 1961, the Public Accountant Act (WPO) stipulated the set-up of a Chamber of Public Accountants (WPK) of which an auditor has to be a member. The WPK, an organization under public law, is responsible for oversight, admission, quality control and the development of auditing standards. The IDW then returned to its original role: being an organization for lobbying on behalf of accountants and for giving advice.

Enforcement in Germany mainly revolved around auditing. The mandatory annual audit was introduced for joint stock companies in 1934. Regulated only on the surface in company law, principles for the audit's scope and content were established by the profession, traditionally by the IDW. This task was transferred to the Chamber of Auditors in 1961, but the latter immediately delegated this responsibility back to the Institute. Quality control was a matter only for the Chamber until 2005 when a newly founded Auditor Oversight Commission (APAK) took up its work. The APAK ultimately oversees the auditing profession. In effect, it merely enhances the public sector's influence on auditing oversight by supervising the WPK's operations and by intervening in its decisions if necessary.

German enforcement never focused much on capital markets. Listed companies never featured high on the agenda as distinctions would be typically made by size or legal status, but rarely by listing status. This changed after a number of high-profile cases of fraudulent accounting in the late 1990s and early 2000s. Listed groups now face random checks by a newly created enforcement panel under private law, modelled along the lines of its British counterpart. Membership of the control authority, Financial Reporting Enforcement Panel (DPR), is determined by the private sector, but staffing decisions at the executive level need approval by the state. The DPR is backed by the Federal Financial Supervisory Authority (BaFin). Despite the legal role it plays in accounting, its factual importance is rather small: the BaFin has so far intervened only occasionally in accounting contexts and focuses mainly on fighting insider trading (see Schüler 2004).[3]

The institutional reforms were accompanied by initiatives that increased the possibilities for legal action by investors. While courts intervened traditionally into questions of recognition, measurement and disclosure, it was comparatively difficult for share owners to sue for liability in cases of misconduct. After the corporation law was amended in 2005 to extend investors' opportunities in courts, this has changed. The amendment increased the risk of board members being held liable for their actions. As a consequence the number of complaints about misleading financial information rose and, in addition to the other reforms, the legislator introduced the possibility of representative law suits (*Musterklagen*) that replace the numerous separate cases on the same issue.

The transformations in Germany also changed the governance of financial reporting. While one could see in the British case that the intervention of the public sector has increased at the expense of the private actors' latitude, in Germany the role of the state has decreased in disclosure and increased in enforcement, but in the latter not at the expense of private actors, who had been largely absent. Germany's traditional governance model is still dominated by the public sector, particularly as the relevance of the accounting profession is still rather low. The modernization of the system not only brought additional state intervention, but also led to additional relative and absolute private-sector participation. New forms of public–private cooperation were set up, both in the field of disclosure regulation and of enforcement.

## 2.3   US accounting: Financial markets, interstate commerce and dominance of the SEC

Financial reporting in the US was initially very similar to the British accounting system. After its final emancipation from these roots in the 1930s, most of the literature sees US GAAP as the dominant power for the modern developments in accounting. Today's system started to evolve in the aftermath of the 1929 stock market crash and is built around strong enforcement. As a reaction to fraudulent financial information, the federal government took significant action and started regulating accountancy for listed companies – a policy field that had been virtually unregulated until then. Before the reforms, accounting was merely an issue of voluntary disclosures or stipulation by the stock exchanges, comparable to the UK's *laissez-faire* approach.

The foundations of today's accounting regulation are federal acts from the early 1930s, determining disclosure and enforcement rules for the securities market. This road to accounting intervention was singular as governments used mostly company law to regulate accounting. In the US, though, company law is not a federal responsibility, and so securities law only allowed intervention into corporate disclosures. Rather than forestalling future crises of the stock markets it is likely that the government's 'will to regulate', which is visible in many New Deal regulations, prompted this action. That the US regulation in accounting took the route via capital markets is more a historical accident than a careful consideration: the financial crisis happened across the globe, but nowhere else was regulation extended to the capital markets. This unique combination of an active administration, a financial crisis and a limiting constitution may be the primary reason why regulation and

institutions differ substantially between the US and our other countries. There, the nation state was not constrained – company law being
a federal responsibility in Germany since 1870/71 and Britain being a
non-federal state – and company law was the interventionist instrument
of choice. Formally, the US federal securities legislation complemented
the rather ineffective individual states' securities laws.

The new federal securities laws initiated the set-up of a governmental
financial reporting and enforcement agency equipped with multiple
competences: the Securities and Exchange Commission (SEC). While the
SEC stands alone when compared cross-nationally, it has counterparts in
the US: five governors running the organization, who are nominated by
the US president and confirmed by the Senate. Examples are the Federal
Trade Commission and the Federal Communications Commission. Like
these, the SEC bundles legislative, judicial and executive functions in one
governmental body (Skousen 1991). It is responsible for disclosure rules,
decides on penalties and investigates into cases of misconduct. Hence,
the SEC is integrated in such a way that it has control over all process
steps in financial reporting and its enforcement.

Since its foundation, the SEC is visible mainly in respect of its registration and filing procedures as well as its wide-ranging enforcement
activities. With its so-called 'forms' (for example Form 10-K for annual
reports) the SEC defines basic disclosure requirements. These forms are to
be filed with the Commission in order to not lose the initial registration
that is necessary for issuing securities and having them traded. Annual
reports (filed in the format of the respective forms) are made publicly
available by the SEC, now on its website. The filing process includes random checks of the reports and is part of the Commission's enforcement
activities. However, the main enforcement activities of the SEC are carried out by its division of enforcement, which investigates and litigates
when accounting fraud is suspected. Here, it may take up actions against
board members and the company's auditors. As a consequence the SEC
may ban securities from exchanges by withdrawing the registration or
decide on debarments from practising as auditor or manager. Next to
the severe penalties that the SEC imposes, sometimes in cooperation
with courts, the negative publicity of SEC investigations has a deterrent
effect.

Although the SEC pronounces fundamental rules for financial reporting, standard-setting is in general delegated to bodies under private law.
Analogous to the British development, the accounting profession set
up and controlled the first standard-setters. Professional bodies issued
their own rules on recognition and measurement regularly. After a

wide discontent with the two first standard-setters, today's Financial Accounting Standards Board (FASB), a non-governmental, not-for-profit organization, was set up and became operative in 1973. The FASB encompasses a wide array of business interests, which are represented by users, preparers and auditors. Although the SEC remains legally responsible for standard-setting, the FASB is officially acknowledged by the Commission as the competent standard-setter. Before, the SEC demanded reports to be prepared according to GAAP, but it left open how these GAAP are established. With the stabilization of standard-setting and the manifestation of basic principles in the conceptual framework, decision usefulness (for investors) became the agreed goal and benchmark of accounting.

Notwithstanding the SEC's interventions, auditing is a major part of enforcement in the US. External verification of accounts had been a common practice among listed firms before the federal securities legislation made auditing mandatory. Firms wanted to capture the positive signalling effect of higher credibility. For instance, about 90 percent of the NYSE-listed companies published audited financial statements before it became a federal requirement (Jennings 1958).

A shock for the globally well-appreciated system came with the series of accounting frauds in 2001 and 2002 that are associated with names like Enron or WorldCom. With the Sarbanes–Oxley Act of 2002, the legislator reacted to what was broadly perceived as a crisis of the world's most advanced financial reporting system. The act mainly contains a further strengthening of internal controls, enforcement, and puts forward harsher penalties for responsible managers. It is commonly understood as the most severe regulatory intervention since the securities regulation in the 1930s when the SEC was set up (Thompson and Lange 2003). An institutional novelty of the act is the Public Company Accounting Oversight Board (PCAOB), which oversees auditing, which was previously done by the profession, the similarity to the British POB and the German APAK being obvious. As all auditors need to register with the board to be allowed to perform audits for listed firms and registration may be cancelled in case of misconduct, the PCAOB is factually equipped with sanctioning powers.

Disclosure regulation changed only in minor respects compared to the golden age. With the stabilization of the private standard-setter FASB, the SEC's need to intervene into disclosure rules decreased. And while the FASB's predecessors were dominated by the accounting profession, the latter's importance was systematically reduced in favour of preparers and users of reports. In enforcement one can see an overall increase in regulative interventions, all of them being connected with the stipulations of the SOA. Here, the foundation of the PCAOB, increased internal controls and increased liability of managers and auditors have to be mentioned. Nevertheless, also in the field of enforcement the general set-up did not change substantially since the golden age of the nation state. What is visible, though, is a trend to strengthen government intervention as a reaction to political pressure, caused by corporate fraud and a stock market crisis.

## 2.4   Conclusion

In this chapter, we provided a brief summary of the differences in disclosure and enforcement regulation as applied in the golden age of the nation state in Germany, the US and the UK. We argued that the British system heavily relied on self-regulation of private actors while governmental initiatives were typical of the US and the German system. However, means of governmental intervention differed considerably in both of the latter countries. Germany relied on code law and jurisdiction, mainly in the area of company law; the US installed a powerful agency regulating all fields of financial reporting using securities law.

The chapter also showed that financial reporting has undergone substantial change since the golden age; this is in particular true for the European countries but also holds for the US. While literature commonly asserts that Germany has seen 'privatization' tendencies in this context and that the changes in the UK and US constitute a shift towards stronger state intervention, already the bird's eye view reveals that this conclusion would be too simple. The only thing that can safely be said is that the field of accountancy shows great regulatory dynamics. Statehood as the complex interplay of different actors requires looking in more detail at the changes and separating the seemingly different regulatory spheres of disclosure and enforcement. This will be done in Chapters 3 and 5.

# Part II

# New Governance Arrangements in Disclosure

The subject of this part is the changing governance of disclosure regulation. Disclosure regulation has witnessed a number of substantial transformations in recent years. The golden-age regulatory models in the respective nation states displayed an idiosyncratic interplay of a number of actors: the state, societal actors and private individuals. These actors' importance and interaction changed over time, partly due to national dynamics and partly due to internationalization and (mostly European) harmonization. New actors entered the stage and supplemented the workings of traditional institutions. The overarching question in this context is, how the governance of disclosure regulation changed and whether this has had implications for the role of the nation state in disclosure regulation? Convergence of regulatory models or abrogation of responsibilities may signal a new constellation of statehood.

Part II is subdivided into three chapters. Chapter 3 covers the golden-age nation state in greater detail and the dynamics of regulatory arrangements over time. Our analysis shows fundamental differences between the three cases: while the US system at the first glance shows a comparatively stable configuration since the golden age, the European systems – and the German system in particular – have experienced profound changes. The European harmonization process plays a decisive role as Europe interferes with its directives and regulations in national disclosure regulation. Chapter 3 provides evidence on how the public–private mix changed. Depending on the country in question, we find a diminished (Germany) as well as an augmented (UK) role of the state.

Governance was most profoundly rearranged with the decision of the EU to introduce internationally uniform accounting standards – now known as IFRS – as mandatory standards for listed groups. Chapter 4 focuses on this issue. The EU has chosen a regulatory concept that combines a transnational – that is, a private and international standard-setter – with a supranational approach. Chapter 4 looks at the new balance of international actors that leaves little regulatory scope for the nation state itself.

Finally, Chapter 5 discusses the struggle between private and public actors on stock exchanges. As the new financial reporting arrangements are intended to facilitate disclosure, its ultimate addressee is the investor, trading in shares. This trade typically takes place on an organized special-purpose market: a stock exchange. Stock exchanges, societal institutions at their inception, have also provided some disclosure regulation for the benefit of their participants, and they may have done this earlier and outside the nation state's scope. The increasing economic importance of stock exchanges and the increase in participation also called the nation state to action. Disclosure regulation of stock markets was now competing against or adding to state regulation. With its supreme powers, the nation state can crowd out stock market regulation or seek cooperation with the societal actors. As will be shown, the three countries in our study display differing regulatory paths. In two of our countries, Germany and the UK, state intervention remained relatively low, and societal forms of governance prevail. The US represents the opposite case. State regulation has crowded out nearly all private regulation.

# 3
# Rise and Fall of the Golden-Age Nation State Model

While Chapter 2 provided a brief overview of accounting regulation in the UK, Germany and the US, this chapter considers the organization of disclosure regulation, and in particular the field of standard-setting in greater detail. Even though accounting rules (standards, broadly defined) can be understood as all kinds of regulation that companies have to consider in their financial reporting, we deal only with a subset of this regulation here. This is due to the fact that we distinguish between disclosure rules of stock exchanges (Chapter 5) and general rules, which have to be applied independently from the listing at a certain stock exchange. The present chapter covers how the latter are determined by the major actors in the three economies Germany, the UK and the US.

Changes in the three countries happened at different points in time. While structural adaptations in the US occurred already in the early 1930s, the two European countries have witnessed a two-stage process. The first steps of European harmonization allowed the respective nation states to hold on to their specific traditions wherever possible and practical. This stage of 'acceptance seeking' will be described here. The second stage of ever-closer harmonization in Europe is deferred to Chapter 4. As the US transformations happened long before the Europeanization, we will first consider to which extent the US model influenced accounting governance in Europe.

## 3.1 Standard-setting in the US: Not quite Europe's precursor

The US entered into regulating financial reporting by creating the SEC with extensive powers to regulate accounting for listed companies. From this beginning, the US has witnessed a trial-and-error process to devise a cooperative model between the state and the actors from the private sector. This model for the capital markets has eventually influenced all types of company accounting in the US as standards for listed companies provided the model for the GAAP. This federal regulation is not fully rooted in written law, and it left company law, which is a matter for the states, untouched. The focus on listed firms forms only one of the major differences between Europe and the US.

The first attempt in developing uniform accounting standards was neither rooted in state intervention nor distinctively in professional self-regulation. Instead, it dates back to an initiative by the New York Stock Exchange (NYSE) in 1917 involving the American Institute of Accountants (AIA) (Wolk and Tearney 1997). This cooperation resulted in basic accounting principles which had to be followed by all the companies listed on the exchange (Hendriksen 1977). The origins of universal financial reporting rules for listed firms can be found in the securities legislation following the stock market crash of 1929 (Morgan and Previts 1984): accounting regulation was ushered in with the Securities Act (SA) of 1933 and the Securities Exchange Act (SEA) of 1934 (primary acts) when the federal government decided to intervene substantially into financial reporting, most visibly with the SEC, which was founded in this context. The legislation puts ultimate responsibility for the development of accounting standards for publicly traded (listed) companies with the SEC. However, the private sector has played a major role in standard-setting from the beginnings of the new model (Sanders 1936). As a result, US GAAP have been influenced substantially by the pronouncements of private bodies.

Even though pronouncements have been promulgated without explicit reference to the SEC, the SEC is no passive bystander during the processes of standard-setting. It had (and still has) considerable influence in the development of accounting practice, and the SEC always made it clear that it would step in and set standards itself if the private-sector standard-setter fails to meet the regulator's expectations (Hendriksen 1977). The SEC primarily participated through comments on drafts of regulations. It also exercised direct influence through the publication of Regulation S-X (covering financial statements), Regulation S-K (covering non-financial disclosure about the operations of business), Accounting Series Releases of the Commission or the Chief Accountant, and official decisions (Roberts *et al.* 2005).

## Towards a stable configuration: Pre-FASB developments

Three episodes of private standard-setting can be observed in the US, involving different institutional structures of the private standard-setter and a different relationship between the standard-setter and the SEC

(Heintges 2005). Those episodes are identified with the following bodies: (1) the Committee on Accounting Procedure (CAP) of the American Institute of Certified Public Accountants (AICPA)[1] (1936–59); (2) its successor, the Accounting Principles Board (APB), which was also run under the Institute's umbrella (1959–73); and (3) the existing independent Financial Accounting Standards Board (FASB), which ended the AICPA's standard-setting responsibility in 1973. While these episodes did not ultimately change the balance between the nation state and the private actors, they saw the emergence, over time, of an acceptable private-sector organizational form: the result of this process is the effective – or at least acceptable – organization of a private standard-setting body in the US. The latest arrangement also forms the blueprint for institutional reform in Europe.

In April 1938, the SEC decided to call explicitly upon the profession in a statement of its administrative policy in the form of Accounting Series Release (ASR) No. 4 (Puxty *et al.* 1987). Subsequent to the release of ASR No. 4, a 21-member CAP was created in 1938 (Wolk and Tearney 1997). Members were predominately active practitioners, and they served without compensation. The CAP originally wanted to develop a comprehensive statement of accounting principles as a general guide to solve specific practical problems. However, it suffered from time constraints and pressures from the SEC (Haller 1994). The Committee's Accounting Research Bulletins (ARB), frequently issued on an *ad hoc* basis, addressed specific accounting issues and allowed the acceptance of alternative accounting practices without an underlying reporting logic.

Particularly during the 1950s, the CAP was criticized for moving too slowly in preparing written expressions of GAAP (Hendriksen 1977), for allowing too many alternatives to accounting methods and for paying insufficient attention to fundamentals. This was partly due to its limited organizational role: the CAP did not have a broadly based authority. In fact, its pronouncements were not even binding for members of the AICPA (Miller *et al.* 1998). Because it lacked authority, the CAP was generally unable to be decisive in its pronouncements.

Criticism of the CAP's operative inefficiency was often accompanied by the claim that its standard-setting procedures were conceptually unsound as they were lacking a theoretical basis. Especially the Institute called for a conceptual approach, and it was decided that an emphasis on research had to be an important feature of a new model to replace the piecemeal method that had been followed for 20 years (Hicks 1969). The Institute set up a Special Committee on Research Program in December 1957. Its report recommended the CAP's replacement by a new institution, the APB (Mutchler and Smith 1984).[2]

The APB, which was also a committee of the AICPA, was established in 1959. To tackle conceptual issues, the Accounting Research Division was founded to accompany the Board's standard-setting process. Particularly in response to complaints about the lack of systematic research, the Board was initially given the task of developing a so-called 'conceptual framework' to provide guidance for the settling of issues and to improve written expressions. The APB's official pronouncements were intended to be based primarily on studies of the Accounting Research Division; its conclusions were to be supported by reasoning. It was given a full-time research staff of six individuals and a director of accounting research. The Board was drawn primarily from the accounting profession but also included members representing industry, the academic community and government. However, none of the efforts made by the research division were particularly helpful to the APB, and the research studies were not accepted by the profession (Wolk and Tearney 1997).

Disapproval was voiced on a number of issues. In regard to the standard-setting process there were two points of criticism: first, the exposure for tentative APB opinions was too limited and occurred too late in the process; and second, the standard-setting process was too long and subject to too many outside pressures (Roberts *et al.* 2005). A major institutional shortcoming was seen in the APB's supposed lack of independence, which allegedly existed due to the part-time nature of the APB (Rockness and Nikolai 1977). While there were many causes for its demise, perhaps the most significant one was the lack of a broadly based mandate: while the Institute prescribed adherence to the pronouncements, the SEC never formally endorsed the Board as a source of authority while it existed. As a result of these fundamental criticisms, the rapid change in financial institutions and the numerous abuses of financial reporting in the 1960s and early 1970s, proposals were made to reconsider the organizational structure for setting accounting principles once more. These proposals also encompassed the study of the basic objectives of financial accounting, which would then serve as guidance for new accounting principles.

When the academic American Accounting Association (AAA)[3] proposed appointing an interdisciplinary commission to consider how accounting standards should be developed in 1971, the Institute reacted promptly by appointing its own seven-men group to study the establishment of accounting principles. That study group became known as the Wheat Committee. Its recommendations included the creation of a Financial Accounting Foundation (FAF) as an institution separated from the accounting profession. Further, the formation of an FASB under the roof of this foundation was proposed, which should be complemen-ted by a Financial Accounting Advisory Council. The almost immediate adoption of the Wheat Committee's recommendations resulted in the creation of the third US standard-setting body that is still active today. The AICPA was instrumental in establishing the FASB as an independent standard-setting body by dissolving its own APB (Sprouse 1987). It also strengthened its institutional commitment: shortly after the inaugura-tion of the FASB, the Institute's Code of Professional Ethics was amended by a rule obliging members to comply with promulgated authoritative financial accounting pronouncements.

During its 14-year-long life, the APB issued 31 authoritative opinions, which the FASB also acknowledges in its Rules of Procedure. The opin-ions were generally more definitive than that of the CAP. The enhanced authoritative status of APB opinions was a critical and important differ-ence in the development of private-sector standard-setting.

### Endorsed cooperation: The FASB

The organizational structure of standard-setting goes back on the pro-positions of the Wheat Committee. Standards are set by the FASB. The Board's members are not serving part time, as did the members of the two previous bodies. Instead they receive full pay and are obliged not to work in their usual businesses while serving on the Board (FASB 2004b; Larson and Holstrum 1973). They are selected by the trustees of the FAF and have a diverse background, consisting of users and preparers of financial statements, academics as well as members of the profession.

The success of the FASB's endeavours has two sources, one being procedural and the other organizational. The Wheat Committee had recommended the set-up of a practice-oriented standard-setter. Theor-etical development of accounting was seen as a task of the AICPA and the AAA (Larson and Holstrum 1973; Zeff 1999). The Board, however, did not want to outsource the foundational parts of standard-setting and decided to work on its own conceptual framework, a collection of broad principles that is supposed to enhance consistency among the binding pronouncements (Zeff 1999). This procedural decision is often considered as the reason for the FASB's success and persistence as it can be interpreted as the end of the predecessors' piecemeal approaches.

The second source of success, not discussed often, is its distance to the accounting profession and its professionalism. A crucial role is played by the FAF. Ownership of the foundation rests with the trust-ees, who were first appointed by the FAF's constituent organizations such as the AICPA, the AAA and other professional bodies. The trustees now typically co-opt future trustees, who are nominated by financial accountancy and governmental bodies such as the AICPA and the AAA (financial) or the National Conference of State Legislators and the US Conference of Mayors (government). The composition of the trustees reflects, like FASB membership, the wider community of financial accounting, including preparers, users, members of the profession and government officials, who are a small minority. The trustees also select all members of the standard-setting body (Miller 2002). Next to staffing the respective bodies, financing the standard-setter was the other important function of the foundation. It has become redundant with a reform in 2004 that introduced a fee-based system amid worries of increased dependence from sponsors. A Financial Accounting Standards Advisory Council (FaSAC) consults the FASB and analyses short-term developments in the financial reporting environment (FASB 2005). Exhibit 3.1 charts the organizational structure of private standard-setting in the US.

In 1973, the SEC issued its ASR No. 150, in which the commission explicitly recognized the FASB's pronouncements as determining GAAP. This backing by the authority established the FASB as the primary agent exercising substantial authority over the determination of financial reporting standards (Morgan and Previts 1984). Practically, the role of the SEC now rests on its veto powers and the participation in the FASB's deliberations (Newman 1981). Ultimately, it took nearly 40 years until the state authorities recognized a private standard-setter officially.

The two most important types of pronouncements from the FASB are the Statements of Financial Accounting Standards (SFAS) and the Statements of Financial Accounting Concepts (SFAC). While the latter represent the Board's conceptual framework, SFAS are the actual accounting standards. Furthermore, there are FASB Interpretations (FIN) and Technical Bulletins that deal with urgent matters or interpret older standards. Since 1984 the Emerging Issues Task Force (EITF) has pronounced its Consensuses and Issues (FASB 2004a). The Task Force is formed by members of the FASB and the SEC and solves urgent issues not foreseen in the standards (FASB 2004a). Meanwhile, the Task Force has become the second most important source of US GAAP.

The development of the main pronouncements, the SFAS, follows a predefined procedure known as Due Process. This process has been adopted by the FASB from the Federal Administrative Procedures Act of 1946, which lays out procedures for federal authorities and departments for developing regulations. The right of interested and concerned parties to

Exhibit 3.1  Organizational structure of US financial accounting standard-setters

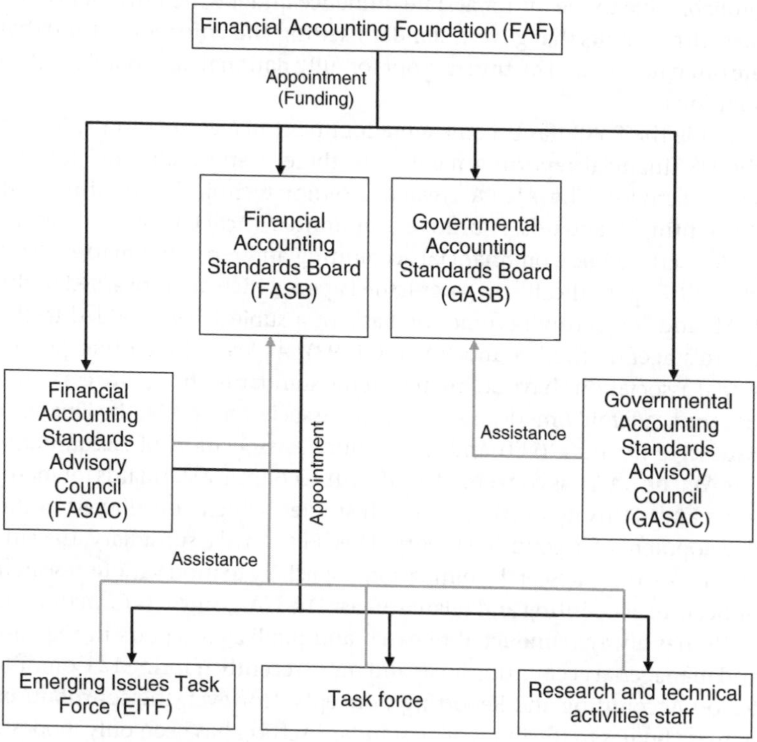

```
                    ┌─────────────────────────────────────┐
                    │ Financial Accounting Foundation (FAF) │
                    └─────────────────────────────────────┘
                              Appointment
                               (Funding)

        ┌────────────────┬──────────────┬──────────────┬───────────────┐

                  ┌──────────────┐  ┌──────────────┐
                  │  Financial   │  │ Governmental │
                  │  Accounting  │  │  Accounting  │
                  │ Standards    │  │ Standards    │
                  │  Board       │  │  Board       │
                  │  (FASB)      │  │  (GASB)      │
                  └──────────────┘  └──────────────┘

┌──────────────┐                                      ┌──────────────┐
│  Financial   │                                      │ Governmental │
│  Accounting  │         Appointment    Assistance    │  Accounting  │
│  Standards   │                                      │  Standards   │
│  Advisory    │                                      │  Advisory    │
│  Council     │                                      │  Council     │
│  (FASAC)     │                                      │  (GASAC)     │
└──────────────┘                                      └──────────────┘

          Assistance

┌──────────────────┐  ┌──────────────┐  ┌──────────────────────┐
│ Emerging Issues  │  │              │  │ Research and technical│
│  Task Force      │  │  Task force  │  │    activities staff   │
│  (EITF)          │  │              │  │                       │
└──────────────────┘  └──────────────┘  └──────────────────────┘
```

*Source*: Pellens (2001), adapted.

participate in the form of submitted comments features prominently (FASB 2004b). With the adoption of this procedure into its due process, the FASB seeks to prevent criticism on legitimacy and transparency issues. Until today, the FASB has pronounced 159 SFAS, numerous EITF Issues and composed a relatively far-reaching conceptual framework. Recently the Board started to cooperate closely with another globally important standard-setter, namely the IASB, which will be discussed in greater detail in Chapter 4. While the first collaboration merely represented an exchange of opinions, the Boards now work together on joint projects with shared results. With this cooperation the FASB increased its effort to achieve the long-term goal of globally converging financial reporting rules. With a set of standards other than the FASB's reaching for global prominence, the Board decided to embrace international cooperation. This is, as will be seen throughout the book, an exception, probably due to the minimal state influence under which the FASB operates. Other actors that govern standard-setting and enforcement and that are often dominated by the state opt for fully national (and public-sector) solutions.

While the FASB has become a predominant player next to the SEC in the US financial reporting regulation, there is still additional private-sector activity. The AICPA created a senior technical committee, the Accounting Standards Executive Committee (AcSEC), to serve as its policy-setting body on financial accounting and reporting matters. This committee periodically prepares Issue Papers which are forwarded to the FASB and frequently become the basis of a subject being added to the Board's agenda (Rodda and Volkert 1993). At least three other professional associations have an interest in the standard-setting process in the US: the academic American Accounting Association (AAA), the Financial Executive Institute (FEI) and the National Association of Accountants (NAA). The AAA has concerned itself with accounting standards for many years and sponsored various research studies, which contributed to the development of accounting theory. The FEI formed a subsidiary, the Financial Executive Research Foundation, especially to fund various research projects in accounting and related areas. The NAA, since its formation in 1919, has always conducted research and published reports in the cost and managerial accounting areas and more recently it formed a Committee on Accounting and Reporting Concepts. However, the contribution of these bodies to the immediate standard-setting has been only modest.

New regulations introduced with the SOA of 2002 had implications for the organization and the funding of the FASB as well as for accounting standards applicable to listed firms under SEC supervision. These developments will be discussed in Chapter 9.

## 3.2   Standard-setting in Europe: National developments and early European interventions

Within the last few decades Europe – be it in the form of the EEC, the European Communities or the EU– has become a major player in the regulation of financial reporting. Particularly accounting rules have been subject to harmonization. These harmonization attempts had already started with the early Treaty of Rome of 1957 ('Treaty Establishing the European Community'), which formulated the goal of establishing 'an economic equal level playing field in the Community' (Haller 2002).

## The company law framework for European interventions

European legislation has mostly seen accounting in the context of company law, and the first harmonization of accounting rules technically took the route of directives. Most EEC members had insider economies and placed little emphasis on the financial markets. With the role of the financier being more pronounced than the role of the shareholder-investor across Europe, company law seemed the obvious field for harmonization efforts. Unlike in the US, the legal arrangements allowed European initiatives in this field. As directives have to be transformed into law by the respective national regulators, accounting harmonization in Europe became a complex interplay between the 'federalist' actor 'Europe' and the member states. Exhibit 3.2 lists the numerous harmonization initiatives in company law. Out of the 12 directives only 2 have an immediate impact on national accounting regulation, namely the Fourth (78/660/EEC) and the Seventh (83/349/EEC).

Active harmonization of accounting regulation started when the Fourth European Council Directive (78/660/EEC) was passed. It established rather detailed minimum requirements for company accounts (individual or single, as opposed to group or consolidated accounts) of certain companies with limited liability. Efforts were made in order to achieve a set of commonly acceptable prescriptions for disclosure levels, formats of accounts and measurement attributes. That harmonization was a contentious issue can be understood from the duration of the legislative process at the European level: the first draft of the Fourth Directive had been published in 1971 and it took seven years to arrive at the final version.

The finally accepted version of the Directive had to combine different traditions and approaches. To achieve harmonization, the Directive incorporated legalistic or procedural approaches such as regulations from the (then) recently modernized German Stock Corporation Act of 1965 (AktG). At the same time an output- and user-oriented true and fair view override was included in the Directive that goes back to UK company law (Alexander 1993; Nobes 1993; Ordelheide 1993; 1996). This diversity of traditions was practically impossible to reconcile as all had strong national lobbies. No side wanted to give in, and the deliberations on European accounting standards led to a great number of options, all of which seemed necessary in order to gain the support of the member states involved. The Seventh Directive (83/349/EEC), which followed in 1983, complemented the Fourth by establishing common rules for consolidated financial reports. While mandatory disclosure of

44

*Exhibit 3.2*  EU company law directives (including draft directives)

| Directive | Date | Subject matter |
| --- | --- | --- |
| First council directive (68/151/EEC) | March 9, 1968 | Disclosure requirements |
| Second council directive (77/91/EEC) | December 13, 1976 | Capital maintenance rules |
| Third council directive (78/855/EEC) | October 9, 1978 | Mergers of public limited liability companies |
| Fourth council directive (78/660/EEC) | July 25, 1978 | Financial statements |
| Fifth council directive (Proposal, not implemented) | | Structure of public limited liability companies, power and obligations of their bodies |
| Sixth council directive (82/891/EEC) | December 17, 1982 | Division of public limited liability companies |
| Seventh council directive (83/349/EEC) | June 13, 1983 | Consolidated accounts |
| Eighth council directive (84/253/EEC) | April 10, 1984 | Statutory audits of financial reports |
| Ninth council directive (Did not reach the Proposal stadium) | | Law of group accounts |
| Tenth council directive (Proposal, not implemented) | | Cross-border mergers of limited liability companies |
| Eleventh council directive (89/666/EEC) | December 21, 1989 | Disclosure requirements by certain types of companies governed by the law of another state |
| Twelfth council directive (89/667/EEC) | December 21, 1989 | Regulation on single-member private limited liability companies |
| Directive (86/EC) | October 8, 2001 | Supplementing the Statute for a European Company, concerning employees involvement |
| Directive (58/EC) | July 15, 2003 | Takeover bids |
| Directive (25/EC) | April 21, 2004 | Cross-border mergers of limited liability companies |
| Directive (68/EC) | September 6, 2006 | Amending council directive 77/91/EEC |

*Source*: European Commission (2006).

consolidated financial reports was introduced, with regard to formats and measurement rules it referred mainly to the Fourth Directive.

As Council Directives have to be incorporated into each member state's legal system, the national parliaments' power to set accounting law at their sole discretion was curtailed. Nonetheless, the directives' scope for choice allowed a decision on many contentious issues in European accounting by national parliaments. Hence, major differences in accounting remained and the goal of achieving comparable statements across Europe was not fully achieved. The directives' effect was mainly the introduction of advanced accounting regulation in member states with underdeveloped laws while the desired harmonization of more advanced systems such as Germany or the UK was limited (Flower 2004). The next section will trace these developments in the UK and Germany in some detail.

While both the UK and Germany use company law to regulate accounting, these countries put different emphasis on the accounting profession. Its role is rather pronounced in the UK and modest in Germany. This also implies that the type and level of private involvement in setting accounting rules differs. We will consider both countries in turn.

### Development of financial reporting rules in the UK

In the UK, accounting rules first emerged from competing professional bodies, whose activities eventually unified into setting standards. Additional legal regulations governing financial reporting requirements are found in the Companies Acts, which are under the responsibility of the Department of Trade and Industry (DTI) (Lamb and Whittington 2001).[4] Currently, UK accounting requirements are laid down in both company law and accounting standards.

In 1844, the British Joint Stock Companies Act required companies to keep books of account and to present a 'full and fair' balance sheet without specifying the content of financial reports (Edey 1979). In a subsequent Companies Act of 1856 the whole legislation on compulsory accounting was deleted from the company law, leaving companies broad scope in accounting matters. Until 1900 there was a complete absence of statutory regulation except for special industries. This left the market to operate freely and, as a result, accounting practice varied considerably over time and over industries (Lee 1984b). The accounting profession – through its self-organizing bodies such as the Institute of Chartered Accountants in England and Wales (ICAEW) or the even older Institute of Chartered Accountants of Scotland (ICAS) – made recommendations on accounting practice, but these were not binding.

Disseminating financial information was not universally regarded as good practice. A consensus in favour of disclosure started to evolve in the UK in the late 1920s. The Royal Mail case of 1931 marked the turning point for disclosure in the UK. The declining fortunes of the Royal Mail Steam Packet Company had been disguised by the use of secret reserves which were fed into the income statement and turned a trading loss into an overall profit. It was agreed that procedures like these should no longer be admitted (even though they were regarded as 'best practice' until then). There were two divergent positions in the profession as to how new rules should be implemented: one group thought that accounting and auditing could be improved by detailed legislative prescriptions; the other group opined that it should rather be the accountancy profession who should seek to achieve improvements, and the legislator might subsequently choose to give statutory support (Lee 1984a). Finally, the tradition of minimal intervention by government prevailed and the second route was taken.

With the imminent accession to Europe, the multitude of accounting rules seemed arcane, and the profession embarked on a journey towards unification. The largest of the professional bodies, the ICAEW, issued a 'Statement of Intent on Accounting Standards in the 1970s'. As a result, the ICAEW set up the Accounting Standards Steering Committee (ASSC), which was soon to be renamed as the ASC. The Institute of Chartered Accountants of Scotland (the ICAEW's sister institution) and the Institute of Chartered Accountants in Ireland (ICAI) co-sponsored the initiative. From its inception, the three most influential professional accounting bodies in the UK were already on board (Leach 1981). The predecessor organizations of the Chartered Institute of Management Accountants (CIMA), the Association of Chartered Certified Accountants (ACCA) and the Chartered Institute of Public Finance and Accountancy (CIPFA) had joined by 1976. This group of professional bodies became known as the Consultative Committee of Accountancy Bodies (CCAB) (Pong and Whittington 1996). The accountancy bodies jointly 'owned' the ASC and each retained the veto power over any standard. In consequence, the ASC had little authority, and this is reflected in its method of operating. The councils of each of the Committee's sponsoring bodies had to adopt each Statements of Standard Accounting Practice (SSAP) before it could be issued in final form.

This setting posed fundamental questions about the interests served by the ASC and its competence to make regulatory judgements in the public interest. These concerns led to a review of the standard-setting process which started in 1978. After an extensive period of consultation and discussion the Watts Report was published three years later. The Report resulted in some widening of the membership of ASC in order to relax the apparent stake of the auditors in the standard-setting process. Generally, the Report maintained the view that standard-setting was the primary function of the accounting profession.

Europe did not loom large in UK accounting until the early 1980s. The first major influence was the transformation of the Fourth Council Directive into national law with the Companies Act of 1981. The corresponding Seventh Council Directive, however, only became law with the Companies Act of 1989. This made the UK a forerunner with regard to company accounts, but not in regard to consolidated accounts of groups. With the transposition of the Fourth Directive into British law, the number of detailed legal prescriptions multiplied. In consequence, both standard-setters and preparers of financial reports found their discretion to act significantly constrained. The European regulation specified in quite some detail which accounting treatments were applicable and how a financial report was to be structured. Contrasting the previous national practice with the new European approach, this constituted a major interference by the law and reflected the procedural notion of accounting regulations that most other member states shared.

The Companies Act of 1989 gave a legal recognition to accounting standards for the first time. The Act defined standards as 'statements of standard accounting practice issued by such ... bodies as may be prescribed by regulations'. The passing of the new Companies Act coincided by no means incidentally with several initiatives by the CCAB. When the EC regulations for company accounts were implemented in 1981, the overall structure of standard-setting had remained the same. In the meantime it was increasingly felt that the rather loose type of cooperation in standard-setting warranted improvement. Controversies about current cost accounting and the overall low credibility of the ASC as an effective means for regulating accounting practice clearly signalled a need for improvement, and only a credible set of standards would help fighting the increased influence of the state sector and leave the accounting supremacy with the profession. The Seventh Council Directive thus proved to be a catalyst for a major overhaul in standard-setting (Whittington 1989). In November 1987, the Dearing Committee was appointed by the CCAB to put forward changes for the standard-setting process (Eccles and Holt 2005).

The Dearing Report, published late in 1988, addressed the issue of authority and proposed a new structure for accounting standard-setting. Dearing proposed a move away from self-regulation by the accounting profession towards wider private-sector regulation (Whittington 1989). The standard-setting body should become independent from the profession, reflecting the move that was made in the US about 15 years ago. However, Dearing recommended that accounting standards should remain, as far as possible, the responsibility of preparers, users and auditors, rather than becoming a matter of regulation by law. The Report provided the blueprint for some sweeping reforms in the area of standard-setting (Fearnley and Hines 2003).

To tackle issues of legitimacy, the standard-setting process was to reach out into the wider policy arena. It was suggested to involve the whole community of interests and to use separate professional capabilities to translate policy into standards. For this purpose, a FRC was set up as an umbrella institution for financial reporting regulators under a private law arrangement (see also Chapter 7 for more detail). With its Directors all being appointed by the Secretary of State for Trade and Industry (except the Chief Executive, who needs approval also by the Bank of England (BoE)), the FRC was placed in the sphere of public-sector influence. The standard-setter ASC was reformed from a committee entirely made up of part-time volunteers into a permanent body with full- and part-time members and renamed the ASB. Membership of the ASB is extended by the FRC to users and preparers of statements, academics and the profession. Its composition, thus, resembles that of the FASB, its US counterpart, with the exception that the latter's members are all full-time. The reformed Board was set up to issue accounting standards for all company reporting – not only for listed companies – and was thus given more authority and independence from the accounting professional bodies than the ASC. The new regulatory structure is shown in Exhibit 3.3.

The Chairman and Technical Director of the ASB serve full-time together with their technical staff and up to eight part-time members of the Board. The ASB also received the legal authority to publish standards in its own name. For this, the Board is acknowledged by the UK government. Still, the ASB's standards are not mandatory, but large companies need to explain whether their reports comply with the ASB's standards. This 'true and fair override' is a legacy of the multiple approaches to financial reporting in the past: if an auditor agrees that the application of a standard does not result in a truthful representation, financial reports may resort to reporting alternatives (Livne and McNichols 2003). The 'true and fair override' is peculiar to the UK and can be explained only by its *laissez-faire* history.

*Exhibit 3.3*   Organizational structure of UK financial accounting standard-setters

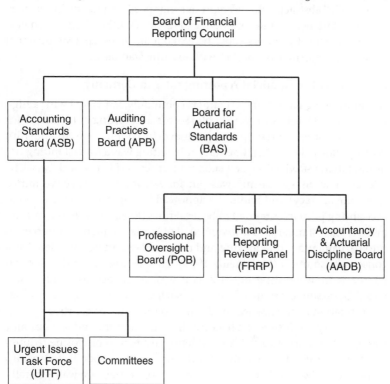

*Source*: FRC (2007b), adapted.

The ASB's due process includes publishing exposure drafts and standards for comment, often after a discussion paper. Although the CCAB bodies are invited to comment, they now have no veto power. The most important pronouncements of the Board are labelled Financial Reporting Standards (FRS). The SSAP as issued by its predecessor until 1990 were adopted by the ASB and have gradually been amended or superseded by new FRS. Since 1999 the Board has a conceptual framework to which it refers in its standard-setting procedures. This framework can be found in the so-called Statement of Principles and, like the FASB's SFAC, it does not contain binding accounting rules for constituents. Next to the FRS, of which the Board has promulgated 29 so far, other pronouncements are relevant to accounting practice. The Urgent Issues

Task Force (UITF) issues interpretations of accounting standards, the so-called 'UITF abstracts'. Bodies representing specific industry sectors may develop Statements of Recommended Practice (SORP). These statements are not specifically endorsed by the ASB but are given an assurance that they do not apparently conflict with existing standards.

## Development of financial reporting rules in Germany

Accounting regulation in Germany is commonly associated with a high degree of state intervention. Public-sector accounting rules date back to the first simple prescriptions included in codified law in the 18th century (Born 2002). Parliamentary rule setting was a long-standing tradition having survived several economic crises and two world wars. The relevant law on accounting was put forward by the respective ministries (bureaucracy) and had to be approved by the parliament. German accounting principles tended to be legal rules (*Rechtsnormen*) rather than professional standards (*Fachnormen*). Lobbyists frequently intervened into parliamentary rule making and the final law can be considered as a consensual solution (Ordelheide 1999). This distinguished the German approach to accounting practice as it was never seen as overly influenced by a single group of interests such as the auditing profession. Interpretation of the law was under the competency of courts.

Mandatory disclosure of a balance sheet and a profit and loss account was first introduced in 1884. Subsequently, numerous disclosure requirements were included, mainly into the commercial code but also into corporation law. While the level of mandatory disclosure was generally high, the requirements to prepare group accounts came relatively late with the AktG in 1965. This is notable as group accounts are the primary informational source for investors on stock markets.

One of the unique features of (traditional) German accounting is its interconnection with taxation. One can easily understand why this is unique within our country set. In the UK, the profession developed competing and often not binding standards, which made the computation of the tax base unreliable. In the US, federal intervention touched only listed firms, and there was no possibility to determine the tax base for all firms. It was in the 1920s when the German legislator decided that financial reports should be the basis for determining taxable income. It was initially intended that company accounts determine the contents of tax accounts, but the underlying economics and some legal regulation made tax jurisdiction a relevant source of accounting rules (reverse determination – *umgekehrte Maßgeblichkeit*). While it would have, in theory, been possible to develop separate accounting rules for group reporting to remedy the adverse effects on financial reporting, this did not happen. Accounting rules for company and group accounts remained fairly similar. A possible explanation for the persistence of this inverse regulatory hierarchy is the low relevance of accounting information for decision-making purposes in the German insider economy (see Chapter 1).

However, even for Germany it would be wrong to assume that laws and regulations were the only source of accounting regulation. In fact, there used to be significant involvement of private actors as the relevant laws stipulate that financial reports have to be rendered according to German Generally Accepted Accounting Principles (*Grundsätze ordnungsgemäßer Buchführung*; hereafter, German GAAP). German GAAP consist of inputs from different sources, which are neither clearly defined nor published as an anthology. In a common understanding German GAAP are made up of jurisprudence, regular practice, academic input and professional opinions. The latter exerted significant influence on financial reporting in practice (Marten *et al.* 2003), albeit in a roundabout way: while no official standard-setter existed, the IDW pronounced standards for auditing, which, in turn, were informative for balance sheet preparers and relevant in court decisions (Schruff 2006). But while private participation in formulating GAAP did exist, it is important to stress the ultimate competency of courts: finally judges decided in their interpretations of law and adjudication of 'good business practice' what was considered to be GAAP.

Germany enacted the Fourth and Seventh Council Directives simultaneously in 1985 by means of an omnibus bill, the so-called Accounting Directives Act. This transposition caused a shift of many regulations from GAAP, but more so from specific company laws, to the commercial code. The commercial code's paragraphs concerning financial reporting skyrocketed, but at the same time the provisions in the corporation laws were reduced. The immediate legislation also applied to more firms. Qualitatively, however, the accounting system remained unchanged due to the wide scope for choice within the accounting directives. Controlling whether the overall aims of the directives were met, the Commission was satisfied with the adopted regulation and the ensuing practice. There was only one significant intervention, which also occurred comparatively late: Germany was ordered by the European Court of Justice in 1998 to mend its transposition of disclosure requirements for public companies (C-191/95). In the court's opinion, Germany had failed to transpose stipulations of the two directives to define appropriate sanctions for companies that are reluctant to obey the respective disclosure obligations. The reason for the Commission's complaint was the fact that only less than 10 percent of the affected companies complied with the disclosure obligations.

Even though the scope of the national parliament on setting accounting rules was diminished through European legislation, formulating accounting rules still remained a duty of the public sector and not of any private actors. The first changes in German financial reporting towards an outsider-oriented disclosure system occurred in the 1980s when the legislator initiated reforms that focused on listed companies and securities trading. In different regulatory waves the legislator tried to improve the legal framework for investors, especially with the so-called Financial Market Promotion Acts (FFG), which are discussed in greater detail in the Chapters 5 and 7. Already influenced by European legislation, an important component of the FFG was the Securities Trading Act of 1994 (WpHG), which introduced additional disclosure rules for listed companies. In the context of insider trading, *ad hoc* publicity was made a mandatory component of disclosure.

A landmark change happened in 1998 with an omnibus bill named the Corporate Sector Supervision and Transparency Act (KonTraG). It contained an amendment to the Commercial Law (HGB) that authorized the Federal Ministry of Justice to accredit a private standard-setting institution, and in the same year the German Accounting Standards Committee (GASC) was appointed. The GASC is an incorporated association under private law (*eingetragener Verein*, e.V.), membership to which is open to companies and the interested public. Its Steering Committee (*Vorstand*), elected by the General Assembly, appoints the GASB, consisting mainly of users and preparers of financial reports as well as members of the profession. The GASB was authorized to develop recommendations for group accounting, advise the Ministry of Justice on accounting legislation proposals and represent the Federal Republic of Germany in international standardization bodies. In the contract with GASC, the Ministry of Justice committed itself to involve the Board in all legislation proposals concerned with accounting. The major task of the GASB, however, was to develop accounting standards for consolidated financial statements independently. These standards would not represent official accounting rules until the Federal Ministry of Justice would review and publish them. While this may sound like a careful scrutiny, the actual process is of a rubber-stamping nature. So far the GASB has pronounced 15 Standards labelled German Financial Reporting Standards (*Deutsche Rechnungslegungs Standards*, DRS), while its Financial Reporting Interpretations Committee (*Rechnungslegung Interpretation Committee*,

Exhibit 3.4 Structure of GASC/GASB standard-setting

*Source*: (DRSC 2007), adapted.

RIC) issued five interpreting documents. The organizational structure of private German standard-setting is shown in Exhibit 3.4.

As with the US and UK boards, the GASB's standard-setting process includes a due process with the publication of exposure documents and the analysis of constituents' comments. An envisaged conceptual framework project has been cancelled, mostly due to the fast-changing focus of the Board: with the rise of the IASB as extraterritorial standard-setter relevant in Germany, the GASB merely participates in the IASB's due process and regulates financial reporting of companies that do not fall into the IASB's scope (DRSC 2007).

The GASB was not the only private standard-setter to have gained importance in German (group) accounting. In the same year when the GASC was appointed, that is in 1998, the Capital Raising Facilitation Act (KapAEG) was adopted and brought further significant change. Listed (parent) companies were now allowed to publish their consolidated financial statements following recognized international accounting standards, in practice either IFRS or US GAAP. The Act was supposed to enhance German firms' abilities to access foreign capital markets (especially in the US) because the widely used reconciliation statements had been proven costly for preparers and puzzling for users. As US GAAP statements of US firms were accepted for listing on Germany's stock exchanges already, the legislator saw its act as abolishing the discrimination of domestic companies. Moreover, the act was intended to strengthen the German capital market by introducing investor-oriented financial reports. Retrospectively, the first intention turned out to be less important, as only a small number of firms found these new rules attractive enough to list in the US. The second reason was more relevant: large listed groups had before repeatedly and with increasing emphasis expressed their concerns that German accounting rules were not informative enough for investors (Schildbach 2002; Thiele and Tschesche 1997). In fact, a large number of companies used the opportunity that they had lobbied for (Born 2002) and applied IFRS or US GAAP after the KapAEG had been passed.

The decision not to require group accounts according to German GAAP any longer was accompanied by strong objections from jurisprudence. Critics pointed to a lack of legitimacy of the externally set rules and to the impossibility of influencing further standard-setting (Bratton 2007; Ebert 2002; Kirchhof 2000; Schildbach 2004). Accounting literature castigated the declining comparability among German group accounts – some being rendered according to German laws and German GAAP, others according to IFRS or US GAAP (Börsig and Coenenberg 1998). As standards for group accounting totally eluded from the influence of German authorities, private standard-setting reached its climax during the period in which this legislation was valid. From 2005 this has become a matter of EU regulation, precluding a further extension of the KapAEG.

## 3.3  Conclusion

There is no unified formal pattern that emerges from the discussion. In the US, legislation does not prescribe standards but instead authorizes a government agency to do so, which, in turn, delegates the standard-setting to a private body, the FASB. In the UK, legislation prescribes some standards – this being a result of European harmonization – and also makes wide-ranging provisions for a private-sector agency, the ASB, to set standards. In Germany, legislation prescribes accounting and disclosure standards to a great extent, relies on outside sources to contribute to German GAAP but does not designate a powerful standard-setting agency at the national level. The GASB never achieved this stature.

A functional perspective allows drawing inferences from these findings. In the US, the state had taken on responsibility for accounting early on. With the securities legislation, the state signalled that the outcome responsibility for functioning capital markets rested there. The creation of the SEC allowed taking over operation responsibility, but this was delegated mostly to the private sector. Today, the FASB serves as the standard-setter under the authority of the SEC, which exercises the state's supervision responsibility. While a closer cooperation between the national and the international standard-setters can be witnessed, significant tendencies in internationalization have not materialized in the US: the standard-setting procedures largely remain at the national level, albeit with international input.

In the UK, the state applied a hands-off approach in the development of accounting standards (Hopwood and Vieten 1999). One could even argue that outcome responsibility for functioning capital markets had not been ascribed to the UK nation state for a long time. While this has now changed, there is still no desire to introduce extensive legislation. The state calls for further engagement of the professional bodies and continues delegating regulation to private-sector bodies and supporting voluntary codes of practice wherever appropriate. Legislation and extensive rules are seen as a backstop to be applied only where everything else fails or when EU legislation requires adoption. Operational and supervision responsibility have been delegated to private actors to the extent that is allowed by the European directives.

Germany adopted the state model of standard-setting early on, and the state had taken on operational as well as supervision responsibility for standard-setting. This changed significantly in 1998. For German GAAP, the nation state gave up operation responsibility by establishing a standards board for group accounting, but it held on tight to its regulatory responsibility: each pronouncement of the GASB was scrutinized by the Ministry of Justice. This response in regard to German GAAP contrasts sharply with the legislator's initiative regarding third-party standards: in the same year, Germany allowed – alternatively, to be decided by the preparer of financial statements – the most sweeping model of internationalization by giving up operation and supervision responsibility altogether. Any respectable third-party standards could be used for consolidated accounts. As a national legislator, Germany had no influence over them. In all of this, though, it must not be overlooked that these developments concern accounting for groups. Company accounts, which are the input in taxation procedures, stayed under German legislation using German GAAP throughout.

While there were changes in all countries, it was most substantial in the two European countries, albeit for different reasons. While the changes in the UK are driven by European harmonization, which ushered in the state, Germany's changes seem to be driven by lobbying of private firms, and they do not take a clear direction with the state simultaneously trying to hold on to its powers, but letting go completely in other governmental initiatives covering the same public policy field. The US shows only minimal variation and no structural change.

One could say that in all considered legislatures the state's interventionist interest is now combined with the flexibility and professionalism of a private standard-setter that initially develops accounting standards. In sum, standard-setting became a much more complex process with multilevel public and professional private actors involved.

# 4
# The New Accounting Procedures in Europe: Combining Transnational Standard-setting and Supranational Rule-making

As discussed in the previous chapter, accounting harmonization in Europe proceeded in two stages. At the first stage, company law directives were used that had to be transposed into national laws. As the early European directives contained much scope for choice, the powers of national legislators were not overly curtailed. Consequently, effective harmonization was not achieved by these directives, and the project of the single financial European market fell short of expectations. Instead of undertaking a second round in harmonizing company law, the EU Commission applied an approach in which the national legislatures could be circumvented on the one hand, but the Commission would not play an overly imposing role on the other. This became possible with the emerging international framework in accounting and an increased emphasis on regulating accounting with a perspective to financial markets (and securities law) rather than to company law.

Mostly unnoticed by state regulation, some users and preparers of accounts had begun to promote the idea of an internationally uniform set of standards in accounting in the early 1970s. This private initiative proceeded very much along the same strategic lines as the European project: first allowing scope for choice to accommodate national peculiarities, then trying to unify practice by eschewing minority choices that had lost acceptance. By the end of the 1990s, the private initiative for setting unified standards had gained sufficient acceptance – particularly among listed firms – to provide a credible framework to which Europe could turn without having to coordinate national regimes. This latest stage of harmonization will be described in this chapter.

However, employing not only the expertise but relying fully on the outcome of private actors raises concerns of input and output legitimacy. This chapter therefore traces not only the private institutions of accounting standard-setting but also how Europe augmented the private standard-setting process with input from its own institutions to achieve procedural propriety and to arrive at standards that regulate accounting in the public interest.

## 4.1   The emerging framework: The IAS

The harmonization of accounting standards has concerned the accounting profession for a long time. The early beginnings of accounting harmonization can be traced back to 1973, when the International Accounting Standards Committee (IASC) was founded by professional organizations from ten countries. In a standard classification, seven are considered having an 'Anglo-Saxon' tradition (Australia, Canada, Great Britain, Ireland, Mexico, the Netherlands and the US) and three a 'Continental European' one (France, Germany and Japan). The IASC's aim was to 'formulate and publish in the public interest accounting standards to be observed in the presentation of financial statements and to promote their worldwide acceptance and observance' (IASC 1992). The foundation of the IASC was mostly a pre-emptive response of the private Anglo-Saxon standard-setters: the drafting of the Fourth Council Directive envisaged a strong role of the state as legislator, which would have considerably diminished the existing responsibilities of the professional organizations, particularly in the UK (Olson 1982).

The last constitution of the IASC, which was in force from 1983 to 2001, stipulated that it had to be run by a board of up to 17 members. The country members were selected by the Council of the International Federation of Accountants (IFAC), discussed later in Chapter 6, and there had to be a representative mix of developed and developing countries. Up to four organizations could be institutional members. These came typically from the IASC's consultative group, with institutions like the World Bank or the International Federation of Stock Exchanges. The IASC's board was charged with discussing developments in standard-setting, establishing working parties to develop exposure drafts and deciding on exposure drafts and eventually an international accounting standard with a qualified majority of votes. Work was mostly done by the so-called Steering Committees, which the Board instituted on an *ad hoc* basis. Since 1994 the IASC was assisted by an Advisory Council to promote IAS, and since 1997 the Board was assisted by a Standards Interpretation Committee.

Four phases of the IASC's operation can be identified (Pellens *et al.* 2006): in the first phase, which lasted until the late 1980s, the IASC developed around 30 standards. These IAS, some of which are still in force, show the highly controversial nature of accounting convergence. They do not rest on a common framework, and most contentious issues are resolved by allowing choices. Most practices were admitted in the respective standards. The second phase lasted from the late 1980s to the mid-1990s. At the end of the 1980s, the IASC published a framework for the development of accounting standards and started a comparability project to eliminate or at least reduce inconsistencies between standards. Its approach was to distinguish between preferred methods (benchmark treatment) and allowed alternative treatments with the goal to eliminate the latter eventually. In the third phase the IASC tried to gain regulatory acceptance. While accounting standards should permeate through the respective national practice, the IASC recognized the limited success as accounting rules were increasingly constrained by national or supranational company and securities laws. The IASC identified the stock exchanges (and reporting under security regulation) as a possible gate to gain worldwide acceptance. Stock exchanges focus on investors and their informational needs. This allows for a clear focus of financial reporting rules and circumvents complications that arise from multiple uses of accounting for conflict-solving in company law. A first success of these efforts was the endorsement of a core set of IAS by the International Organization of Securities Commissions (IOSCO).

To ensure eventual success, a more professional organizational structure, which also signalled greater distance from the accounting profession, was deemed necessary. The US experience had highlighted the precarious balance of a private standard-setter and state authorities when the latter bear the ultimate responsibility for financial reporting: political concerns can only be dispelled when the private body show sufficient distance to a specific interest group. It seemed therefore advisable to follow the FAF/FASB model in designing an international standard-setting body. In 2001, the International Accounting Standards Committee Foundation (IASCF) was established to replace the former organizational structures and institutions. The Foundation, legally established under US private law, has the twofold task of financing and staffing the standard-setter. It is, like the FAF, effectively owned by the trustees. Trustees come, again following the US model, from the financial reporting world at large; this means the group is made of users, preparers, academics and members of the profession. A regional mix of the trustees is mandated by the IASCF's constitution. The trustees appoint the newly created IASB and select all future trustees.

The IASB decides on accounting standards and their non-binding precursors, the so-called 'exposure drafts'. It receives input from the

Standards Advisory Council (SAC), and interpretations of standards are provided by the International Financial Reporting Interpretations Committee (IFRIC). The IASCF appoints the IFRIC and an Advisory Council, with which national standard-setters liaise. Technical staff supports the board members. The structure of the IASCF is shown in Exhibit 4.1. To mark the new organizational structure, the IASCF decided to change the name of the promulgated accounting standards: International Financial Reporting Standards now refer to the new numbered series of pronouncements that the IASB is issuing, as distinct from the IAS series issued or initiated by its predecessor.

The IASB consists of 14 members, of which 12 serve full-time and 2 part-time. In selecting Board members, the trustees need to ensure that the board is assembled in a balanced way with members appointed from an auditing background and with others chosen from the respective groups of preparers and users of financial statements. At least one member must come from academia. The IASB members are supposed to be independent, to have professional competencies in the field of financial reporting and practical experience. Members agree contractually

*Exhibit 4.1*   Organizational structure of the IASCF

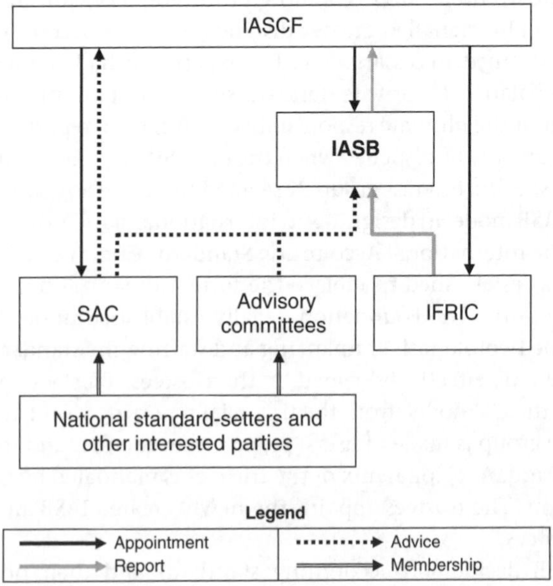

*Source*: IASB (2007), adapted.

that they will act in the public interest and follow the IASB Framework in their regulatory decision-making on accounting standards.

One of the main concerns with private standard-setting is to ensure that decisions are taken in the public interest, and this requires that processes are transparent and accessible to a wider public. This thinking is reflected in the IASB's due process which is now regulated by the IASB's Due Process Handbook approved in 2006. Again, the due process is modelled very closely along the lines of its US counterpart. The IASB's standard-setting process usually has six stages (from here following IASCF 2006). At Stage 1 the IASB deliberates and decides in public meetings which items should be put on its agenda. At Stage 2 the IASB first decides whether it wants to involve another standard-setter, and it takes the necessary steps to establish cooperation. At Stage 3 – this stage may be passed over – the IASB publishes a discussion paper as its first publication on any new major topic. A discussion paper is released with a simple majority vote by the Board, and it is usually out for a 120-day period for comment. The usual inputs in this period are comment letters, which are published by the Board. The comments play a decisive role in the Board's deliberations, and they are also used at Stage 4, the publication of an Exposure Draft (ED). A draft standard already has the final format of an IFRS and also contains a basis for conclusions, which explains the IASB's decisions and reveals the views of dissenting IASB members. After the comment period, the respective project team collects, summarizes and analyses the feedback received for the IASB's final deliberations and prepares for Stage 5, when the standard is completed and pronounced after passing a vote in which at least nine members have to be in favour of the draft. While earlier stages of the process may be controversial, the final vote on standards typically sees a wide majority. The time after the pronouncement is still perceived as a component of the due process: At this stage, Stage 6, regular meetings with interested parties follow in order to discuss and resolve unexpected issues, not so much by means of a quickly redrafted standard but rather by means of interpretations.

## 4.2 The European use of the framework

European efforts in financial integration were stepped up after the Lisbon Special Summit early in 2000. In November 2000, the 'Initial report of the committee of wise men on the regulation of European securities markets' (Lamfalussy Report) was published, highlighting the need for a better integration of the European financial markets. In the wake of these developments, the EU Commission took a big step towards harmonization of European accounting practices with the IAS Regulation (EC 1606/2002) on the application of IAS. Both the European Parliament (EP) and the European Council decided that '[f]or each financial year starting on or after 1 January 2005, companies governed by the law of a member state shall prepare their consolidated accounts in conformity with the International Accounting Standards adopted [...] if, at their balance sheet date, their securities are admitted to trading on a regulated market of any member state [...]'. In contrast to the accounting directives, it was not necessary for this regulation to be transformed into national law as EU regulations are directly relevant for all constituents in the member states.

Delegating standard-setting to the IASB does not mean, however, that the EU has given up its influence on accounting rules for listed groups. While discharging authority to the IASB, Europe has recognized the risk of being faced with policy outcomes that could differ from the favoured policy choice. To ensure at least some political oversight, the IAS Regulation established a screening mechanism: each individual standard has to be endorsed by the European Commission in accordance with a specific committee procedure to become European law (Schaub 2005).

To oversee and control the Commission's implementation powers, the Council has established oversight committees (Ballmann *et al.* 2002) as the Council only delegates the responsibility to enact legislative measures to the Commission. These oversight committees form the intermediate level of governance between the Community and the member states (Vos 1997). The term 'comitology' refers to the resulting processes (Joerges and Neyer 1997; Nugent 2003).

A Council Decision (1999/468/EC) laid down the procedures for the exercise of implementing powers conferred upon the Commission. It also introduced guidelines as to which procedures should be used in particular cases and policy areas. Three different types of comitology committee procedures exist: advisory, management and regulatory committees. These three procedures can be ranked according to the increasing level of member state control over the implementation process, from the advisory committee procedure (representing the lowest) to the regulatory committee procedure (representing the highest). The principal difference between the advisory committee and the other two committees is that management and regulatory committees can block a measure proposed by the Commission and thus act as gatekeepers (Steunenberg *et al.* 1996).

For the adoption of accounting standards, the EU has chosen to use the highest level of state control: the regulatory committee procedure applies. Before a standard is forwarded for endorsement by regulatory committee, the Commission receives input from the European Financial Reporting Advisory Group (EFRAG). EFRAG was founded in 2001 to provide appropriate technical input from the very beginning of the standard-setting process (Scheffler 2004). EFRAG plays a somewhat awkward dual role. On the one hand it delivers input to the IASB, and on the other hand it gives endorsement advice to the European Commission. EFRAG's role is rather technical and helps the Commission with technical expertise. The decisive control committee is the Accounting Regulatory Committee (ARC). The ARC was set up according to the requirements of the IAS Regulation. The committee decides on Commission proposals to endorse IFRS. The ARC consists of representatives from the European member states' governments and is chaired by a representative from the European Commission. To adopt an IFRS, the Commission's proposal must be passed by a qualified majority vote (QMV) in the Regulatory Committee, which applies the procedures of the EU in its respective current form.[1]

The endorsement process is thus as follows: after the adoption of an IFRS by the IASB, the European Commission asks EFRAG for its view on whether an IFRS should be endorsed. EFRAG undertakes a due process involving primarily its own consultative network, among them the national standard-setters of Europe, such as the ASB and the GASB. As soon as the opinion of EFRAG has been delivered, the European Commission puts the standard forward for adoption. The ARC subsequently discusses the proposal and takes a vote. In case of rejection, the Commission takes its proposal to the EU Council. The Commission will automatically endorse the standard if the Council has no opinion on the standard in question. In case of rejection by the Council, the Commission can change or amend its proposal (Council Decision 1999/468/EC: Article 5, No 6). An adopted standard is published in the official EU languages and becomes Community law. This also creates a role for the European Court of Justice in the future.

The case of IAS 32 and IAS 39 showed how member states (Belgium, France, Portugal and Spain) expressed strong opposition to IAS 39 and to the proposed changes in the ED (Brackney and Witmer 2005). The French president Jacques Chirac joined the debate to discuss how to pressure the IASB into eliminating the fair-value reporting requirements with the reasoning that it would be destructive to EU banks and national economies.

In the aftermath of this controversy the ARC unanimously gave a non-endorsement advice, but endorsed a carved-out version. However, this controversy was exceptional. In general, the ARC accepts the proposed full IASB standards forwarded by the Commission.

## 4.3   Shifting responsibilities from the nation state: The legitimacy issue

Public compliance and the legitimization of those governed are based on the general acceptance of the procedures by which laws are formulated. This makes legitimacy a measure of social consensus about how standards or rules are developed. Demonstrating legitimacy involves the use of assumptions, principles and arguments in terms of which authority is justified. In international governance, a combination of rational–legal conceptions (control and accountability) and those of discourse may serve as sources for legitimacy (Steffek 2003).

### Legitimacy in mixed governance models

Legitimacy is always mediated through a composite of principles. We employ two fundamental approaches taken from theory: the first one is participation and public debate (deliberation) and the second one is control and accountability. In distinguishing private standard-setting and public rule-making/implementing procedures it is conceivable that those principles are not equally important and applicable. The IASB itself has no authority to make the adoption of international standards binding, and Europe has developed a system to decide whether a particular standard is suitable. In that light, accountability in the most traditional sense lies primarily with the bodies that are responsible for adopting legally binding IFRS. These two distinct stages in European accounting standard-setting imply that the focus for assessing the private setting of standards should be on participation and public debate, whereas the rule-making authority should be assessed in terms of accountability and control.

The underlying idea of participation and deliberation is that constituents are more likely to accept the resulting norms when they were involved in their formation (Craig 1997). Indeed, the involvement of interested parties and the consideration of divergent views are seen as a necessary condition for a privately organized body without democratic legitimacy (Heuser *et al.* 2005). Participation can also be justified in terms of functional requirements (Birch 1993): those who have the authority to take decisions will do so more effectively if they are well informed about the problems of the community they govern. Deliberation requires a public process through which reasons can be debated, revised or rejected (Dryzek 2000). Deliberative processes seek to increase the quality of judgements through widespread citizen participation in multiple spheres, both within and between the institutions of state, economy and civil society.

Accountability and control are the second issue. In Europe, member states have delegated significant powers to the Council, which, in turn, conferred responsibilities to the Commission, which resulted in a 'dual executive' (Hix 2005) with shared responsibilities of 'government'. In consequence, the policy formation and implementation procedures are disconnected from immediate electoral and parliamentary control. In this context, legitimacy may derive from (at least) one fundamental type of control: (1) procedural safeguards; (2) procedural control; and (3) a balance of procedural and outcome controls (Johnson and Solomons 1984). Procedural safeguards presuppose a reasonable distribution of access to decision-making power among members of the constituency. This is partly covered by the notion of meaningful participatory rights. A procedural control mechanism requires that 'outsiders' identify the infrastructure and individuals behind the decision-making process. This requires openness and transparency, as well as a right of public access to documents and information. Finally, it is possible to assess the extent of control in terms of whether a balance of procedural and outcome controls (for example voting rules) exists.

## Assessing the IASB procedures

The analysis of the IASB, its structure and working procedures illustrated the steps in developing a standard: issuing a document, inviting comments, holding public hearings, reviewing the comments received and then revising the document. This allows constituents sufficient time to put forward their views. After the evaluation of the statements and a final consultation, the IASB publishes the standard. In the appendix of a standard a basis for conclusions, illustrative examples and dissenting opinions is published. The IASB's primary means of publishing its consultative documents and standards is through the IASB's website to ensure up-to-date information about its working process and progress. Consultative documents in their electronic form are available free of charge.

The descriptive analysis of the infrastructure and due process of the IASB has shown that many possibilities for participation exist. Further, the IASB seems willing to consider the views of parties with an interest in and affected by standard-setting. With often diverse and conflicting interests regarding financial reporting, there rarely exists an accounting standard that is acceptable to all parties involved – and it would be unreasonable to expect all parties to agree on the final outcome. By giving interested parties the opportunity of voicing their objections, the IASB increases the chance of finding a compromise that is acceptable to all parties. At the very least, the IASB allows the discussion of alternative solutions in the development of accounting standards and can claim that it has acted reasonably, which, in turn, meets the conditions of a deliberative procedure. Input from interested constituents assists the IASB and helps to prevent the promulgation of standards that are unworkable (Tandy and Wilburn 1992). Through its due process the IASB tests its arguments and implements an additional element of procedural control. It is also important to note that accounting standards do not evolve automatically out of this process, and the IASB does not expect them to come into force unchanged.

The amount of information that is published by the IASB allows 'outsiders' to identify what kind of interests are represented during the formulation of an accounting standard and how they might affect the outcome of the discussions. This enables interested parties to identify the actors behind each procedural step, the represented interests and the procedural steps.[2] It is an often-heard objection that a standard-setting body lacks independence and objectivity due to a biased influence of 'big' corporations or institutional organizations (Schildbach 2004) which, in turn, flaws the 'conditions of equilibrium'. However, empirical studies did not demonstrate that the IASB is substantively biased by any particular interest group (Giner and Arce 2004; Kwok and Sharp 2005).

Due to the importance of financial reporting, scholars have also analysed a number of aspects concerning participation in the due process. Such studies mainly explore the diversity of participation (Schmidt 2002), observed levels (Harding and McKinnon 1997; Kaplan and Fender 1998; Larson 1997; Nakayama *et al.* 1981; Weetman *et al.* 1996), how the diversity changes over time or how it differs from issue to issue (Tandy and Wilburn 1992). A low level of participation (mostly observed in the written response stage) is generally associated with equally low level of legitimacy (Larson 2002). Adequate representation, however, does not necessarily need to equate to direct involvement. Rather, the interests of users or other interest groups may be adequately represented by other parties who are directly involved, and besides, one should not confuse the presence of more actors with an actual increase in the diversity of ideas. Additionally, one could argue that a low response rate just reflects the fact that a proposed standard is not at odds with the various interests of the financial community, just as a lower turnout in elections can mean a relative satisfaction with the political developments (Grofman 1983). Non-participating companies that do not try to influence the standard-setter may simply be in agreement with the standard-setter's proposal.

Effective participation, however, must allow for the involvement of participants throughout the process of collective decision-making, including the stage of putting matters on the agenda (Dahl 1982). As stated in the Due Process Handbook for the IASB, the IASB makes from its earliest deliberations considerable use of outside sources in order to recognize and accommodate policy preferences of others. The procedures seem to strike an adequate balance in the democratic dilemma of participation versus system effectiveness (Dahl 1994): participation must be limited to ensure working procedures which allow the development of accounting standards in a timely manner.

Finally, the voting rule for issuing an ED or IFRS constitutes an important outcome control element. The majority voting requirement decreases the possibility that a standard which is only marginally acceptable to the Board is approved. This also tends to produce a process of compromise when a new standard is created.

## Assessing the European comitology procedure

The comitology procedure to endorse an IFRS is designed as an outcome control element before the standards become European law. From this it follows that the second stage of the procedure should be assessed more in terms of control and accountability. The role of EFRAG and the ARC will be considered in turn.

The EFRAG contributes technical expertise to the IASB's working process and represents Europe by cooperating with the respective national standard-setters in the EU. The public can access information on the Group's activities through its website. EFRAG professes to act from a position of technical expertise, which is unaffected by sectional interests, thus acting as a procedural safeguard. The second actor in the European screening mechanism is the ARC, which plays a major role due to its legal status. The ARC publishes its agenda items, a summary record and the final voting results. Additionally, information about the rules of procedures and member state delegations are available. Yet discussions – as well as the voting itself – are kept confidential and the individual positions of member states are not published. Non-European countries or organizations may be granted an observer status, but they must withdraw when the committee moves to a vote. The Commission can enact the standard only if the Committee supports the standard by a QMV, which ensures that the decision, although not necessarily unanimous, has to take into account the interest of minorities. The ARC fulfils a significant task as an outcome control element by assessing and overseeing the Commission's implementing function. Yet, under the regulatory committee procedure, the QMV rule poses the danger that national experts easily open the gates – for example, to refer the decision to the Council and make them political (Steunenberg *et al.* 1996).

## 4.4   Conclusion

It is hardly surprising that the new accounting procedures in Europe have generated a lot of interest and debate. In most cases, the debate in traditional accounting research revolved around the contents of the promulgated standards and not so much around the institutions that set them (Nobes and Parker 2004). This is somewhat baffling as it is in this area that the national constellation has truly changed. The first harmonization effects already had seen some competencies shifted to the supranational actor 'Europe'. The early wave of harmonization did not imply much institutional change for Germany, as operation (and the ensuing supervision) responsibility was only minimally curtailed by European law as the Council Directives simply proposed a minimalist Continental European model. This is also why UK witnessed a stronger influence of Europe from the first wave as the directives established minimum standards and a bigger role for the state. The second wave of harmonization by means of the IAS regulation is now a double blow to the nation state: the operation responsibility in regard to standards for listed groups is transferred to a transnational, that is an international, and private actor. The supervision responsibility is also transferred, this time to the supranational European level.

Despite the declared goal of a single financial European market, the outcome responsibility, though, rests with the nation state. This is visible in the case of accounting scandals and the malfunctioning of capital markets. After the financial crises of the early 2000s, the public turned to the nation state with a call for action. Actual financial reports are a product of design and implementation, and here it was thought that the implementation of rules could be improved, not that the rules as such were faulty. With the nation state as the primary addressee of the criticisms it is therefore unsurprising that its role in enforcement was even increased, which will be discussed in Chapter 7.

# 5
# The Struggle between Private and Public: The Case of Stock Exchanges

Capital markets are now an essential component of a strong economy. They facilitate the formation and allocation of capital, which is necessary for economic growth (Healy and Palepu 2001). Capital markets function well only if they can trade on information. This information can reach the market as insider information or as disclosure. The use of insider information, knowledge particular to a subset of owners and managers, puts some buyers and sellers at an advantage: informed insiders can exploit knowledge that they only received due to their privileged position in the company at the expense of outside shareholders. Disclosure, the simultaneous release of information to all market participants, forestalls these windfall gains. Making markets thus attractive to outsiders, disclosures, both mandatory and voluntary, play an important role in strengthening stock markets.

Stock markets are not merely abstract places where shares are traded. They are societal arrangements whose participants have an active interest in their well-being (Huddart *et al.* 1999). This means that stock markets should have an interest in stamping out insider trading and in furthering disclosure. A low level of insider trading and increased disclosure may boost the revenues and profits from organizing trade in securities, making the public interest in improving capital allocation only a side issue. This will be even more the case when stock markets compete with each other for trade in shares when the flows of capital are liberalized. These organized capital markets can require additional regulations for all participants or for some market segments only, resulting in transparency standards different from those required by law.

With the rise of the shareholder model in regulating financial reporting, many rules of stock exchanges were gradually superseded by state regulation in regard to insider trading and disclosures. Currently, mandatory disclosure dominates, crowding out the societal arrangements.

Today's mandatory disclosure stipulations are predominantly defined by legal frameworks that focus more strongly on financial markets than before and specified by private-sector standard-setters who had made disclosure for capital markets a key concern for themselves (see Chapters 3 and 4).

This chapter discusses the interplay of the state and stock exchanges in regulating these markets. Two observations are common to all of them. First, increased state participation has limited the influence of private regulation. Second, all countries show a three-tier regulatory structure. The first tier, which is historically the oldest, corresponds to private regulation by stock exchanges. These regulations mostly evolved from the origins of stock exchanges but – as will be shown with the stock exchange in Frankfurt – could also be established on behalf of the state (for example for operating and regulating a particular stock market segment). Later, the state provided the second tier of regulation by establishing a regulatory framework, which is mostly concerned with the overall development of the national capital market. Additionally, supervising authorities such as the US SEC, the UK FSA and the German BaFin have been installed, representing the third and most recent tier of regulation. These agencies operate by order of the state, but at least in the UK case it is debatable whether this is an original state system. Altogether, regulation and oversight of stock exchanges have changed significantly over time.

An additional aspect is the globalization of capital markets. Allowing investors to choose between markets, the legislator indirectly introduced competition between stock exchanges. To become more attractive, stock markets can not only resort to listing, trading and disclosure regulation; they can also become more commercially attractive by providing a competitive fee structure, swift trading mechanisms or longer trading hours. As will be shown, stock markets often use trade-offs between these parameters, for example by trading off lower fee levels against a weaker disclosure regime.

This chapter first tracks general changes in the organization and the business model of stock exchanges themselves. Then the legal framework and private regulations by stock exchanges in Germany, the UK and the US will be discussed. Here, the different regulated and unregulated listing categories are considered. They entail different disclosure consequences for issuers and allow for choice of different transparency levels. The chapter closes with a discussion of similarities and differences in the organization of the national stock markets and analyses the different public–private arrangements in the regulation of listing and disclosure requirements.

## 5.1 The business model and organizational form of stock exchanges

The institution of stock exchanges or bourses appeared as early as in the 14th century, and the first bourse is supposed to have existed in the Belgian city of Bruges (Deutsche Börse AG 2006; Ehrenberg 1885; Walter 1992). Emerging financial instruments as well as rising financing needs of nation states (especially for wars) and risky businesses of private bodies (for example the East India Company) fostered the establishment of big fairs in Lyon, Frankfurt and Antwerp, where interested traders regularly met during the 16th century (Michie 1992). Today's understanding of stock exchanges varies significantly from these meetings, even though it was only 300 years later when traders began to meet more frequently throughout the year and established stock exchange buildings.

Traditional floor-based trading shaped the picture of stock exchanges until the 1980s, when electronic trading gained importance (Théodore 1997).[1] Although electronic networks cannot be differentiated from conventional stock exchanges on a functional basis, this change had a significant impact on the way business is conducted. On the one hand, trading is no longer necessarily linked to the physical location of market actors. This increases the mobility of trade and puts pressure on the way in which business on the stock exchanges is organized. On the other hand, electronic trading did not dissolve the stock exchanges as local foci. While there is no longer a physical need for a nexus, the informational requirements – absence of insider trading and provision of disclosures – make the existence of institutions as anchor points for regulation even more necessary.

Another substantial change in the role and function of exchanges happened when exchanges converted from non-profit, member-owned ('mutual') organizations into for-profit, investor-owned corporations in a process that is called 'demutualization'. Demutualization requires the separation of the operational and of the oversight role that an exchange possesses, as the regulator, working in the public interest, cannot operate with a profit motive. The possibly ensuing commercial success of the operational segment, in turn, has further consequences for the role of the public sector since regulation has to be adequate to its importance (Mues 1999). The effects of demutualization will be discussed in the national contexts subsequently.

The history of exchanges shows that the shape of stock exchanges developed towards organized and complex entities, for example with own funding needs to finance investments in trading technology.

The view that treats stock exchanges simply as markets is reductionist and falls short of a crucial element explaining current trends. Existing stock exchanges can be described with a set of three basal variables:

1. the main type of trading featured (that is physical vs electronic trading);
2. the type of market featured (auction vs market maker system);
3. its internal structure and governance (public vs private entity/non-profit vs for-profit).

We are primarily interested in the latter point, that is we are interested in the question as to who owns an exchange and how this translates into governance structures. This will have implications for the role stock exchanges play in setting disclosure regulations, especially in the form of listing rules.

Traditionally, most of the world's stock exchanges were organized as non-profit organizations or cooperatives that were considered to perform public functions (Lee 1998). In the Continental European countries, exchanges were generally set up as public entities while their Anglo-Saxon counterparts usually were private bodies, in some cases regulated publicly (Di Noia 2001). Regardless of their original legal set-up, these institutions were located between state and society, being largely characterized by extensive self-regulation. Providing what became seen as public services and still being privately governed, exchanges usually became at least indirectly part of the public sector by official recognition or registration. This administrative act simultaneously made them legal monopolists; and stock exchanges were lacking market orientation.

With globalization and technology progressing, the formerly unrivalled national exchanges witnessed pressures resulting in major organizational and operational change (Aggarwal 2002). The trend of demutualization started in the early 1990s and gave stock exchanges more features of private firms. Stock exchanges became private companies themselves, which were often listed at their own market in order to satisfy their funding needs. However, as their profit orientation might interfere with a regulatory functioning, exchanges were often split into an entity operating the exchange and a regulating unit, to which we will refer as 'the bourse' in the following for reasons of terminological clarity. The bourse and the operating entity together form the stock exchange. The bourse can be the former exchange body (as in the example of the Frankfurt Stock Exchange, FSE) or a separated but still exchange-owned regulatory department (as in the case of NYSE Regulation Inc.).

We will now take a closer look at the developments in our sample countries. Germany, having a focus on the Frankfurt Stock Exchange, will be treated first; the UK, with the London Stock Exchange (LSE), second. A description of the developments in the US will follow, focusing on the New York Stock Exchange (NYSE), the American Stock Exchange (AMEX) and the National Association of Securities Dealers Automated Quotations (better known as NASDAQ). The analysis will proceed along historical lines, and the major capstones of reform – which differ in the three countries – will be discussed.

## 5.2 Germany: An active role for the private sector

German stock market regulation is an awkward melange of federal and single state (*Länder*) regulation, having its roots in the foundation of the Reich in 1870/71. In a non-competing environment, the single state's own stock markets could survive despite clear competitive disadvantages. This has now changed and established the supremacy of the FSE.

### Stock market regulation prior to the demutualization of the FSE

Due to its annual trade fairs, Frankfurt had become the most important centre for financial and commercial transactions in Germany as early as in the 14th century (Deutsche Börse AG 2006). In 1585, the FSE was established in order to set uniform exchange rates for the range of different monetary systems within the predecessor states of today's Germany. Until the introduction of the first official exchange rules in 1682, the FSE merely existed as an unorganized market without any element of stock exchange administration. Private investors discovered the possibility of wealth formation through the introduction of bonds and promissory notes at the end of the 17th century.

In the beginning, trading in Frankfurt was solely based on rules of conduct between merchants, thus being a sphere free from governmental influence (Lütz 2002). The transition towards tighter organization typically marks the switch from autonomous stock exchanges to state institutions. In the case of Frankfurt, this was a very gradual and protracted change: in 1707, the exchange members of FSE created an official institution labelled Deputies of the Merchants (*Deputierten der Kaufmannschaft*), which in 1808 was transformed into the Chamber of Commerce (*Handelskammer*). In the same year, the Chamber of Commerce took over the operations of the FSE. Other German exchanges switched to the same governance model subsequently (Mues 1999). Being a professional statutory body under public law, the Chamber is no part of state administration but has been assigned sovereign competences within the public sector (Avenarius 1997). Regulatory bodies under public law are a peculiarity of code law countries. They are entitled to self-regulation, equipped with regulatory competencies exceeding private law and operate under their own constitution (Zänsdorf 1937). Thus, the exchange was no longer privately owned by a group of merchants, but a public institution, and members had to comply with statutes. However, while the chambers and exchanges moved into the regulatory scope of the state, their organizational features remained dominated by self-regulation.

In contrast to many other jurisdictions, regulation of securities trading did not appear as a state reaction to market malfunctions but rather on demand from the participating traders. Even the market crises of 1873 and 1891, partly driven by dubious reporting practices, had no effect on disclosure regulation and investor protection.

The first regulatory action was taken by the legislator in 1896, when the Stock Exchange Act (BörsG) created the first uniform regulation of all existing 29 stock exchanges in Germany. It outlined the first formal listing standards and made arrangements for price quotation by official brokers (the Official Market). It thus dismantled the system that buyers and sellers negotiated individually on prices. Moreover, liability for disseminated information was codified as a first step by the federal government towards higher investor protection. These requirements were rather liberal, however. Mandatory disclosures for listed companies were not introduced. The legislator relied on the rather minimal stipulations in company law, which applied regardless of listing status (Chapter 3).

The stock exchanges were brought under legal oversight of the German states (*Länder*) in 1896 – corresponding to the federal nature of the *Reich* – but the states' intervention remained rather formal and no active control was executed. The single states were simply authorized to establish stock exchanges within their territory by granting licences, while the internal governance was left to the self-regulated exchanges. This fragmented regulatory system, under the patronage of the universal banks as its key actors, was re-established after the Second World War, but it now provided the federal government with the right to intervene (McCraw 2000; Steil 2002). However, non-intervention of the federal state prevailed for a long time. Legal disclosure rules were still determined by company law, and they were not set in a way that particularly benefited investors in shares. The universal banks, interested in extending credit to listed companies rather than in what is now called 'investment banking' and placement of shares, did not press for increased levels of disclosure either. Without competitive pressures, the system ticked along.

The further development of capital market regulation in Germany was strongly connected to supranationalization. Next to the US intention of coordinating capital market oversight across borders, the initial creation of the integrated financial market and the necessary implementation of European directives put most pressure on the German system of informal self-regulation. Three EC directives that aimed at enhancing investor protection were passed in 1979 (79/279/EEC: Admission Directive), in 1980 (80/390/EEC: Listing Particulars Directive) and in 1982 (82/121/EEC: Interim Reporting Directive). The German legislator transposed these directives into national law (mostly using omnibus bills) only in 1986 (Möller 2006). Resistance from the financial sector, not fully convinced of the supply-side arguments of disclosure, partly explains the substantive delay. While in accounting regulation and the company law framework the Continental European view had been paramount, the financial market regulations showed a stronger Anglo-Saxon handwriting, requiring eventually an entirely new legal approach with the WpHG. But while the UK coped with the changes by adapting their organizational structures, Germany – also then being an insider economy – dragged its feet.

Instead of competing on high levels of disclosure, the financial system lobbied for a statutory market segment with lower legal requirements in which features of the old system could persist. This segment was established as the Regulated Market. Its official reason was to facilitate equity financing, and this facilitation took the form of lower listing requirements than the traditional Official Market. Both markets are regulated; the listing and disclosure requirements of the two segments Official Market and Regulated Market are governed by law.

The regulations of 1986 also officially acknowledged the existence of an Open Market as a third market segment (Kümpel 2004), which had coexisting right from the beginning of stock markets. Neither does the state interfere with disclosure rules nor does the Open Market represent an organized or regulated market according to the WpHG. Hence, its listings are no listings in the sense of the AktG. Trade takes place at the exchange only factually; legally the Open market is an off-exchange arrangement. This allows – at least in theory – to forego admission and disclosure requirements. The Open Market at the FSE had been fully established in 1987. Before, it had been virtually unregulated. A distinctive feature is that securities can be included by a financial institution without permission of the underlying company. Although being organized in a legal framework, the listing requirements of the Open Market emphasize its private-law character, and it appears to be rather a market established in the interest of securities dealers than for the funding needs of the listed companies.

After 1986 the integration of the world's capital markets gained momentum and more and more EC directives had to be adopted. However, the German capital market was not prepared for the change. As an example, the Insider Dealing Directive of 1989 (89/592/EEC) was transposed only five years later due to a massive blockade by business and politics (Hopt 1991). The Directive demanded an institutional setting similar to the US that is able to enforce regulation and to sanction market abuses undertaken with insider information. Germany was not yet ready for such a change. Instead of a transposition, the legislator tried to promote the German stock market with an amendment to the Stock Exchange Act in 1989 as well as the First Financial Market Promotion Act of 1990. The act of 1989 set the legal stage for electronic trading, particularly for derivative activities, and facilitated the market admission of securities and dealers. The First Financial Market Promotion Act of 1990 abandoned turnover and note taxes, also transposing the Investment Directive of 1985 (85/611/EEC).[2] The two legal initiatives thus intended to decrease transaction costs of the German exchanges while their overall structure was not changed or amended towards more transparency and credibility. Market fragmentation, low disclosure levels and a subordinate role of small investors left Germany with a capital market that was rather underdeveloped, at least in a regulatory sense.

### Demutualization and further regulatory developments

In the early 1990s, technological developments brought the stock exchanges the opportunity to reap huge economic benefits or the risk to fall substantially behind. With a single European market on the horizon, trade in shares now saw the opportunity to relocate to attractive market places. Additionally, advanced Information Technology (IT) started to shift the balance from floor-based towards automated trading (Williamson 1999). As a result, larger exchanges could achieve economies of scale, which allowed lowering the investors' transaction costs. In this competition, the German stock markets were in danger to fall behind. This is why a number of private actors made substantial efforts in order to strengthen the securities markets. All of this was driven by economic motives: the commercial banks tried to enter the promising investment and IPO market, and firms were seeking to become less dependent on bank financing (Deeg 2005). Yet these attempts were constrained by odd cartel-like relations that benefited the smaller regional exchanges, for instance by mandating regional listings of large companies in order to protect revenues within the system (Lütz 1998). The federal states' (*Länder*) governments had no incentives to increase competition between the exchanges. This left the system to operate at comparatively high costs as issuers and brokers had to pay additional related fees to comply with duplicating regulation.

The FSE decided in an early move on demutualization, as this facilitated the raising of outside funds for further investments in technology. In turn, demutualization requires changes in the regulatory structure so that regulation in the public interest is decoupled from the profit motive. The FSE is a showcase for these developments: it was one of the first exchanges that demutualized, splitting the institution into an operator and the self-regulating bourse in 1993 (Deutsche Börse AG 2006). Deutsche Börse AG took over the role of an operator, issuing its shares to the former exchange's members, mainly large banks.

Shortly after the demutualization of FSE, the Second Financial Market Promotion Act of 1994 transposed the above-mentioned Insider Directive (89/592/EEC) and the Investment Services Directive (93/22/EEC) into German law. In a massive re-organization of public oversight, the federal states were stripped of most powers and a new centralized market supervisory agency was created, the Federal Securities Supervisory Office (BAWe), having a focus on tackling insider trading (Möller 2006). The BAWe monitored and enforced insider offences and acted as the competent authority regarding international coordination (for example with the SEC). The bourses held on to the oversight of the market and monitored listing and disclosure requirements. They were supported in this by bodies that monitored trading activities and were overseen by the federal states. These new organizational structures were placed in the Stock Exchange Act. The reorganization of 1994 also saw the creation of an entirely new act: the WpHG was introduced, governing the competences of the BAWe as well as disclosure requirements concerning insider dealings and *ad hoc* reporting. By the end of 1994 a complex oversight structure had evolved. The need for an increased public role was satisfied with the establishment of the BAWe at the national level, and the self-regulation of exchanges was curtailed to compensate the *Länder* for powers that were shifted to the federal level.

Demutualization and regulatory reform also touched on the Open Market. After the demutualization in 1993, the Open Market has been regulated by the Directives of the Regulated Unofficial Market of Deutsche Börse AG. This means not the bourse, but the operator sets the rules for this off-exchange trading arrangement. In addition, the BaFin monitors the Open Market with a view to the rules on insider trading and market manipulation. Although the latter was not required for unregulated markets by the relevant EU legislation (Directive 2003/6/EC, Market Abuse Directive), the German legislator believed that a collapse of the Open Market would reduce investor confidence in other segments, damaging the whole financial market. It therefore opted to extend the regulation to this segment. But issuers must fulfil only few inclusion requirements (such as disclosing annual reports and filing approval applications), and there are so far no follow-up obligations. Listed companies are even exempted from *ad hoc* disclosure in order not to dry up the Open Market and not to reduce the exchange's international competitiveness (Kümpel 2004).

Due to the increasing competition among the world's stock exchanges, the FSE decided to complement floor trading by electronic trading early on. The introduction of the electronic XETRA trading system in 1997 increased the funding needs of the exchange. Deutsche Börse's initial public offering in 2001 and subsequent capital increases have thus been logical economic consequences leading to an integrated financial company (for example by the takeover of Clearstream in 2002). In 1998, the Third Financial Market Promotion Act adopted existing regulations, in particular concerning electronic trading, prior to the approaching introduction of the Euro currency. The federal states conditioned their consent on the participation of regional exchanges in the XETRA system although this diluted the competitive position of the FSE as Germany's most prominent stock exchange.

Finally, the Fourth Financial Market Promotion Act of 2002 was to remove the remaining parts of the fragmented oversight structure that appeared to be inefficient. Competences shifted towards the federal state while disclosure requirements also increased as a result of the Consolidated Admissions and Reporting Directive (2001/34/EC). The BAWe was transformed into a uniform regulatory authority, the BaFin. Additional directives concerning investor protection have been transposed subsequently. Besides the Prospectus Directive of 2003 (2003/71/EC), these include the Market Abuse Directive (2003/6/EC) as well as the Transparency Directive of 2004 (2004/109/EC), which tightened disclosure requirements. Exhibit 5.1 summarizes the most important developments in the history of German stock exchange governance.

### Disclosure rules set by stock exchanges: The case of FSE

The above discussion of the FSE has so far mainly revolved around the attractiveness of the stock exchange, and in this discussion the lowering

79

*Exhibit 5.1* Changes in the German model, demonstrated for the FSE

| Time | Main business (and capital needs) | Organization | External oversight | Regulated markets — By law | Regulated markets — By exchange | Unofficial markets |
|---|---|---|---|---|---|---|
| Traditional model (since 1896) | Floor trading (low) | Public law entities | States | Official Market | | Open Market (unregulated) |
| 1986 | *Stock Exchange Admission Act (Amendment of the Stock Exchange Act of 1896)* | | | Official Market, Regulated Market | | |
| 1987 | | | | | | Open Market (governed by FSE) |
| 1990 | *First Financial Market Promotion Act (Erstes Finanzmarktförderungsgesetz)* | | | | | |
| 1993 | | Deutsche Börse operates FSE | | | | Open Market (governed by Deutsche Börse) |
| 1994 | *Second Financial Market Promotion Act (Zweites Finanzmarktförderungsgesetz)* | | | | | |
| | | | BAWe, States | | | |

*Exhibit 5.1* (Continued)

| | *Third Financial Market Promotion Act (Drittes Finanzmarktförderungsgesetz)* | | |
|---|---|---|---|
| **1997** | Electronic trading: XETRA, later Clearstream (high) | | Neuer Markt and SMAX (governed by Deutsche Börse) |
| | *Fourth Financial Market Promotion Act (Viertes Finanzmarktförderungsgesetz)* | | |
| **2002** | | | |
| **2003** | BaFin (and States) | Prime Standard; General Standard (equal to Regulated Market) | |
| **2005** | | | Entry Standard (governed by Deutsche Börse) |

*Note:* Dotted lines indicate that the arrangements before are not interrupted.

of transaction costs and the eradication of insider trading were decisive. Disclosures played a smaller role in the legal activities. As was shown in Chapter 3, the German legislator only used the 1994 Securities Trading Act and the 1998 reforms to the Commercial Code to differentiate between disclosures of listed and unlisted firms. It was not that these regulations crowded out private initiatives; quite to the contrary, with an increased emphasis on capital markets, the state gave rise to further disclosure initiatives of the operators under private law, especially the FSE's operator Deutsche Börse AG.

Deutsche Börse AG has been setting disclosure standards both formally and informally. Two early examples of private regulatory arrangements are the *Neuer Markt* and the Small-Cap-Segment (SMAX). Although these markets have been terminated in the meantime, they represent an outcome of the unique features of the German regulation and warrant further discussion.

In 1997, the FSE introduced a new model of an independent 'market segment' referred to as *Neuer Markt* (Kersting 1997). Initially intended to act as the European equivalent to the high-tech-oriented NASDAQ, the project gained notoriety around 2000 and was finally abolished in 2003. Being established within the legal framework of the Open Market (that is under private law and beyond the Stock Exchange Act), the *Neuer Markt* demanded higher regulatory standards particularly with regard to disclosure. First, issuers had to fulfil a rather sophisticated procedure to be admitted. After formally applying to the Regulated Market, candidates had to resign their official listing immediately and were subsequently admitted to the *Neuer Markt*. Hence the applicants had to meet all legal regulations for the Regulated Market segment including those from the Stock Exchange Act and the WpHG. Secondly, Deutsche Börse AG set additional rules in a private law constitution which were stricter than the rules for regulated markets in most other European countries. Among these requirements, Deutsche Börse AG demanded financial reporting according to international standards, for example quarterly reporting according to IAS or US GAAP. The FSE's SMAX was also a private market segment outside the regulated markets that may be compared to the *Neuer Markt*. Having the same structure and demanding the same requirements, it rather focused on established companies with lower growth opportunities and having less volatile shares (Baumeister and Werkmeister 2001).

In its beginning, *Neuer Markt* was a success story. Then, in 2000 the dotcom bubble burst and prices dropped. More importantly, a number of financial reporting abuses within the segment became publicly known and had serious consequences. Deutsche Börse AG as the regulator of *Neuer Markt* and SMAX had neither enforced its rules nor the accuracy of disclosure but had simply controlled the complete publication of required information. Thus, credibility of these private law segments suffered from the lack of an independent supervisory and enforcement institution. The exchange reacted finally and reconsidered its market segmentation. *Neuer Markt* and SMAX were closed and the remaining listed companies transferred to other segments. While especially the *Neuer Markt* strengthened the popularity of securities trading and investments in Germany, it became a symbol for the inadequate control mechanism of German capital market regulation (Vitols 2005).

Since the Fourth Financial Market Promotion Act of 2002, the bourse has been assigned regulatory competences to demand additional disclosure requirements (setting transparency levels) within certain statutory market segments.[3] The operator can also directly act as a standard-setter by creating and regulating market segments under private law. As it earns money with the prosperity of their respective exchanges, Deutsche Börse AG has a natural interest in enhancing the listing quality. It used a provision from the Fourth Financial Market Promotion Act which allows the creation of self-governed transparency standards within the statutory market segments. In 2003, Frankfurt established two sub-segments in the Official and Regulated Market called Prime Standard and General Standard (Spindler 2003). These two levels of regulation provide companies with a customized access to the capital market: the General Standard does not exceed the legal requirements; the Prime Standard contains additional regulations beyond legal stipulations. This differentiation enables issuers to choose a preferred transparency level beyond the choice of the market segment (Regulated or Official). As the legal requirements of the German Regulated and Official Markets have converged the choice of a segment hardly allows for any signalling. The additional Prime Standard requirements in the Exchange Rules contain quarterly reports in English, a financial calendar and analyst conferences. Exhibit 5.2 provides an overview of disclosure regulation by the three regulators: EC, national legislator and the bourse.

With its rule that only Prime Standard issuers are considered for the Deutsche Börse AG's indices DAX, MDAX, TecDAX and SDAX, the operator established a strong incentive to comply with the additional requirements. However, the increased disclosure obligations may squeeze some firms out of their initially chosen market segments. This happened, for example, when the German sports car manufacturer Porsche AG refused to publish interim reports and was consequently

*Exhibit 5.2*  Disclosure regulation in Germany (bourse: FSE)

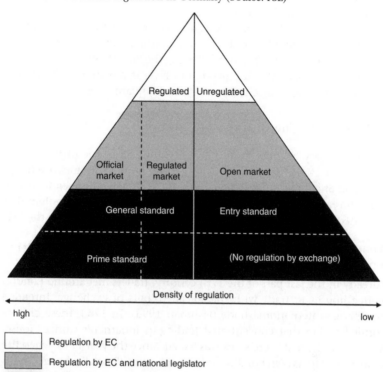

transferred to the General Standard (The Economist 2004; Zimmermann and Abeé 2007).

Analogous to the regulated markets, the Deutsche Börse AG established the so-called Entry Standard at the Open Market, accessible to all companies that wish to position themselves by providing additional information to the investors. It may thus be regarded as an entry segment for the Official and Regulated Market. Inclusion criteria vary from those of the Open Market quite significantly and mainly in regard to transparency requirements. Besides audited financial reports, publication of interim reports, mandatory immediate publication of significant company information, a brief, up-to-date company profile and a calendar of corporate events are required. The specific characteristics of the Entry Standard demand issuers to have an applicant trading member monitoring the fulfilment of transparency standards. Moreover, a so-called 'listing partner' has to be chosen in order to guide the issuer in admission and continuing disclosure procedure.

All this gives rise to a complex regulatory structure that allows for firms to choose between different levels of disclosure. A minimum level is the listing on the Open Market, not following the Entry Standard regulations by Deutsche Börse AG. The maximum level is a listing at the Official Market following Deutsche Börse's Prime Standard rules.

## 5.3   The UK: The shift to state control

With a history of more than 300 years, the LSE is one of the world's oldest and at the same time *today's* most important stock exchange (London Stock Exchange 2006; Smith 1929). It gained pre-eminence in England early on, and this pre-eminence in trading scope and volume has persisted until today. We will therefore focus our discussion on the LSE.

### London Stock Exchange: Developments and listing requirements until the Big Bang

Already in the last part of the 17th century, traders met around London coffee houses to trade with the so-called 'bills of exchange' intended to finance international trade (Fishman 1993). In 1763, these brokers formed a club that concentrated trading at Jonathan's Coffee House, where also the first list of stock was issued. Since the year 1773, when the club moved to its own building, it bears the name 'Stock Exchange'. With the 'Deed of Settlement' on 3 March 1801, the business became the first closed and self-regulated exchange working under a formal membership subscription basis and with annual member fees (Michie 1999).

At first, trading rules had been imposed and enforced by the Board of Trustees and Managers, which could withdraw membership in case of misconduct. Several years after the settlement, the exchange created its first code, 'Rules and regulations for the conduct of business on the stock exchange', in 1812. This code still applies today in a modified version. While it did not contain listing rules for issuers at first, rights and obligations for the growing number of exchange members were specified from the outset. Thus the LSE was largely entrusted with organizing its own affairs.

While the LSE's establishment was connected to the growth of international trade, the BoE quickly gained importance from its foundation as a private institution in 1694 with the purpose of financing the Crown's capital needs (Moran 1991). Through the exclusive business with government bonds, the BoE as a credible issuer of securities and the LSE as an organized trading place consistently contributed to the development of a strong national securities market. However, the British system was mainly built on restricted competition through market segregation between the LSE and other regional exchanges, which preserved the dominance of the London financial community. This very fact and the organization of securities dealers as an exclusive club with 'Oxbridge background' gave the LSE a rather negative image in the public.

The statutory framework governing LSE's affairs was marginal. In particular, the Companies Act of 1900 set minimum disclosure standards for issuers. The Prevention of Fraud Investments Act (PFI) of 1958 demanded traders to be member of an exchange or at least to be registered with the DTI. Overall, these arrangements underline the limited importance of state intervention until the Big Bang in 1986 (Fishman 1993). Also, the LSE in particular actively lobbied against broader state intervention and instead fostered the development of self-regulation in the field of investor protection. The self-regulatory activities also forestalled legal regulation: amongst others, LSE introduced the first simple listing requirements for issuers and their prospectuses into its Rules and Regulations in 1919. After 1973 these rules became known as the LSE Admission of Securities to Listing or, in short, the Yellow Book. Also the LSE established instruments of investor protection aside from disclosure regulation and set up a compensation fund for victims of misconduct by exchange members in 1950.

As late as in the 1970s the LSE's business was still largely based on a trading cartel exempting non-members. Even in 1978 the LSE responded to the Wilson Committee, assigned to analyse the shortcomings of the British system, that 'the authority of the supervising bodies is drawn not from statute but from the consent of the users of the market' (Taylor 2000). However, despite the merger of the LSE with some regional exchanges in 1973, the exchange suffered more and more from isolation from the world capital markets due to cartel-like trading arrangements and marginal disclosure requirements. At the same time the US capital market was already sophisticated concerning disclosure requirements and exchanges were comparatively open.

In order to re-establish the connection to the international capital markets, the exchange introduced comprehensive reforms in 1986, known as the Big Bang (Michie 1999). These reforms were triggered by government, as officials had realized the LSE's growing difficulties in competing internationally (Vogel 1996). As with Germany, the cosy arrangements of the established firms started to generate windfall profits at the expense of the public interest and the societal arrangements were unable to initiate reforms of their own accord as their environment was not (yet) competitive. While Germany needed the harmonizing influence of Europe, the UK's stock market was reformed in the de-regulating spirit of the Thatcher era. Unsurprisingly, therefore, the eventual execution of reforms was left to the LSE after the deadlock was dissolved. The most important changes liberalized trading and especially opened the exchange for outsiders. The Big Bang deregulation, moreover, set the stage for the modernization of trading, particularly the transformation of the LSE into a privately held company in the form of a public company limited by shares.

### Shaping today's regulatory structure: Developments towards state regulation

Only in the beginning of the 1980s the British legislator discovered investor protection as a genuine task and identified the existing system of self-regulation as an obstacle in the intensifying competition of international capital markets (Alcock 2000). Also a number of fraudulent malpractice cases shook the system. The growing urge for reforms coincided with initiatives of EC harmonization. In particular, the three already-known EC Council directives – 79/279/EEC (Admission Directive), 80/390/EEC (Listing Particulars Directive) and 82/121/EEC (Interim Reporting Directive) – had to be transformed into national law (Fishman 1993).

This required the British government to take significant action in order to codify capital market regulations. The Financial Services Act of 1986, not incidentally coinciding with the Big Bang reforms that the LSE undertook, augmented the formerly marginal state regulation by establishing a three-tier oversight system. The state took on the general oversight but delegated certain statutory regulatory powers to the privately organized and privately funded Securities and Investment Board (SIB). The board's main task was to supervise the Self-Regulatory Organizations (SROs), which accounted for an overall number of 22 organizations. Being one of them, the Securities and Futures Authority (SFA) took over personnel as well as regulatory objectives of the LSE in order to monitor all firms taking part in trading in all kind of securities. In contrast to several other investment and commodity futures exchanges, the LSE did not receive SRO status but restricted itself to supervising trading processes (Moran 1991). The new system aimed at maintaining some parts of the former self-regulatory regime within the new statutory framework. Neither the government (DTI) nor the BoE wanted to take oversight itself. The

SIB was established for setting up adequate rules of overseeing securities trading, but it did not possess enforcement competences. The supervision of compliance was left to the SROs, but rule violations could only be prosecuted by disciplinary courts. Therefore, the SROs refereed the SIB's binding rules by granting and revoking licences to their members. But the actions taken in the middle of the 1980s rather intended to fight insider trading and spent comparatively little time and effort on establishing transparency (Fishman 1993).

The new three-tier system did soon prove to be unsuccessful in dealing with the converging financial industry, namely banks, brokers and insurance companies (Howells and Bain 2004; Taylor 2000). Different actors often interfered in controlling integrated financial companies, and the various rule books of the SIB and the SROs accelerated in their extent and complexity. A financial institution, for instance, may trade in shares, derivatives and provide retail financial services. These activities necessarily overlap in an integrated institution but would be regulated by different SROs. The splintered nature of the system gave the SEC no natural counterpart to consider the regulation of an increasingly globalized financial market, a situation similar to the one described in Germany. Last, but not least, the dissembled regulatory bodies could not tackle the uniform problem of insider trading, which needed to be dealt with in transposing the Insider Dealing Directive (89/592/EEC).

In 1997, the structure was streamlined with the foundation of the FSA, whose nature oscillates between a private and a state institution and which will be discussed in greater detail in Chapter 7. The Financial Services and Markets Act (FSMA) of 2000 abolished the remaining fragmentary self-regulatory arrangements (Fleischer 2001; Ryder 2000). The fundamental change of policy included the complete abandonment of self-regulation of the LSE. Disclosure and other transparency rules would now be set by the FSA, which aimed at maintaining market confidence (Möller 2006). The British three-tier model became similar to that of the US by establishing a system of cooperation between a supervisory institution and private organizations. However, it differs remarkably in its definition of the extent of state influence and discretion (Lütz 2002).

With the enactment of the FSMA, the remaining listing authority functions of the LSE were transferred to the FSA (see Chapter 7). Thus, the disclosure regulation moved from self-regulation by the LSE's Yellow Book towards state regulation by common law executed through the FSA. The FSMA now also specifies general rules for admission of securities to trading on stock exchanges, and it allocates the task of working out detailed listing rules to the listing authority. This institutional name remained when this function was transferred from the exchanges to the FSA. As a tradition, when acting as the competent authority for listing of shares on a stock exchange, the FSA is referred to as the UK Listing Authority (UKLA). The FSA also now maintains the so-called Official List, containing all securities issued by companies to be traded on a UK regulated market such as the LSE.

In order to get listed, issuers have to fulfil disclosure requirements stipulated in the Listing Rules of the FSA/UKLA. Being accepted for listing, the company has to comply with continued disclosure requirements, which also include *ad hoc* reporting as defined in the Listing Rules (Alcock 2000).[4] In order to comply with the listing, the applicant must disseminate information concerning changes in capital, major interests in shares and reporting transactions principally relating to acquisitions, disposal and related parties. Moreover, issue of semi-annual interim reports as well as preliminary full-year results are required, while demanding quarterly reporting is still a matter under review. Overall, the disclosure requirements by the FSA are not much stricter yet than those of the traditional Yellow Book, which were simply taken over and remain valid until they are amended (Keßler 2004). Exhibit 5.3 summarizes the development in the UK's stock exchange governance.

### Market structure and disclosure requirements after the FSMA

While state intervention and rule codification appeared rapidly with the developments in 1986 and afterwards, the LSE only lately developed a market orientation and electronic trading (Lütz 2002). When the FSA took over the listing authority function from the LSE in 2000, shareholders finally voted to incorporate LSE plc as a limited company, which listed on its own exchange the following year. Today, the LSE offers two markets, somewhat analogous to the German regulated and unregulated segments: since 1995, the Main Market, regulated by the FSA/UKLA, is supplemented by the so-called Alternative Investment Market (AIM), which is not in the UKLA's scope. Primarily international emerging or smaller companies with higher investment risk list on the AIM. Opened and operated by the LSE plc, it replaced the former LSE Unlisted Securities Market (USM) that was set up in 1980 to provide an organized market without demanding listing requirements.

While the regulation of disclosure standards in the Main Market has fully eluded from the LSE's authority, the exchange still regulates the AIM. Issuers listed at the Alternative Market underlie the AIM Rule Book. These rules contain considerably less onerous listing and disclosure

*Exhibit 5.3* Changes in the UK model, demonstrated for the LSE

| Time | Main business (and capital needs) | Organization | External oversight | Regulator | | |
|---|---|---|---|---|---|---|
| | | | | **Offical markets** | **Unofficial markets** | |
| **Before 1986** | Floor trading (low) | "Club" | Trade Secretary and DTI | LSE | Unlisted securities market (governed by LSE) | |
| 1986 | | | *"Big Bang"* | | | |
| | | | *Financial Services Act of 1986* | | | |
| **Since 1986** | Electronic trading (high) | Member-owned cooperative | SIB | LSE and SFA (SROs) as UKLA | | |
| 1995 | | | | | AIM (governed by LSE) | |
| 1997 | | | FSA | | | |
| 2000 | | | *Financial Services and Markets Act of 2000* | | | |
| **Since 2000** | | LSE plc | FSA | FSA as UKLA | | |
| 2004 | | | | | | |

*Note:* Dotted lines indicate that the previous arrangements persist.

requirements than those of the Main Market, leading to higher hetero-geneity of listed firms (Goergen *et al.* 2003). However, the AIM Rule Book contains a number of requirements especially concerning disclos-ures. For instance, audited annual reports according to IFRS (for issuers from the European Economic Area, EEA) and semi-annual reports are required. Beyond these financial reporting requirements, the overall dis-closure requirements are commonly regarded as modest, although they contain duties of notification on any substantial or price-sensitive event concerning related parties, reverse takeovers or fundamental changes of business.

The AIM is not only the world's first, but the most successful market for emerging companies (measured in terms of listings and market cap-italization). This can be seen as confirmation that its regulatory level is appropriate for the firms targeted (Löhr 2006). Despite its success, the AIM's requirement for each listed company to have a Nominated Advisor (NOMAD) turned out to be its major weakness. The NOMAD, chosen from an official LSE list by each company itself, organizes the listing process and acts as a market maker. In some cases this depend-ency has led to serious abuses and thus provoked calls for stronger oversight.

While the LSE plc does not regulate the Main Market anymore, it still introduced market partition indices labelled 'techMARK' and 'techMARK mediscience'. In doing so, LSE tried to increase the visibility of innovative firms for a greater public. However, these indices are not related to stricter disclosure standards as in the case of the FSE's Prime Standard. The LSE does not possess the required regulatory competences and was not as successful as Deutsche Börse AG to set stricter disclosure rules out of its own market power.

## 5.4   The US: Crowding out the private sector

The US was long thought of as having the world's strongest and most innovative capital market. American institutions and stock exchanges such as NYSE and AMEX – and later also the NASDAQ – achieved cutting-edge positions in the struggle for equity and venture capital. Unlike in Germany and the UK, the number of successful stock markets was higher. This can be explained by the functional differentiation of some exchanges, applying different and non-competing business mod-els, which warrants the discussion of all the above-mentioned stock exchanges instead of just one.

## Pre-SEC arrangements

The NYSE as the oldest organized stock exchange in the US traces its origins to 1792, when 24 stockbrokers signed the original Buttonwood Agreement (Geisst 1997; NYSE 2006). The subscribers agreed to trade securities on a commission basis while demanding minimum provisions from outsiders (Werner and Smith 1991). Trading in stocks grew rapidly: more than 100 local exchanges had emerged all over the country, 24 of them located in New York. In 1817, brokers formed the New York Stock & Exchange Board (NYS&EB), adopted a statute and established a permanent trading place on Wall Street. Since 1863 trading occurs under the official name New York Stock Exchange.

Analogous to the developments in the UK, cartel-like relationships were established, which prohibited trading of stocks listed at NYS&EB on other exchanges and restricted exchange access by membership in order to enhance the individual gains for its members (Blume *et al.* 1993). Besides monitoring trading rules and orders, the board could impose fines or even bans in case of misconduct. In other words, the exchange built up a structure of self-regulation and restricted competition that determined the further development of the NYSE throughout the subsequent century (Lütz 2002). Next to the dominant NYSE – where approximately 75 percent of all US securities transactions took place – a number of 32 other organized stock exchanges had remained on the market by 1933 when the new securities regulation was ushered in.

Among these traditional exchanges, the AMEX deserves a particular mention. The history of the AMEX dates back to the 1800s when it was known as the Curb Market. Rapidly growing with the Gold Rush of 1849, the Curb Exchange positioned itself as a non-competitor to the NYSE because AMEX styled itself as a place where innovative traders conducted unconventional businesses with mostly young or marginal firms (Sobel 1972). Many of those companies sooner or later disappeared through mergers, bankruptcies or liquidation.

In the absence of legal disclosure or financial reporting regulations, the exchanges started introducing listing requirements analogous to the developments in the UK (Smith 1936). In particular, NYSE and AMEX initiated formal listing requirements including disclosure duties that were scrutinized by their own committees. Already since 1869 the NYSE had recommended that listed companies publish annual statements on a firm's financial condition to its shareholders (Hilke 1986; NYSE 2006). However, the standards were barely enforced and companies could easily avoid compliance by switching to other exchanges (Seligman 1995;

Smith 1933). Still, some companies began to extend the publication of financial reports to its shareholders (McCormick 1960). This very situation provided the capital market with different degrees of transparency at different exchanges and hence contributed to its growth by means of competition (Di Noia 2001).[5] The NYSE's disclosure requirements at that time were principally related to financial reporting and immediate issuance of information on material corporate events. Issuers were required to publish interim and annual reports to the exchange as well as to their shareholders. With the upcoming private regulation at the stock exchanges, the difference between issuers of listed and unlisted stocks increased. While issuers of listed stocks had to fulfil listing and disclosure requirements, issuers of stocks traded over the counter (OTC) were not regulated.

As in the previously discussed jurisdictions, a series of frauds and financial crises accompanied the era of self-regulation until the beginning of the 1920s. In particular, incidents in 1869 and 1873 provoked legal action in regard to the structure of the US capital market. In these years, stock prices escalated and presumptions on manipulation spread. As a reaction, the federal states began to impose the so-called Blue Sky Laws in order to protect investors against fraudulent securities practices. Not being company but securities law, the Blue Sky Laws were intended to enhance disclosure regulation in the respective states. In practice, however, the states lacked the ability for enforcement since their equipment with funds and personnel was not sufficient and companies had the opportunity to opt out by moving to other jurisdictions. Moreover, companies operating across the single states' borders could hardly be regulated at all. After a short period, these laws were understood as inefficient (Tiedeken 1999). In an uncontested application of the interstate commerce clause – much different from other measures taken during the New Deal – the federal government stepped in, regulating the stock exchanges and, this is novel, the disclosure rules of companies listed on them. In a relatively short time span today's financial reporting system evolved, which is dominated by the SEC (see also Chapter 2 and Chapter 7). The developments are summarized in Exhibit 5.4, which provides an overview of the most important developments before and after the enactment of the federal securities regulations.

Contrary to conventional wisdom, the federal regulatory reforms of securities trade in the 1930s are not only a result of the capital market's collapse in 1929 and the accompanying Great Depression (Skousen 1991). In fact, these events represent only the final trigger for a transformation of securities regulation that had its origins in the experiences of the

*Exhibit 5.4* Changes in the US model, demonstrated for the AMEX, NASDAQ and NYSE

| Time | Main business (and capital needs) | Organization | External oversight | Regulator | |
|---|---|---|---|---|---|
| | | | | Offical markets | Unofficial markets (OTC) |
| Traditional model | Floor trading (low) | Unincorporated associations (most important bourses are NYSE & AMEX) | Exchanges (NYSE, AMEX) | | OTC |
| Since 1911 | | | States (Blue Sky Laws) | | |
| 1933/34 | *Federal Securities Regulation (SA und SEA)* | | | | |
| Since 1934 | Floor trading (high) | SROs | SEC | SEC (additional to stock exchange's regulation) | NASD and OTC |
| 1971 | *Electronic trading (high) (Floor trading at NYSE)* | *Incorporation (NYSE)* | | | First electronic stock exchange (NASDAQ) starts to operate |
| 1975 | *Re-regulation by the SEC: Amendmends of the Securities Laws* | | | | |
| Since 1975 | | | | SEC (NASDAQ starts to operate listed segment) | |
| 2002 | | NASDAQ-going public | | | |
| 2005/2006 | | NYSE-going public | | | NASD and OTCBB takeover |

*Note:* Dotted lines indicate that the previous arrangements persist.

late 19th century. The US needed to stamp out the practice of shopping for regulation as particularly the enforcement still varied widely between the states. This helps to explain the strong enforcement culture of the SEC (see Chapter 7). The detailed requirements for disclosures, though, remain remarkable. It can be seen as a means to regulate business nearly to the extremes of the interstate commerce clause.

## Stock exchanges under SEC regulation

With the SEC becoming the omnipresent regulator of the US stock markets from 1934, the exchanges' disclosure stipulations lost their importance. In the fragmented market and during the Great Depression, this new financial regulation and the shift of competencies met with little resistance. After being registered with the SEC, which necessitates further continuing disclosure requirements, a company may enter into admission proceedings at US stock exchanges. While the system of competition between the exchanges has been of particular importance for the development of the US capital market, the SEC got more and more involved in regulating disclosure, accounting standards and corporate governance (Bishop 2001; Lütz 2002). Shortly after its foundation, the SEC codified disclosure requirements at a basic level for all issuers listed on national exchanges. And because issuers have to file ever-increasing amounts of financial and non-financial information on a regular basis with the SEC since then, virtually no room for private law disclosure requirements has been left. Especially after the Securities Act Amendments of 1975, the Commission extended the scope and extent of its disclosure forms (Küting and Hayn 1993; Moran 1991). These forms predefine the content of financial reporting and registration documents. They have to be filed for registration as well as for meeting ongoing disclosure requirements (see also Chapter 2).

Next to the regulation of issuers and its enforcement activities, the SEC supervises all stock exchanges, which are obligated to maintain a set of rules that promote good conduct in trading. Next to stock exchanges, there are other organizations such as the National Association of Securities Dealers (NASD) as well as the clearing sites that are supervised by the SEC. They are often referred to as SROs. In practice, the SROs need to register with the SEC and are in permanent interaction with the Commission (Seligman 1995). Every new rule that is intended to be pronounced by the SROs needs approval of the SEC and is subject to a due process with commenting opportunities.

The regulatory arrangements in the US are a three-tier oversight system. For the US, one sees government/state as the first, the SEC as the second and the stock exchanges as the third tier of oversight supervising its members in turn (Moran 1991). The three-tier classification of stock market oversight, albeit commonly used, reflects neither historical developments nor regulatory might: in the US the SEC holds the key position with its statutory powers delegated from the US Congress. The SROs are often presented as the third tier, but they represent the much older stock exchanges.

To maintain the quality of their markets, US exchanges require issuers not only to meet original (SEC-approved) listing criteria but maintain their own continued listing standards. Here, the NYSE's standards are perceived as being among the highest of any market in the world (Shapiro 1998). These listing criteria ensure that disclosures can quickly be priced into shares by means of trading. Criteria include earnings, cash flow, ownership structure, trading volume, market value and share price. By signing the listing agreement, issuers also commit to follow NYSE's practices and procedures regarding disclosing and reporting material information, all of which is to be found in the exchange's listing manual. The Listed Company Compliance division of the NYSE reviews the submitted disclosure documentation. In case of violations, the exchange may suspend the security and remove it from the list.

Today's stock exchanges in the US differ from the organizations they used to be in the early days of the SEC. Since the Buttonwood Agreement, the NYSE had been an 'unincorporated association', and its membership has been tradable after 1953. By 1971, the exchange incorporated into a non-profit company and members obtained the status of partners with voting power (NYSE 2006). The SEC forced the exchange in May 1975 to abstain from requesting minimum provision fees, an event that critical members later recorded as May Day (Geisst 1997). Finally, in December 2005, the NYSE's governing board announced its acquisition of the electronic-based exchange Archipelago and became a for-profit public company that now features both floor and electronic trading. The large amount of smaller exchange members hampered demutualization for a long time, and larger exchange users such as investment banks gained influence in the explicit exchange bodies only in recent years. Trading of NYSE's shares began only in March 2006, which is late when compared to Deutsche Börse's demutualization in 1993. NYSE still remains the United States' biggest market place for shares, covering a trading volume of more than 60 percent.

The AMEX as the second traditional stock exchange in the US is handling a small amount of the North American share trades. Registered with the SEC as a regular exchange, AMEX is known to have the least strict listing requirements among the three top American exchanges, resulting in many small domestic companies being listed on it (Sobel 1972). While listing requirements are less demanding than those of the NYSE, there is a notable difference between the OTC market, that is trade between individuals not using an organized market, and the AMEX, not at least due to the different legal requirements. In fact, AMEX is often seen as a transition step from OTC trade towards an NYSE listing (Aggarwal and Angel 1999). However, since disclosure requirements of the SEC apply to all issuers listed on a regulated market, differences between the exchanges have diminished, similar to the Regulated Market in Germany.

Turnover-wise, the NASDAQ is today the second most important stock exchange in the US following the NYSE and leading before the much older AMEX. It holds a share of more than 30 percent of the organized trade. Today, among these three large US institutions, the NASDAQ is the only exchange to offer two segments on which to list and trade stock, each with its own set of listing requirements. While larger, established companies are more likely to list and trade on the NASDAQ National Market, smaller, emerging companies usually opt for the NASDAQ SmallCap Market with less-demanding listing criteria. Although founded only in 1971 to service a much different target audience, NASDAQ has become the NYSE's biggest rival in the meantime.

The dealers' association NASD is originally the relevant body to regulate OTC trading. When the members of the dealer's association NASD created NASDAQ, the market was intended to enhance OTC trading by providing the first purely electronic market without floor trading (Sharpe *et al.* 1995). Over the years, NASDAQ enhanced the information and automated trading system and developed into an alternative market specialized in stocks of high-tech companies. Still, the market itself did not gain the status of an SRO as it was operated by the NASD. In 1975, NASDAQ separated its market into two segments: OTC and listed. For the latter segment, the NASD not only provided listing requirements (Löhr 2006), but also ruled that the disclosure requirements of the SEC had to be met by issuers, thus voluntarily transferring its operational responsibilities to the SEC.

Listing requirements were tightened in 1982 when larger companies were concurrently moved to the National Market system that provided continuous price quotation. The NASDAQ was demutualized by NASD in a series of sales in 2000 and 2001 and became listed on its own exchange in 2002. In order to achieve the desired exchange status as an SRO, the NASDAQ transferred its OTC business back to the NASD and the Over the Counter Bulletin Board (OTCBB) in 2005. Although NASDAQ received SEC approval as a national securities exchange only in 2006, the exchange had started to operate an organized market before.

In contrast to the European exchanges discussed before, today's US exchanges show one significant difference. While the German and British exchanges operate both regulated and unregulated markets, there is no unregulated OTC trade on the three big US exchanges. This fact limits the regulatory discretion of the institutions significantly. However, this implies by no way that the OTC market is of marginal relevance in the US. From its beginning, OTC trade has been conducted by professional traders outside the Regulated Market without imposing any listing or disclosure requirements (Küting and Hayn 1993; Sharpe *et al.* 1995).

The OTCBB continues to provide trading services formerly executed by the NASDAQ. The OTCBB is not an exchange in the sense of an issuer listing service but a quotation medium for subscribing members, not charging listing fees or demanding for disclosure requirements itself. However, the NASD as the owner of the Board changed the rulings significantly when the NASDAQ was still conducting OTC trade. Since 1999, all firms traded on the NASD's systems (today the OTCBB) have to file (and publish) annual and quarterly financial reports with the SEC following the Commission's special rules for OTC issuers that have to meet certain criteria. This rule coming from NASD therefore also applies for entities that are legally not obliged to comply with SEC regulation, illustrating that all significant securities trade in the US is under the SEC's supervision today.

## 5.5   Conclusion

The struggle between public and private arrangements in the governance of stock exchanges has been a continuous one in all three countries. Private trading activities of merchants were the foundations of organized capital markets. The traders built their own private institutions mostly as exclusive clubs to systemize trading. For a relatively long period these institutionalized capital markets remained predominantly self-regulated. In the golden-age nation state, cartel-like rules supported the existence of the nationally prevalent exchanges: by restraining competition between regional exchanges (Germany), by demanding minimum trading provisions (the US) or by having the monopoly on trade in government funds (the UK). Security trading was based on informal codes of conduct, that is some type of mutual self-surveillance (Ouchi 1979), rather than on transparency and abstract rules of behaviour.

Until the end of the 19th century, the state resisted to assume outcome responsibility for the provision of welfare in capital markets. Neither was the state initially interested in their functioning, nor did it seem overly perturbed by the monopolistic arrangements and the distribution of rents that could be extracted from organizing share trade. Insider trading was of no concern.

The New Deal set an end to this in the US. The SEC was established to ensure transparency of market transactions and to punish market abuse. The state took on outcome and supervision responsibility for the stock markets. Inasmuch as the state was lacking essential skilled knowledge, private actors were included in the regulatory process. Consequently, the SEC offered a 'public status' to private associations such as stock exchanges. They became autonomous SROs provided with regulatory competences in order to enforce rules autonomously against their customers. They were private organizations operating on behalf of the state. In Germany and the UK, the lack of state interference persisted until pressures from global share trade, a daunting dominance of the US and European harmonization, forced governments to take up outcome and supervision responsibility. They responded mostly by providing listing rules and regulating against insider trading. Some operating and supervision responsibility for the share trade still rest with the exchanges, more so in Germany but also in the UK. In both countries, the stock markets organize unofficial segments in which they exercise regulating powers.

The shift from different self-regulatory approaches towards state intervention has recently accelerated further. In the US, the SEC has tightened already rigid regulatory standards, further diminishing the influence of stock exchanges in self-regulation. Motives for expansion of state intervention have been the growing lobby of institutional investors as well as several business scandals. In the UK, far-reaching changes from liberal self-regulatory arrangements towards a strongly hierarchical organization of securities markets have taken place. Here the FSA has been established as an independent rule-setting and enforcement agency that largely rules out stipulation of listing rules by private actors. In Germany, the changes are least pronounced, partly because stock market regulation is shared between the federal government and the single states. Exhibit 5.5 provides a compressed perspective on the different phases within the three countries considered.

Having examined the regulation of stock exchanges, the emphasis on financial reporting as such seems rather limited. The state typically set minimum rules for disclosure. While some additional regulations were

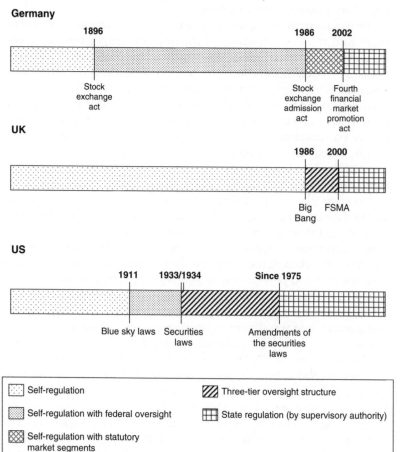

*Exhibit 5.5*  Different phases of regulation in Germany, the UK and the US

put forward by the exchanges before the national governments augmented their interventions, systematic and comparatively reliable corporate disclosures were provided to investors only after government intervention. Thus, stock markets typically did not compete by increasing levels of disclosure but by lowering transaction costs. Liquidity of the market was rather enhanced by tightening listing rules such as requiring a minimum free float than by reducing insider trading, which should entice more people into the financial market. Insider trading regulation has been a state concern and has, apart from egregious cases of wrongdoing, been forced onto the stock exchanges.

The regulatory changes, which were traced in this chapter, go hand in hand with the transformations of the stock exchanges' business models and organizational forms, in particular the privatization of stock exchanges' operating entities. The process of demutualization is most advanced in Germany, having already started in 1993. Meanwhile, the US-American NYSE and NASDAQ as well as the British LSE have also been transformed into for-profit companies under private law. The process of transforming exchanges into listed for-profit organizations led to a refreshed intrinsic interest of the institutions to foster listings and trade by establishing different levels of transparency at their markets, especially in Germany but also in the UK.

This competition is possible due to a remaining degree of discretion among European exchanges and operators. Hence, the Deutsche Börse AG and the FSE introduced supplementary market segments with additional transparency regulations in all legally defined segments, namely the Prime Standard or the Entry Standard. In the UK the LSE still regulates the AIM and provides the market with a predominantly privately governed exchange. This market is highly successful with (non-UKLA-listed) issuers worldwide because it demands only a minimal level of transparency that is sufficient to boost credibility among investors and to reach an international audience. In contrast, no such arrangement can be found in the US. The NASD as the relevant player within the OTC market had at least the theoretical latitude to establish a comparable competitive setting but decided to delegate disclosure rulings to the SEC. Almost no competition exists in the US.

Perplexingly, financial information does not seem to play such an important role for those that trade on it. If the opposite were the case, stock exchanges would have interfered earlier with additional disclosure rules. Regarding accounting, therefore, as a part of company law rather than an integral part of securities regulation does not seem to be an entirely incongruous approach. This underscores the observation that regulating accounting by means of the SEC is a singular accident due to the constitutional arrangements in the US. Even though Europe has now followed the US model, it may have altogether taken the wrong junction to the path of progress.

# Part III

# The Role of the Nation State in Enforcement

The subject of this part is the role of the nation state in enforcing the accuracy of financial reports. As financial information is prepared inside the reporting entity, users of accounts are likely to question the credibility of the information conveyed to them. They thus might require attestation of the reported results. Typically, a firm appoints an independent auditor who testifies that the reports were prepared according to accepted principles or that the published accounts give a 'true and fair view' of the firm's financials. Auditing is the private enforcement solution of choice, often also required by stock exchanges. Another possibility to enforce existing accounting rules is to police them. Such policing is typically done by state agencies. At the moment, both solutions complement each other in the countries under consideration.

A further strategy to enhance the credibility of financial reports is to expose preparers of financial reports to litigation risk. We do not consider this strategy in Part III, as litigation risk does not arise from specific institutional structures. Instead, we treat litigation risk as an element of the corporate governance system that is operating in a particular country, and we will discuss this issue in Chapter 9.

As in the previous part, taxation plays no role in this story: enforcement has its necessary precondition in prepared reports, and as accounting for tax is by and large independent from devising financial reports for the information of investors (group accounting), enforcement for taxation purposes has very little influence on the enforcement of financial reports. While it may contribute to the overall accuracy of the reporting system, it does not align with the other types of accounting, managerial and financial, and therefore does not complement the other activities in a systematic fashion.

Part III is subdivided into two chapters. Chapter 6 deals with the attestation of financial reports by means of auditing. The demand for auditing was first articulated by private actors and later institutionalized by stock exchanges and in the law. Regulating the standards of statutory audits was left to the professions for a long time. It was relatively late – many legal disclosure regulations were already developed – when the nation state started to intervene in the auditing process either by setting minimum standards or by shaping the organization of the profession. A major involvement in the institutional structures of the profession happened after the wave of accounting scandals of the late 1990s and early 2000s. It was mostly the auditing profession that was blamed for superficial and inaccurate checks, and at times members even advised firms how to bend accounting rules. As a response, the state created oversight bodies in all three countries under consideration, stripping the professions of powers at least partially. The nation state has expanded in this domain. Regarding the procedural rules, though, the nation state's scope for influence on auditing is on the retreat: increasingly, auditors use International Auditing Standards, which are set by a transnational body. This only seems to copy the developments in disclosure, but with one important exception. While, in disclosure, firms were compelled to report under national rules due to earlier government interventions, the detailed procedures of the audit were not regulated by law. Unrestricted by legal stipulations, the profession has voluntarily turned to applying international norms. In the meantime, the EU has used this institutional set-up to harmonize auditing standards across Europe, following the private-sector developments more than leading them. This means that the state's influence will be superseded by supranationalization, in which the role of the public sector increases as transnationally set rules will be mandated by the EU. As with financial reporting standards, the US does not follow this route; it relies on national solutions.

While auditing has become increasingly international, the national 'policing' of financial reports, which we cover in Chapter 7, has gained in importance. All three nation states rely on different institutional arrangements to enforce the material correctness of published financial reports. The oldest enforcement model, built around the SEC in the US, has not provided a blueprint for enforcement. Each nation state implements its own preferred model. Not even Europe has achieved a consistent solution: unencumbered by binding European regulation, Germany and UK have developed institutions that are somewhat similar in organizational form but differ significantly in regulatory competence.

# 6
# Dawn and Dusk of the Nation State in Auditing: From Supervising Private Arrangements to Transnational Governance

Auditing is the oldest mechanism to enforce the quality of financial disclosures. Audits are performed by external accountants, who are appointed by the firms that prepare and submit the reports. As a result of this process, attested financial reports are published. In this particular situation, the credibility of the auditor and of the methods employed for the audit plays a decisive role. If the auditor is not sufficiently independent or if the methods employed are not effective for detecting shortcomings, the accreditation of the accounts will not be of much value. For a long time, it was the accounting profession that established standards to maintain the quality of audits. These standards comprised organizational mechanisms such as access to the profession and procedural regulation on how to conduct the audit itself. Increasingly the stock exchanges and the state have relied on the mere existence of audits as an enforcement mechanism but abstained largely from setting detailed regulations on how the audits should be done. In most cases, the self-regulatory nature of the profession stayed intact. The profession reached out internationally and developed a framework for setting International Auditing Standards early on. While the US largely ignored these developments, the EU has used the profession's transnational arrangements in its attempt to harmonize auditing standards.

In the wake of recent accounting scandals, the reputation of the profession was tarnished. In many cases wrongdoings were not discovered in the auditing process, faulty reports were cleared and sometimes firms were even advised how to bend the regulation to achieve desired reporting results. The boundary between an independent auditor and a paid advisor had become increasingly blurred. With the melange of conflicting interests, self-regulation was not likely to be successful. To maintain the credibility of audited accounts, the respective nation states had to tighten their grip on the professions and introduced increased state oversight. The transnationalization of setting and using International Auditing Standards – the procedural aspect – goes hand-in-hand with an increased role of the state in the organizational set-up of the auditing profession.

The chapter is organized as follows. The first section will take a look at the role of auditing in the accounting process, also covering the potential role of the state and international actors. The developments in auditing from the golden age until today are then described for the US, UK and Germany. The latter two countries will be analysed in the context of the ongoing Europeanization in financial markets. The chapter will close by discussing perspectives of future internationalization in auditing.

## 6.1   Auditing: A supply and demand analysis

Auditing is one of the most important enforcement mechanisms. As will be shown, the genesis of the statutory audit and the relative importance and size of audit professions differ across nation states. Primarily, economic crises and increasing capital needs led to the formation of external auditing and, finally, can be seen as the main drivers for the annual audit becoming mandatory between the late 19th and early 20th century. The UK was a pioneer in prescribing external audits with the Companies Act 1844, which required the publication of *audited* financial statements for certain companies (Vieten 1995). In Germany, for instance, it was the crisis of Nordwolle AG in 1931 that triggered a banking crisis and finally led to the introduction of statutory audits for joint stock companies by the Emergency Decree on Stock Corporation Law in the same year (Quick 2005). In the US, it was the federal reforms of the 1930s that made auditing of financial statements by an independent certified public accountant (CPA) compulsory for listed companies (Zeff 2003).

### Demand for auditing services: Some theory

Ensuring the credibility of financial statements is the main task of statutory audits (Marten 2006). Auditing complements financial reporting and adds credibility to financial statements, which enhances their usefulness. Hence, it can be supposed that economic incentives would lead to a demand for audit services even in cases of absence of any regulation: as it cannot be taken for granted that managers report truthfully, addressees cannot fully trust the published numbers. In economic terms, the basic problem is one of information asymmetry between the preparers and the users of financial reports (Ewert and Stefani 2001). Such information asymmetries may lead to opportunistic behaviour of the party with information advantages. Obviously, the managers have such advantages as they are the preparers of financial reports. Suppose that managers follow opportunistically their own interests, they might in many cases have incentives to overstate the company's financial situation (Bazerman *et al.* 1997). For example, managers would benefit from such behaviour when compensation plans tie their remuneration to financial results. While some level of earnings management might be inevitable (or even desirable as a signalling device), problems occur when accounting standards are eventually violated and the company's financials become misrepresented. Such behaviour will often be unobservable for outsiders, who have no information about the workings of the accounting system. Given that there is a positive probability that financial reports will become less informative, their usefulness for addressees is lowered. For example, financial reports might thus be no longer useful for evaluating the stewardship function of the managers and for assessing the financial position of a company for valuation purposes.

Principal–agent theory sees this mechanism as a driver for the demand of auditing services (Herzig and Watrin 1995). Financial reporting itself is intended to lower the information asymmetry between preparers and users of financial reports. Consequently, independently 'verified' financial statements are better capable of reducing the agency problem. Auditing, in particular the checking of financial reports, increases the likelihood of a truthful representation (Scheffler 2005). A high level of trustworthiness of financial reports again reduces the perceived investment risk of the principal. This allows for lower capital costs, and it ascertains the usefulness of earnings for the valuation of the firm (for the role of annual reports in financial analysis see, for example, Meitner *et al.* 2002; Nichols and Wahlen 2004). However, there always remains a gap in expectations: auditors mostly perform plausibility checks on the financial reports, they do not and cannot fully verify the information. Risks of misrepresentations remain, and they increase with cost and time pressures on the auditor.

So far there have been several empirical studies in which the capital market perception of audits was addressed. Most of these studies tried to find evidence for the relevance of information for investors provided in the auditor's report and found (at least some) relevance in such disclosures. Early examples for this strand of research include the studies by Firth (1978) and Ball *et al.* (1979).

In recent research, a further approach was used to test for the value increment connected to credible audits. The hypothesis is that if accounting misrepresentations accompanied by audit failures are revealed, this may lead to a loss in reputation for the audit firm in question (Gelter 2005). These effects may extend to third parties, namely other clients of the audit firm involved in these scandals. If negative consequences can be detected, this allows to measure (by default) the value increment from a fault-free statutory audit. Using this methodology in the case of the Enron collapse, Chaney and Philipich (2002) found that other clients of the involved auditor, Arthur Andersen, experienced a negative market reaction around the event date. Investors seemed to downgrade the quality of the audits performed by Andersen. This can be explained by the argument that there is a lower level of assurance for such firms that financial statements are prepared under a true and fair view.

The observable capital market reactions to audit reports and to audit firms as well as the widespread use of audits in the unregulated phases of the British or the US setting (see also Chapter 5) allow the conclusion that market forces lead to the demand and the supply of audits with high quality: there is evidence that proper audits are priced by the market with a value increment. However, there are also some arguments that state interventions into auditing are nonetheless necessary.

### The role of the state in auditing

Despite the demand for and the supply of auditing services, one may doubt whether market forces alone would lead to an optimal level of audit quality (Kirsch 2004). Miller and Bahnson (2004) point to managers having certain incentives to demand lower-quality audits so that they can pay as little as possible. These incentives may in fact be so strong that the state needs to ascertain minimum quality levels.

Another concern is that the auditor themselves is a provider of services and a customer of the firm that they audit. This means that the auditor has to act in the (articulated) interests of their clients. Depending on who is perceived to be *their* principal, independence of the auditor becomes a material concern (Ballwieser 2001). Traditionally, the managers (in particular the management board in the German corporate governance model or the managing directors in the Anglo-Saxon one-tier system) were influential players in the selection process. Hence, there might be a tendency for a coalition between managers and auditors which is not necessarily in the interest of shareholders or other outsiders. State interventions thus can try to enhance auditor independence.

A lack of auditor independence might also occur when auditors provide additional consulting services to the firms that they audit (Meitner *et al.* 2002). In this case, the auditor becomes a commercial contractor of the management not acting in the public interest. Their material independence may then be reduced as the auditor often has to verify procedures that they have suggested for implementation themselves: this is what happened in the Enron case, the trigger for wide-ranging institutional reform in the early 2000s. Here, the auditor devised mechanisms of 'double-counting' in group reports, where otherwise unearned profit – because business was conducted between dependent entities and thus within the group – could be reported as if they were outside earnings. The auditor's economic independence may also be reduced if she receives a comparably high sum for auditing and consulting services. In the latter case, the management has power to pressure the auditing company. It may threaten to terminate the profitable business relationship if the findings of the auditor compromise the actions (or the financial results) of the management. As the profession had used exactly this route to shore up its earnings, often using audits as a loss-leader for the acquisition of profitable consulting opportunities, the threat seemed increasingly real.

From an economic perspective, the demand structures for auditing services work against these developments. If the audit becomes dubious, it loses its value increment. At least to the outside, management needs to keep up the impression that the audit does what is expected from it. Still, informational asymmetries exist. An external shareholder will have difficulties in assessing how trustworthy the auditor really is.

The state sector's intervention should not be understood as market-braking, but rather as market-backing.[2] Interventions are generally intended to strengthen audit quality, which can, for example, be achieved through regulation of auditor quality and independence. Historically, the scope and intensity of audit regulation varied across nation states. Vieten (1995) sees the differences in where the responsibility for regulation is located on an axis between the state and the profession. In his study, he compares the cases of Germany and the UK. His analysis concludes that even the definition (or self-conception) of the profession differed in both countries. However, the author sees some kind of convergence between the two systems as early as in the 1990s. Particularly the British system changed and moved away from its traditional *laissez-faire* approach towards more statutory controls, in particular an increasing role of the state in the UK. This tendency continued in recent years and can also be detected in the US. Additionally, there are political aspects in connection with the crisis theory of interventions (Owen and Braeutigam 1978). When market failures occur, the state may have to intervene early, even in the auditing process, before the crisis actually happens to signal its outcome responsibility. This is particularly the case when the financial reporting standards are either state-set or state-backed: here, audit failures put the state's legitimization at stake.

With standard-setting leaving the national arena (see Chapter 3), the state's task of intervening into auditing may also be internationalized. At least three reasons suggest that this is very likely to happen. First, the big (four) audit companies already act globally. First, mergers between the previously nationally organized firms occur; and these legal developments are themselves only a reflection of previously harmonized practice between the national partnerships that operated under a 'brand umbrella'. Uniform approaches to financial reporting allow to realize economies of scale in such companies – the more so when auditing requirements are also harmonized. As auditing companies have significant lobbying power (Hopwood 1994), this 'demand' can be a driver of internationalization. Second, harmonizing regulation also makes sense for the audited firms themselves: recent regulations, discussed in more detail in Chapter 9 of this book, make top managers of holding companies responsible for the accuracy of accounts even of foreign affiliated companies. Hence, it is likely that managers have incentives to demand auditing standards of the same quality in each country where affiliates are domiciled. Third, as in financial reporting, the EU undertakes efforts to harmonize auditing regulation within the Community. This not only leads to a 'regional internationalization' of auditing within the EU but can also be a driver for further global convergence.

In the following sections, the developments in audit regulation will be described for the US, the UK and Germany. As the latter two countries are member states of the EU, Community regulation of auditing will also be addressed. Before summarizing our findings, we will look at the increasing role of the IFAC, an organization of the national professions. The IFAC is going to provide the structures for an emerging global framework of audit regulation and thus can be seen as an institution analogous to the IASCF.

## 6.2   Audit governance: Institutions and procedures

The previous supply and demand analysis has revealed the multiple interests driving the auditing process. As auditing is intended to strengthen the purposes of the financial report, the use of the financial report will shape the audit governance. If these reports are primarily used to solve conflict between the financiers, then auditing becomes an issue of company law and will be regulated there. If the emphasis lies on investors, the quality of audits becomes an issue of securities regulation. And when there is strong enforcement, this may crowd out the need for intense auditing. Further, the 'variety of capitalism' plays a role: as auditors enhance the value of reports for outsiders, who did not participate in its preparation, insider economies such as (traditional) Germany will place a lower emphasis on audits than outsider economies such as the UK and the US.

## Developments in the US

The US has long applied a multilevel governance mode to auditing. An individual who wishes to practise as a CPA has – after passing an exam – to register with one of the State Boards of Accountancy, which have been regulating the profession of public accountants since the beginning of the 20th century. The state locus of regulation shows the origins of auditing in company law–type 'problem solving', and this access route for the audit of public firms still exists.

Significant changes have, however, happened in the way that the quality of the audit is controlled. Prior to the corporate scandals which shook the foundations of the accounting profession, the AICPA was setting standards on auditing, quality control, independence and ethics. The quality of audits and the quality of firms conducting these audits were reviewed by the private POB, which did this under the remit of the SEC for audits conducted for an issuer of shares. The SEC set requirements for quality control and stipulated peer review for the audit firms. As with the development of US GAAP, the federal government used listed firms to intervene in the audit governance, and a role model evolved that was eventually applied for all firms throughout the country, thus circumventing the states' powers in company law.

The SOA of 2002 led to major changes in the regulation of the auditing profession (see also Chapter 9). While the overall regulatory oversight now still rests with the SEC, the SOA shifted the organizational responsibilities to the PCAOB. The PCAOB is a quasi-governmental organization with extensive powers. It registers firms that conduct audits for listed public companies, sets standards for the quality of audits and establishes rules for quality control, pronounces rules on auditor independence and inspects registered audit firms. The Board is staffed with five persons, who are appointed on a full-time basis by the SEC after consultations with the

Federal Reserve and the Secretary of the Treasury. The PCAOB reports to the SEC, which reports to various congressional committees in turn.

Establishing this quasi-governmental agency does not only effectively end the self-regulation of the profession but it also alters the framework in which auditing standards are set. The PCAOB had, upon its inception, kept the AICPA standards on auditing in force as 'interim standards', but it soon signalled its intent to develop auditing standards further. The release 2003–2023, 'Proposed Auditing Standard on Audit Documentation and Proposed Amendment to Interim Standards on Auditing' confirmed that the PCAOB would take a national focus and would be working independently of other international actors, and raised concerns that the PCAOB standards may differ from those outside the US. As the profession increasingly internationalizes in its procedures, a US-only regulation would forestall reaping economies of scale and would not be in the interest of the profession.

This concern was not entirely unfounded as the PCAOB has a strong US focus. This may be 'normal' for the US, but it seems increasingly arcane in the globalization process of financial reporting. The Standing Advisory Group, which assists the Board on standard-setting, has a purely national make-up of academics and practitioners from the auditing profession, publicly listed companies and investors. Out of the six organizations which have observer status only one is denominated as international: the International Auditing and Assurance Standards Board (IAASB). The other observers are the Financial Accounting Standards Board (FASB), the Government Accountability Office, the SEC, the Department of Labor and the Auditing Standards Board of the AICPA. So far, the PCAOB has set four auditing standards, all of which have received SEC approval and became effective. These standards not only cover formal issues such as references in the financial reports (Auditing Standard No. 1) but also material rules on how to audit internal control systems (Auditing Standard No. 2) and what to do when weaknesses persist (Auditing Standard No. 4).

The new auditing standards have already been facing criticism as being unduly burdensome. This has led the PCAOB to consider easing its regulations. In December 2006, the Board proposed a new standard on internal control, effectively redesigning Auditing Standard No. 2 only after two years. The new draft standard is more principles-based and allows the auditor to implement own strategies to increase the likelihood to detect material weaknesses. The proposed standard also simplifies and shortens the text of the previous Auditing Standard No. 2. However, this should not be seen as a first step towards internationalization but more so as a pragmatic response to the profession's pressuring.

## Developments in the UK

The UK had long followed a model of self-regulation in auditing as well. Audits could be conducted by an accountant who was registered with one of the chartered accountancy bodies, the professional associations which were described in greater detail in Chapter 3. They laid down their own audit regulation and guidance. A registration with a state agency was not necessary. This model was established in the outgoing 19th century and was practised for nearly a century. The first major change occurred with the Companies Act of 1989, requiring the DTI to monitor company audit work. The regulation coincided with the transposition of the Seventh (83/349/EEC) and Eighth (84/253/EEC) Council Directives into UK law (using the Companies Act of 1989), which established minimum state regulation and thus reflected what was common in Continental Europe (see Chapter 3).The subsequent monitoring was undertaken by the institutes/societies such as the ICAEW or the ICAS, which were discussed in more detail in Chapter 3. Thus, 'a multiplicity of dual capacity professional bodies exist in Britain' (Vieten 1995), which acted simultaneously as professional associations and supervisory organizations. The use of the existing private infrastructure with an increased state recognition parallels the role of the ASB as the official standard-setter for UK GAAP.

The regulation of the auditing profession in 1989 led to the eventual set-up of an APB. The APB was established in 1991 to further auditing practice and to establish unified standards of auditing. The APB promulgated Statements of Auditing Standards (SASs) containing principles and procedures to be complied with by auditors in the statutory or any other audit. Again, this reflects the experience from rule-setting, where the multiplicity of standard-setting bodies was eventually replaced by a single national regulator, the ASB.

The APB had 16 voting members, half of whom were auditing practitioners while the other half were individuals who were involved in financial reporting as users or preparers. Among concerns that the APB was tied too closely to the profession (Sikka 2002), a slightly remodelled APB moved under the umbrella of the Accountancy Foundation as an independent oversight body in 2001 (Fearnley and Hines 2003). While the new APB had a similar remit as its predecessor, the majority of voting rights now were outside the auditing profession. Increasingly, the

APB made use of International Auditing Standards instead of developing its own. In 2004, the board adopted and supplemented the existing framework of International Standards on Auditing (ISA) for Britain.

In part as a response to the wave of reporting scandals in the early 2000s, the DTI initiated a series of further reviews which resulted in some institutional re-arrangements (Dewing and Russell 2003). The Accountancy Foundation was moved to the FRC and a Professional Oversight Board for Accountancy (POBA) was established as successor body to the Accountancy Foundation's Review Board (Fearnley *et al.* 2005). In 2005, the Companies (Audit, Investigations and Community Enterprise) Act was passed in order to restore investor confidence in companies and financial markets (Beal and Bennett 2005). This act granted augmented powers to the FRC and to its operating bodies. The POBA was given more rights to oversee regulatory activities of professional bodies. It was renamed into Professional Oversight Board (POB) since it became responsible body also for the actuarial profession. The newly installed Audit Inspection Unit (AIU) is assigned to monitor audits of listed and other major companies. Further, a board now named as Accountancy & Actuarial Discipline Board (AADB) was founded. This body is assigned with carrying out independent investigations into the discipline of accountants and actuaries involved in matters of public interest nature (FRC 2007a). The AADB operates and administers an independent disciplinary scheme and can exert regulatory actions against members of the chartered institutes and societies.

## Developments in Germany

Germany has a chequered history when it comes to the governance of the auditing profession. In the beginning of the 20th century, access to auditing and its quality control was in the hands of the profession. After 1933, the state started to squeeze individuals out of the profession using membership rules to the Institute of Accountancy. After a brief interlude of direct state involvement from 1943–1945, when the Chamber of Auditors existed, the profession regulated itself; after the war it was under the supervision of the respective state (*Länder*) authorities. In 1961, the WPK, a professional organization governed by public law, was established. To conduct annual audits, every auditor has to pass an exam set by the WPK and then to sign up as a member. The WPK is assigned by law to regulate the accreditation of public accountants, supervise the profession and operate a system of quality controls, which includes pronouncing auditing standards (Marten *et al.* 2003).

Germany does not have a unified system of auditing standards but relies on a strict screening system to the profession. Auditors have to observe a number of regulations, not unlike the system of German GAAP. Of highest importance are regulations by law, which can primarily be found in the Commercial Code and in the Public Acountant Act (WPO). The development of further auditing standards is the task of the WPK, which has largely delegated this authority to the IDW. Its pronouncements are intended to fill gaps in (legal) auditing and accounting regulation (Born 2002). The IDW publications (*Verlautbarungen, Fachgutachten, Stellungnahmen*) and the Principles of Proper Auditing (GoA) constituted the system – or rather the compilation – of auditing standards until 1998. GoA claim to be a behavioural guide to auditors; however, they lack explicit legal codification, and are rather fragmented instead of presenting a complete framework (Marten 2006). In 1998, the IDW began to transform the existing system to IDW Auditing Standards (PS) and IDW Audit Guidelines (PH). IDW PS and IDW PH are highly detailed and uniformly structured for a better understanding (see, for example, Böcking *et al.* 2000). They bear close resemblance to the ISA promulgated by the IFAC.

In the German model, there is a clear regulatory separation between the WPK and the IDW: the former acts as a supervisory body, the latter as trade organization (Vieten 1995). While quality control was traditionally the exclusive remit of the WPK, this changed in the wake of corporate scandals. The Act on Auditor Oversight (APAG) implemented a public oversight body in the German regulation system, namely the APAK. The APAK consists of experts selected by the government, is independent of the profession and bears the overall responsibility for quality control. The APAK does not intend to substitute the existing oversight system executed by the WPK, but to complement it by an additional layer of oversight (Böcking and Dutzi 2006).

## The Eighth Council Directive of 1984 and 2006

European legislation influences the UK and Germany. This is why we will now take a closer look at the developments at the European level in regard to audit regulation. This field is largely covered by the Eighth Council Directive (84/253/EEC), which first came into effect in April 1984. A preliminary draft had already been devised in 1972, and the first official proposal was published in 1978 (Evans and Nobes 1998). The Eighth Directive complemented the Fourth (78/660/EEC) and

Seventh Directive (83/349/EEC), which require statutory audits on financial statements for annual and consolidated accounts (Grundmann 2004).

The Eighth Directive harmonized minimum requirements for auditing and auditors so that auditors could make use of the Common Market. It also enhanced trust in cross-border relationships through legal certainty in intra-Community operations. The harmonization achieved by the Eighth Directive was rather minimal and it soon fell short *vis-à-vis* other initiatives in regard to the free movement of goods and services. In 1996 the Commission published a Green Paper about 'The Role, the Position and the Liability of the Statutory Auditor within the European Union', which indicated the need for action regarding statutory audits (COM (96) 338 final, 24 July 1996). A Committee on Auditing was working on the quality of statutory audit, based upon the priorities identified by the Financial Services Action Plan (FSAP) (IP/99/327), and its work covered external quality assurance, auditor independence and auditing standards. The Committee's work resulted in 'Recommendation on quality assurance for the statutory audit in the European Union' (2001/256/EC), which was promulgated by the European Commission. Based on the Committee's work in 2002, a further recommendation was published in 2002 by the Commission ('Statutory auditors' independence in the EU: A set of fundamental principles'; 2002/590/EC).

The accounting scandals of the early 2000s were reasons to reconsider EU priorities on the statutory audit. The Commission's Communication 'Reinforcing the statutory audit in the EU' refers to this incident and contains a '10 point action plan on statutory audit', in which the Commission proposes, amongst other measures, the modernization of the Eighth Directive of 1984. In 2006, the Council agreed on a modernized Eighth Company Law Directive, and it accepted all alterations from the first reading (Downes 2005). The modernized Directive (2006/43/EC) has to be transformed into national law of the member states within two years. The modernized Eighth Directive extends the harmonization to most areas of auditing. Its 12 chapters cover the following: (1) Subject Matter and Definitions, (2) Approval, Continuing Education and Mutual Recognition, (3) Registration, (4) Professional Ethics, Independence, Objectivity, Confidentiality and Professional Secrecy, (5) Auditing Standards and Audit Reporting, (6) Quality Assurance, (7) Investigations and Penalties, (8) Public Oversight and Regulatory Arrangements between member states, (9) Appointment and Dismissal, (10) Special Provisions for the Statutory Audits of Public-Interest Entities, (11) International Aspects and (12) Transitional and Final Provisions.

Chapter 5 now requires auditors to apply 'international' auditing standards. The term 'International Auditing Standards', by definition of Article 2, paragraph 11, refers to standards set by the IFAC, which are denoted as ISA. However, to become effective within the EU, these standards first have to be adopted by the Commission and have to be published in the Official Journal of the EU. This will provide ISA with authority of law (Brinkmann and Spiess 2006). Additionally, the Directive demands a system similar to the PCAOB in the US. But while the PCAOB is only responsible for auditors of listed companies, in Europe all statutory auditors and audit firms are required to be subject to such public oversight. This, yet again, reflects the different inroad to accountancy regulation taken in the US: In Europe, there is no need to bypass the member states and company law can be regulated by means of directives. This also implies that the rules of the statutory audit will have a broader scope, applying to all firms, not merely the listed ones.

National public oversight systems have to cooperate at Community level. This generates a demand for the establishment of a single body which ensures this cooperation. For this purpose, the Commission founded the European Group of Auditors' Oversight Bodies (EGAOB) in December 2005 (Tiedje 2006). This body, which has to be governed by non-practitioners, deals with the approval and registration of auditors, the adoption of ethics standards, internal quality control, as well as continuing education and quality assurance for investigative and disciplinary systems.

For adopting auditing standards, the European Commission has established a screening mechanism to ensure that each standard has 'been developed with proper due process, public oversight and transparency, and are generally accepted internationally; contribute a high level of credibility and quality to the annual or consolidated accounts [...] and are conducive to the European public good' (Article 26.2 of the Eighth Directive). For assisting the adoption procedures the Commission has installed the Audit Regulatory Committee (AuRC), which consists of representatives from the member states. Additionally the EGAOB will provide support for the adoption of ISA. However, once an ISA is adopted, the Eighth Directive still allows member states to deviate from it under certain conditions: if national requirements are opposed to ISA provisions, supplementary provisions may be added or carve-outs may be accepted (Lanfermann 2005). Carve-outs underlie specific conditions. For example, they have to be explained to the Commission and to the other member states six months before national application.

## 6.3   The emerging global framework: The IFAC

The IFAC was founded in 1977. This institution is more akin to the German Institute of Auditors as a lobbying institution rather than the UK institutes/societies or the AICPA in the US, as both have some regulating powers over the profession. The IFAC solely consists of institutional members, and membership is not limited to one per national jurisdiction. Germany, for instance, is represented by the WPK and the IDW; five institutions from the UK are members, namely the already-discussed professional organizations. The US is represented by the AICPA, the CIMA and the National Association of State Boards of Accountancy (NASBA).

The IFAC has a wide institutional mission. The organization concerns itself with ethical standards and education, but its currently most important objective is to establish and promote high-quality professional standards and to further international convergence in auditing. IFAC's international standards on auditing are currently transmitted into auditing practice by the respective member organizations, but IFAC's standards do not override national professional regulations, which may also be restricted by (unharmonized) national legislation. Even though IFAC does not have any power of sanctions if standards are not adopted by its members (Chandler 1990), more than 70 countries apply ISA or standards with no material difference to the ISA (IFAC Annual Reports 2002 and 2003).

The IFAC has witnessed a substantial structural reform somewhat similar to that of the IASCF, the organization that promulgates IFRS, and was described in Chapter 4 in some detail. The reform programme was driven by external pressures, as concerns were raised in regard to independence and transparency by regulatory organizations, particularly the SEC when it came to the issuance of an ISA (Loft *et al.* 2006). In 2003, the Council of the IFAC approved reforms designed to strengthen the international audit standard-setting processes. The new procedures aimed at convergence to international standards and at being more responsive to the public interest. The new constitution was approved in November 2006.

According to the IFAC's Constitution, it is now governed by a Board elected by a Council in which every member organization represents one vote. It therefore still differs from the standard-setting arrangements where ownership has effectively been transferred to the trustees (like the organizational structure of the IASC, see Chapter 4). IFAC is still owned by the member organizations and is, in that sense, not fully independent from the accounting profession. The Board sets the policy, staffs the committees and operating boards and supervises their functioning.

The operating boards include the International Accounting Education Standards Board, the International Auditing and Assurance Standards Board, the International Ethics Standards Board for Accountants and the International Public Sector ASB. ISA are promulgated by the IAASB. To ensure that the IAASB operates in the public interest, IFAC has established a Public Interest Oversight Board (PIOB), whose work also covers the other operating bodies. Nominations for PIOB membership come from international organizations and regulatory bodies.

The issuance of ISA follows a due process, which is modelled on the IASB's and was developed by the PIOB. It reflects what is now considered 'best practice' in accountancy, and there seems to be consensus that this 'best practice' needs to be in place for a private organization to become recognized by state body: again, the relationship between the FASB and the SEC shaped this model, which was first used in setting accounting (disclosure) standards from the mid-1970s in the US and which is now applied to auditing as well. The due process is followed by all of IFAC's public-interest committees. A due process has the following seven steps: (1) project identification, prioritization and approval, (2) development of a proposed pronouncement, (3) public exposure of a draft, (4) consideration of respondents' comments on the exposure draft, (5) re-exposure, (6) approval of a final pronouncement and (7) voting. Each member of the IAASB has a vote, and a standard is approved by a majority of two-thirds of the votes.

In recent years, IFAC has gained increasing support for its endeavours. For instance, the IOSCO, the stock market regulators and the World Bank supported its work even though none of these organizations has been involved in systematically implementing IFAC's standards as global standards. The global role of the IFAC is likely to increase further with the adoption of ISA as European auditing standards.

## 6.4 Conclusion

Auditing has been one of the strongholds of professional self-regulation in the public interest. This self-regulation has an institutional and a procedural component. The first consists of the organization of the profession, access to it and disciplinary procedures; the second comprises the rules and regulations on how the audit is done and which procedures (standards) should apply as well as the ongoing quality control. In the golden age, the profession governed the whole regulatory arena of auditing with only minor exceptions, and the state merely signalled its outcome responsibility or constructed weak forms of supervision responsibilities (US POB or the German WPK) and mandated minimum levels of the statutory audit. Despite these common roots, recent developments saw changes in governance of both components, which differ from country to country, both on the public–private and on the national–international axis. This applies to standard-setting and quality control of the audits as well as to professional oversight, all of which now display different degrees of public-sector intervention and internationalization.

First, the systems of ongoing quality control saw a major overhaul. Professional bodies as the communitarian form of accounting governance remained the same, but competencies were shifted towards state oversight agencies: Germany established the APAK, the US created the PCAOB and the UK extended the activities of the FRC. These oversight bodies increase control over auditors directly or indirectly with a special focus on auditor independence. While there are gradual differences in the national responses, which seem to depend on previous traditions – the more self-regulating British are more reluctant to increase state control than the Germans or the US –the overall structural responses are the same. National bodies that are stipulated by law and that are closely linked to the public sector were set up. National governments have decided to increase intervention and to intensify supervision responsibilities.

Second, the procedural side is currently witnessing a major change. The setting of auditing as well as financial reporting standards has become an increasingly global phenomenon. At the international level, the IFAC has started playing a decisive role in shaping uniform auditing standards first with its rules being transformed into national regulations by the respective organizations in the UK, Germany and many other countries. Recently, the ISA's previous recommendation–only character changed. With the amended Eighth Directive the use of IFAC's auditing standards is not merely a commitment of professional bodies, but will be – once transformed into national laws – a state requirement. Soon, ISA will be

*Exhibit 6.1* Localization of audit governance

|  | **National** | **International** |
|---|---|---|
| Private | *Auditing standards* | Auditing standards |
| | *Oversight* | |
| Public | Oversight | Endorsement |

*Note*: Text in italics refers to golden age.

established (privately) and endorsed (publicly) in the way that IFRS are. In consequence, Europe and its national governments will shift operation responsibility to a transnational body and retain some supervision responsibility by means of a supranational committee. To what extent the international structures for developing auditing standards will be used outside Europe remains open, particularly in the US as it remains reluctant to rely on transnational arrangements. Exhibit 6.1 charts the changes.

# 7
# The Stronghold of the Nation State: Enforcement Agencies

In this chapter, we will discuss enforcement beyond the statutory audit and litigation lawsuits. These are policing arrangements in the form of systematic and institutionalized reviews of previously audited financial information, performed by one or more bodies. These enforcement mechanisms are an additional safeguard in financial reporting. While audits and lawsuits relate to individual financial reports, policing arrangements are addressed to the community at large. Financial statements that have been cleared by the auditors are re-examined in the context of policing arrangements to detect fraud overlooked or possibly condoned by the auditor. Re-examinations can be instituted upon suspicion or they can take place regardless of the presumed quality of the reports. The first approach is commonly referred to as reactive, the second one as proactive. Such an additional mechanism was first introduced by means of the US SEC in the golden age of the nation state, while similar arrangements appeared in Europe only recently. Being institutionally a part of capital market oversight, enforcement systems have been developed very heterogeneously in Germany, the UK and the US: While the US system relies on a strong public agency, the former two countries established additional private bodies, which are cooperating closely with the public sector.

In the following sections, the diverging developments of enforcement agencies are portrayed. We will show how these institutions are embedded in capital market oversight systems and analyse their specific modes of operation. The differing arrangements beg the question as to whether some kind of convergence of the European systems towards the US arrangements can be observed. We address this issue by examining the governance modes employed.

## 7.1   The US case: A comprehensive policing role for the SEC

Until the 1930s neither a legal framework nor any kind of supervision for interstate transactions existed in the US (Kiefer 2003). The Securities Act of 1933 and of the Securities Exchange Act of 1934 as part of the New Deal regulations and government activism served as the legal basis for the set-up of the SEC, which was established in 1934. This point was a watershed in US securities regulation: invoking the interstate commerce clause, the federal level took competences from the states for listed companies, and established a comprehensive framework and a significant role of the public regulator in this domain for the first time (Cioffi 2006).

The SEC is responsible only for trade in securities. It is a federal regulatory agency that reports to the Congress and is controlled by the United States Government Accountability Office. Although the Commissioners are appointed by the President and confirmed by the Senate, the SEC works without any governmental interference in its day-to-day business. The five Commissioners, including a Chairman, are jointly responsible for the agency's operation (Kiefer 2003). This makes the SEC typical of the federal agencies established in and after the New Deal legislation. As to the finer organizational structure sketched in Exhibit 7.1, the SEC is made up of four divisions, namely the Corporation Finance, the Market Regulation, the Investment Management and the Enforcement Division. Additionally, there are 18 Offices responsible for enforcement and improvement under the remit of federal securities law, amongst them

*Exhibit 7.1*   Organizational structure of the SEC

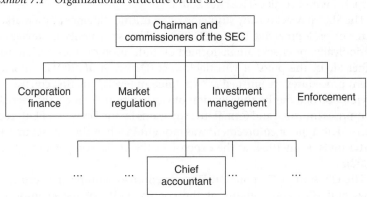

*Source*: SEC (2006), adapted.

the Office of the Chief Accountant. The SEC is funded by fees collected by the national securities exchanges and by fees payable on special transactions such as securities registration. The SEC cannot use these fees directly; they must be released to the SEC by US Congress for each fiscal year. This happens by applying the general appropriations procedures for government expenditure (SEC 2006).

The Commission is endowed with extensive legislative, executive and judicial competences concerning securities regulation (Hazen 2002). As both the SA and the SEA are to be regarded only as a basis for more detailed provisions, the SEC is empowered to enact any rule or regulation in its domain, being published as Code of Federal Regulations (CFR; Skousen 1991). In particular, comprehensive rules on the minimum information content and the form of prospectuses, registration statements and financial statements are described in Regulations S-X und S-K, exceeding the requirements of US GAAP (Kiefer 2003). Disclosure requirements like these are issued by the Division of Corporation Finance in accordance with the Office of the Chief Accountant (Altendorfer 1995). These broad legislative competences are accompanied by respective executive powers which relate to the supervision of the SROs such as the stock exchanges or the stock dealer associations, which were already discussed in Chapter 5.

Finally, there are the Commission's judicial competences: it may set up an internal tribunal dealing with administrative proceedings that may impose sanctions and financial penalties on SROs or its individual members (Hazen 2002). Furthermore, it may pursue a lawsuit to impose civil penalties. However, the Commission does not have available penal sanctions; instigating these types of proceedings is left to the Federal Department of Justice (Fleischer 2001).

The SEC may act on any suspicion of an untrue statement by a market actor or on a proactive basis (SEC 2006). Filed statements are reviewed periodically, or checks are performed on indication of stock exchanges, other SROs, the press or whistleblowers (Dickey *et al.* 2001). Enforcement procedures are pursued at two different levels. The first consists of reviews carried out by the Division of Corporation Finance; the second comprises informal and formal investigations by the Division of Enforcement. This type of enforcement was brought in when the SEC set up the latter division in 1964, at the expense of the SROs' competences (Lütz 2002).

The Division of Corporation Finance enforces both federal securities laws and US GAAP, aiming at the comparability of issued information (Kiefer 2003). This extends to both filed prospectuses for initial offerings and financial statements, as well as to *ad hoc* publications of listed firms. In the first case, the provided prospectuses and registration statements are examined regarding their legal, financial and non-financial aspects (Skousen 1991). In the second case, regularly filed financial reports are reviewed reactively on indication of any market participant. The SEC's Division of Corporation Finance may take no further action, send a Comment Letter to the concerned firm to achieve a correction of the defective statements or forward the case to the Division of Enforcement (Kiefer 2003). An investigation by the Division of Enforcement is not only opened on indication from the Division of Corporation Finance, but also in case of information conveyed by investors, competitors, lawyers or the press. Generally, not only potentially defective financial statements are subject to enforcement but also any suspected violation of rules and regulations issued by the SROs.

All investigations of the SEC at an informal stage first seek the (alleged) offender's cooperation, having no powers to subpoena (Kiefer 2003). In case of failure, proceedings on a second, the formal, stage are started after the authorization by the Commission (Hazen 2002). The Division's actions aim at collecting evidence for a future lawsuit in assessing relevant documents and subpoenaing witnesses, such as chartered accountants or business partners. Generally, these investigations remain under the pledge of secrecy (Dickey *et al.* 2001).

If the SEC comes to the conclusion that a listed firm contravened against securities law or listing rules, it can deny, delay or suspend registration of primary offerings. The latter become commonly known as a 'stop order' (Skousen 1991). In all other cases, the Commission may commence a Cease-and-Desist Proceeding at its internal tribunal, for example as prosecution of the breach of disclosure requirements, with listing suspensions as a possible sanction (Altendorfer 1995). Furthermore, the SEC may institute a civil lawsuit against any person or entity. The respective court decides, for example, on a financial penalty, an injunction or an order to bar an offender from engaging in the responsibilities of an officer or a director. The SEC often seeks the possibility of achieving a settlement irrespective of the type of proceeding.

Detailed information regarding the outcome of administrative proceedings, lawsuits, opinions on appeal of SROs' decisions and trading suspensions is immediately provided on the Commission's internet site. Thus, especially the publication of corrected financial statements is used as a means for investor protection and as a deterrent (Hazen 2002). This last instrument is said to have more impact on decisions of market actors

*Exhibit 7.2*   Competences of US-American enforcement authority

|  | SEC |
| --- | --- |
| Type of incorporation | Federal regulatory agency |
| Political responsibility | Congress |
| Funding | Fees |
| Objectives | Protect investor rights, guarantee integer share markets |
| Fields of supervision | SROs in share market sector; for example,<br>1. National stock exchanges<br>2. Dealers<br>3. FASB |
| Industries supervised | Listed firms |
| Objects of enforcement | 1. Listing requirements: prospectuses, *ad hoc* publications<br>2. Accounting standards<br>3. Rules of SROs |
| Working approach | Reactive and proactive |
| Investigations | Cooperative on informal stage, non-cooperative on formal stage |
| Statutory powers | Civil sanctions:<br>1. Publication of enforcement cases<br>2. Administrative proceeding: Cease and Desist Order<br>3. Civil lawsuit: Injunction, financial penalty |

(such as potential investors) than any kind of penalty imposed. For an overview of all discussed enforcement competences, refer to Exhibit 7.2.

During the fiscal year 2006, the SEC reviewed 4485 financial reports, leading to 914 investigations. On the whole, the Division of Enforcement conducted 356 administrative proceedings, 218 civil proceedings and 30 listing suspensions (SEC 2006).

The US system of enforcement is, due to its roots in the interstate commerce clause, geared towards listed companies. It relies on a dominating public institution as shown in Exhibit 7.3. The federal government only enacts a legal framework, and the SEC, operating under a public governance mode, is entitled to issue a broad set of rules. Almost every facet of enforcement is regulated by the SEC; even the stock exchanges, dealers' associations and other SROs are responsible to the Commission. Its powers of thorough examination extend to both prospectuses and regularly filed statements. While accounting standards and listing rules are

*Exhibit 7.3* Regulatory framework of enforcement in the US

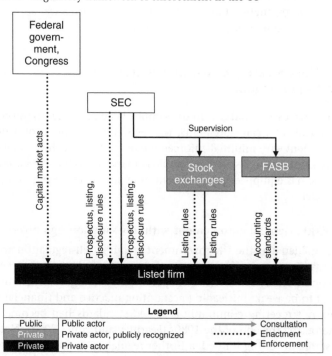

issued by the FASB and the stock exchanges as the relevant SROs, these bodies remain under the strict supervision of the SEC.

Institutionalized enforcement commenced systematically in 1964 with the SEC. Its *modus operandi* remained practically unchanged until the early 2000s, making it one of the most stable institutions in the regulation of accounting and the stock markets. The SOA of 2002, discussed in more detail in Chapter 9, even strengthened the role of the already-dominating SEC. It entitles the Commission to issue additional rules and amends existing regulations, ranging from auditor supervision by the SEC to increased enforcement powers for the SEC. The policing of financial reports has been stepped up with the introduction of risk-based assumptions and requirements of a periodical check within every three years. The frequency of reviews depends on the firm's market capitalization, its stock price volatility and recent restatements of financial reports (Heeren and Rieckers 2003).What started out as a model with a strong nation state became even stronger after the wave of accounting scandals. Not questioning whether the current system, which had actually produced a higher share of scandals than any other, was appropriate, more of the same seemed the right way forward.

## 7.2   The UK case: Coexisting variations of the private–public mix

The UK makes a special case in the sample. When it comes to the general policing of financial statements, the legislator has opted for a private arrangement with minimal enforcement powers. While the regulation of financial markets is also left to a publicly mandated private organization, the state has equipped it with sanctioning powers that even exceed the US model.

### The FRRP: General enforcement with low sanctioning powers

In the golden age, the UK government favoured self-regulation and left the organization of enforcement to the profession. Further enforcement was conducted by the LSE (see Chapter 5).The self-regulatory framework proved to be weak: misleading accounting practice and financial statements not meeting commonly accepted standards had become more numerous by the end of the 1980s (Fearnley and Hines 2003). Not only was standard-setting unified, a further regulatory consequence was the institutional reform of enforcement. This also happened when the Companies Act of 1989 (CA 1989) was passed, transposing the Seventh and Eighth Council Directives (83/349/EEC and 84/253/EEC) into UK law (see Chapter 3). The FRC was created in 1990 as the major player in accounting regulation. It was incorporated as an independent company limited by guarantee and funded mainly by the DTI , the accountancy profession and the supervised firms (FRC 2007a). Several regulatory bodies were established under the FRC's umbrella in a short time span, among them the FRRP in 1991. Previously, there had been no systematic policing of reports. In the case of misstatements, the members of the profession would face disciplinary proceedings in their respective accountancy bodies, but there was no institutionalized mechanism to correct the financial reports. From an enforcement perspective, the creation of the FRRP marks a significant institutional overhaul.

   The staff of the Panel consists of both legal practitioners and accountants, who are equally represented in order to foster different methods of analysis and argumentation related to these professional associations (Zimmermann 2003). To ascertain the correct application of accounting rules across the board, balance sheets and profit and loss accounts of major private limited and publicly traded companies were examined. Initially, the Panel worked on a reactive basis, as accounts were reviewed only in case of information on non-conformal practices by whistleblowers or the press (European Federation of Accountants (FEE) 2001; Zimmermann 2003). This approach was revised with the enactment of the Companies (Audit, Investigations and Community Enterprise) Act of 2004 (CAICE), and requirements concerning a proactive review were adopted into British law, also allowing for a prioritized review of specific industry sectors.

When combating bad accounting practice, the Panel seeks at first the firm's cooperation. If the FRRP is not satisfied, a formal enquiry is opened, in which a company or its auditor in question may be forced, under the threat of lawsuit, to pass documents or further clarification to the Panel (Brown and Tarca 2005). In case of deficiencies, the statutory powers of the FRRP allow privately demanding the offender to restate the accounts, and making a public announcement concerning the case. In more serious cases, as well as in cases when the cooperative model fails, the FRRP goes to court to obtain a legally binding decision. Corrected statements are sometimes issued only in the forthcoming report of a firm if the FRRP considers the deficits as being of minor significance. Overall, the FRRP has to rely on cooperation, adverse publicity or the courts. Its sanctioning powers are therefore minimal, and so is its connection with the state sector.

### The FSA: Stock market focus and high sanctioning powers

The FSA was established in 1997. Its predecessor organization was the private SIB, which had to supervise the numerous Self Regulating Organizations such as the LSE, the SFA or Personal Investment Authority. With the bundling of different product lines in the form of innovative products in the financial services industry, the old regulatory structure was no longer able to cope. Additionally, the BoE had to shed some supervisory competences after it gained autonomy in monetary policy (Blair and Walker 2006).This gave rise to the integrated supervisory authority of the FSA. It is an independent non-governmental body with statutory powers as laid down in the FSMA of 2000 (Turkington 2004). The Authority is responsible for the supervision of, among others, commercial banks, insurance companies and stock exchanges (Keßler 2004). Although the FSA is to fulfil public functions, it is a non-profit private limited company. The Authority is governed by a board of directors, and its chairman and members are appointed and dismissed by the Treasury. While this places the FSA under the influence of the public, its staff are not to be regarded as civil servants (Fleischer 2001). There are two main reasons for this specific private character: it facilitated, first, the merger of the former oversight institutions, and secondly, it allowed involving practitioners in regulation (Keßler 2004). However, the objectives of the FSA are laid down by law, and it is directly responsible to the Treasury, which also receives an annual report (Turkington 2004). The FSA's budget consists solely of fees arising from the regulatory work so that it is completely independent from government funding (FSA 2006). This is modelled along the lines of the SEC and this sets it apart from the FRRP, which does not provide services that can be charged out and which must therefore rely on other forms of financing. As can be seen in Exhibit 7.4, its organizational structure is shaped by vertical business units and horizontal (cross-sectional) sectors.

The FSA's competences combine legislative, executive and judicial powers, which is somewhat similar to the US model. As to the legislative competences, it is allowed to enact rules, issue codes and give guidance.

*Exhibit 7.4*   Organizational structure of the FSA

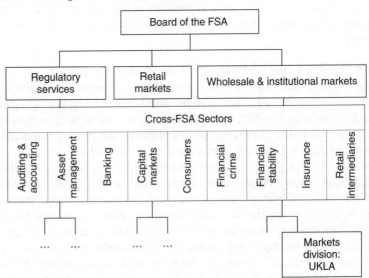

*Source*: FSA (2006), adapted.

Moreover, it is empowered to create binding regulations to improve market confidence, public awareness, protection of consumers and to reduce financial crime (Keßler 2004). The FSA's powers to enact rules are confined, however, by EU legislation, in particular recently by the Prospectus Directive (2003/71/EC) and the Transparency Directive (2004/109/EC). With regard to executive functions, the FSA is competent in authorizing and supervising capital market issuers, and it now maintains the Official List consisting of all securities traded on a UK regulated market, which is a function that had traditionally been performed by the LSE (as discussed in Chapter 5). A firm whose shares are included in the Official List is obligated to issue *ad hoc* publications in case of changes in capital or directors' details. Additionally, the FSA requires publication of audited financial statements, and auditors must notify the FSA in some special cases (Keßler 2004). However, the Authority has no comprehensive remit to check the material accuracy of disclosed financial information: the approval of a prospectus, for example, is only subject to completeness – the figures given are not verified by the Authority (Fleischer 2001).

Its judicial competences comprise all offences relating to the FSMA 2000 and the rules issued by the FSA. It is able to impose civil and penal sanctions (Fleischer 2001). To obtain relevant information, the FSA may initiate investigations, even supported by the police. As a penalty, the Authority may publish a Statement of Misconduct, alter or suspend a listing, take a case to court for an injunction or impose financial penalties (Blair and Walker 2006). The latter mainly applies to contraventions against the Listing Rules, to obstructing investigations by the FSA and to market abuse or market manipulation (Keßler 2004). Furthermore, the independent Financial Services and Markets Tribunal deals with cases arising from actions taken by the FSA (Martin and Turkington 2004).

It may be no coincidence that it was the New Labour government which strengthened the role of the state by creating the FSA. The state has tightened its grip on enforcement by making the regulator directly answerable to the Treasury. Nevertheless, the UK government has kept a more self-regulatory course than the US as it has given its powers of capital market regulation to a publicly recognized institution run under private law. This legal construction – the use of a private arrangement mandated by the state – is unique not only for an oversight institution but also with regard to its powers consisting of issuing and exercising regulations, and in particular in imposing penalties, including penal powers.

## The interrelation of FRRP and FSA

The powers of the FRRP and the FSA (in particular in respect to its role as the UKLA) overlap in several enforcement areas. Both bodies issued a Memorandum of Understanding in 2005 clarifying their respective competences. The most fundamental principle of their task-sharing is that only the FRRP is competent for the enforcement of information conveyed by financial statements, whereas the UKLA has to verify the additional disclosures as required by the Listing Rules, covering, for example, prospectuses and *ad hoc* publications (Fearnley *et al.* 2002; Zimmermann 2003). The FRRP is responsible for both listed and unlisted firms.

Overlapping competences can be observed in the field of audited annual reports that are to be prepared according to IFRS with the FRRP as enforcement authority. Annual, interim and preliminary financial statements have to follow the Listing Rules as well, in accordance with the responsibility of the FSA. This matter has been resolved with the CAICE 2004 and specified by the Supervision of Accounts and Reports (Prescribed Body) Order 2005. In effect, any annual and interim report prepared under the Listing Rules is to be reviewed solely by the FRRP. In all other cases of task-sharing, both authorities declared to designate one of them to pursue this case, depending on, among others, 'the scale of any misstatement [...] and the severity of the consequences' (FRRP and FSA 2005). The FRRP's and FSA's cooperation extends to cases of concurrent investigations, since both bodies agreed to share information, and the FSA provides assistance with the development of a risk-based proactive enforcement model for the FRRP (Brown and Tarca 2005; FRRP and FSA 2005). However, the statutory powers of both authorities differ significantly, as can be seen in Exhibit 7.5. Whereas the former can only pass severe cases of misconduct to the court, the latter has the power to issue regulations, exercise them and impose penalties in its own right. Hence, in this system, capital market malpractice can be prosecuted with more effective deterrents than before.

In the fiscal year of 2006, the FRRP conducted 284 examinations, of which 79 percent were on a proactive basis and 21 percent on indication. About 16 percent of all financial reports contained minor deficiencies, whereas in 1 percent of all cases the Panel either demanded a restatement of accounts or made a press release (FRRP 2006). During the same period, the FSA completed 227 enforcement activities, out of which only 1 percent dealt with listing rule breaches (FSA 2006).

*Exhibit 7.5* Competences of the UK enforcement authorities

|  | FRRP | FSA |
|---|---|---|
| Type of incorporation | Private limited company, authorized by law | Private limited company, authorized by law |
| Political responsibility | Department of Trade and Industry | Department of Trade and Industry, and Treasury |
| Funding | Sponsors, and Department of Trade and Industry | Fees |
| Objectives | Ensuring conformal application of accounting standards | Improving market confidence, public awareness, protection of consumers and reducing financial crime |
| Industries supervised | No specification | 1. Commercial banks<br>2. Insurances<br>3. Stock exchanges |
| Subjects to enforcement | Major public companies and private limited companies | Listed firms |
| Objects of enforcement | Annual and interim financial statements | Listing requirements: prospectuses, *ad hoc* publications |
| Working approach | Reactive and proactive | Reactive and proactive |
| Investigations | Cooperative | Non-cooperative |
| Statutory powers | 1. Require to correct account<br>2. Make public announcements<br>3. Make an application to court | Civil and penal sanctions:<br>1. Require to make a corrective announcement<br>2. Publish a Statement of Misconduct<br>3. Impose a financial penalty |

## 7.3 The German case: A public–private mix with low sanctioning powers

During the post-war period, institutionalized capital market regulation in Germany was relatively underdeveloped. There existed no systematic review of accounting information beyond mandatory audits. An examination of supposedly deficient company accounts prepared according to the HGB had to be conducted in the courts by the shareholders (Baetge and Lutter 2003). Furthermore, all matters concerning the enforcement of listing rules were taken care of by the stock exchanges, which, in turn, were supervised by the respective governments of the German federal states (see Chapter 5). Disclosure requirements and enforcement for listed firms were relatively weak, neither mandating interim reports nor *ad hoc* publications. Sanctions against market abuse did not exist.

## The emergence of enforcement institutions: BAWe and BaFin

The absence of comprehensive regulation in Germany ran counter to the efforts of the European Commission to form an integrated capital market in which member states would assign the respective national bodies with supervisory duties. Until the 1980s, self-regulation by the German federal states and the exchanges did not allow for any centralized national approach. Without EU initiatives the fragmented structures remained, and no institution represented the country in international organizations like the IOSCO (Lütz 2002). First changes happened in 1986 when Germany adopted the Listing Particulars Directive (80/390/EEC) and the Interim Reporting Directive (82/121/EEC), aiming at broader market transparency.

In Chapter 5, we described the national initiatives to make the domestic stock markets more attractive without altering their regulatory structure. Ultimately, this position proved untenable. The need to comply with the European approach to create a competent national regulatory authority to be integrated into a network of European financial oversight institutions, and to rearrange the inefficient and ineffective supervision of securities trade, made the states and the federation enact the Second Financial Market Promotion Act in 1994, transposing the Insider Directive (89/592/EEC) and the Investment Services Directive (93/22/EEC). This amendment led to the establishment of the BAWe, which was to oversee trade in securities (FEE 2001). EU regulation let significant competences in this domain move from the states to the federal level of regulation (Cioffi 2006).

Only seven years after the BAWe had started its operations, the Federal Financial Supervisory Authority Act (FinDAG) was enacted in 2002, founding the first single capital market regulator in Germany. The BaFin was created by merging the BAWe with two other federal offices in charge of capital market supervision, namely the Federal Banking Supervisory Office and the Federal Insurance Supervisory Office. The main factor for merging the three authorities into a single regulator was the convergence of capital market segments, which happened across Europe, illustrated, for instance, by the takeover of Dresdner Bank by Allianz, Germany's biggest insurance company, in 2001. This convergence had

*Exhibit 7.6*   Organizational structure of the BaFin

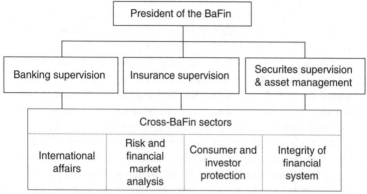

*Source*: BaFin (2005), adapted.

led – as in the UK – to heavily overlapping competences among the supervisory offices. However, the competences of the three former supervisory offices still dominate the present BaFin's organization, which is shown in Exhibit 7.6.

The BaFin is an administrative branch of government, being an executive organ answerable to the Ministry of Finance. Its President and their deputies are appointed by the President of Germany at the Federal Government's suggestion. The staff are made up of civil servants (*Beamte*) and of employees. The main purpose of the BaFin is to guarantee a stable and transparent capital market in Germany, resulting in the remit of protecting consumers and investors (Schüler 2004). Being endowed with the power to conduct its own investigations (Möller 2006), the BaFin pursues both a proactive and preventive approach. First, it may enact directives in coordination with the Ministry of Finance or the German Central Bank, covering rules on detailed issues such as trade in derivatives. Secondly, it autonomously imposes sanctions, which range from financial penalties to moving for a firm's liquidation in the courts. Severe capital market offences have to be officially prosecuted by the state attorneys (Martin and Turkington 2004). The BaFin's budget is completely made up by compulsory contributions from capital market participants (but not, unlike in the UK or the US, fees for services), enabling the authority to operate autonomously from the federal government and also allowing for enrolment of practitioners at higher salaries than those paid to other civil servants (Möller 2006). Overall, however, the BaFin does not have the same degree of sanctioning powers than its British counterpart, the FSA (Martin and Turkington 2004).

There are four general functions of the BaFin with regard to the supervision of the securities market: First, any kind of prospectuses required for the emission of securities is surveyed according to the Securities Prospectus Act (WpPG). However, only formal requirements are subject to this review; no verification as to the information conveyed is performed (Möller 2006). Secondly, being a capital market supervisor, funds and capital investment firms are overseen, and thirdly, market transparency and integrity have to be guaranteed by creating deterrents for insider trading and market manipulation. Particularly, the Investor Protection Improvement Act (AnSVG) prescribes listed firms to publish *ad hoc* notices if necessary (BaFin 2005). Whereas the BaFin is the competent authority to enforce this law, its powers do not extend to the supervision of listing rules: the general oversight of stock exchanges is still within the competence of the federal states (Deutsche Bundesbank 2006; Martin and Turkington 2004). Fourthly, acquisitions of large holdings according to the Securities Acquisition and Takeover Act (WpÜG) are monitored in order to protect minority investors (BaFin 2005).

### The new two-tier enforcement system in Germany

The creation of the BaFin as a federal capital market supervisor did not lead to a systematic and comprehensive enforcement of disclosed financial information. The possibility of contesting financial reports in court did, for example, not apply to standards with relevance only for group accounts, like IFRS or US GAAP (Baetge and Lutter 2003). This was to be changed by the Financial Statement Control Act enacted in 2005, amending the Commercial Code and the Securities Trading Act. The German legislator chose to create a hybrid enforcement system consisting of two tiers. At the lower level operates the so-called Accounting Police (Financial Reporting Enforcement Panel or *Deutsche Prüfstelle für Rechnungslegung*, DPR). At the upper level, the already-existing federal authority BaFin took on enforcement as a fifth competence. This model is envisaged to incorporate the advantages of privately and publicly run enforcers, meaning that in case of failure of the first tier, the DPR is to give the matter to the BaFin as an authorized body of sanctioning (Baetge *et al.* 2004; Zülch 2005). Additionally to its de-escalating momentum, the first, self-regulatory tier was set up to save cost and time (Baetge and Lutter 2003). An overview of the essential characteristics of both institutions is given in Exhibit 7.7.

*Exhibit 7.7* Competences of German enforcement authorities

|  | DPR | BaFin |
|---|---|---|
| Type of incorporation | Registered association, authorized by law, recognized by treaty | Federal authority |
| Political responsibility | Ministries of Justice and Finance | Ministry of Finance |
| Funding | Contributions and disbursements | Contributions |
| Objectives | Ensuring conformal application of accounting standards | Maintaining market transparency and integrity, guaranteeing protection to investors and minority holders |
| Industries supervised | No specification | 1. Commercial banks (shared with the Deutsche Bundesbank)<br>2. Insurances<br>3. Stock exchanges (excluding enforcement of listing rules) |
| Subjects to enforcement | Listed firms | Listed firms |
| Objects of enforcement | On the 1st tier: Annual financial statements | 1. Supervision: Prospectuses, *ad hoc* publications<br>2. Enforcement (2nd tier): annual financial statements |
| Working approach | Reactive and proactive | Only if involved firm or BaFin intend to review results of 1st tier |
| Investigations | Cooperative | Non-cooperative |
| Statutory powers | 1st tier of enforcement:<br>1. If proposal to amend accounts is accepted by firm, it has to publish corrections<br>2. Otherwise, case is assumed to the BaFin | Civil sanctions:<br>1. Supervision: minor share market offences – various sanctions; major offences – to be prosecuted by justice<br>2. Enforcement (2nd tier):<br>  a. Require to amend accounts and to publish corrections<br>  b. Impose a financial penalty |

The DPR is a private body having competences in reviewing financial statements to solve possible deficits collaboratively with the firms in question (Baetge *et al.* 2004; Gros 2006). The Panel, an incorporated association under private law (*e.V.*), had to be recognized by the Ministries of Justice and Finance by a treaty, its code of procedures guaranteeing an independent, competent and confidential review (Zülch 2005).

Similar to the BaFin, the DPR is funded by compulsory contributions (Baetge 2004). Currently, the Panel's members comprise professional associations and other interested groups. Its permanent responsibility is to review annual financial statements published by firms operating in the regulated German capital market. In accordance with the Committee of European Securities Regulators (CESR) 1.13, the DPR examines statements reactively, for example on indication of whistleblowers, the press or on demand of the BaFin, as well as proactively. If it is about to take an action in reviewing a financial report, the DPR is empowered to demand from the firm all information and documentation necessary. The panel is free to employ experts for questions of detail which arise during its enforcement actions. On detection of an erroneous or manipulated financial statement, the DPR may propose to fix the deficiencies, and it has to report its findings to the BaFin. If the offender accepts the ruling of the first tier, the BaFin orders the firm to state the corrections publicly. Otherwise, the BaFin directly assumes the case (Zülch 2005).

The second tier of enforcing financial reporting exists only within the German framework. The BaFin begins its own investigations if a firm does not cooperate with the DPR or if either the offender in question or the BaFin itself doubts the ruling of the first tier. In the end, the BaFin is the only authority within this process having full statutory powers of a public authority (Baetge *et al.* 2004). It has the power to force an offender to change defective accounts and to enforce the publication of these corrections. Further, the BaFin can impose financial penalties and perform investigations against firms or auditors. The whole two-tier enforcement system, however, relies in the first place on the preventive power of adverse publicity (Baetge *et al.* 2004; BaFin 2005) as the correction of financial statements has to be publicly announced at the end of a review performed either by the DPR or by the BaFin. Generally, both enforcement bodies are obliged to contact any competent institution if offences or breaches of duty are suspected; with regard to the BaFin even in cases of possible breaches of listing rules.

The DPR completed 116 examinations in 2006, of which 90 percent were performed on a proactive basis and 10 percent on indication. Of all financial reports reviewed, 17 percent showed erroneous accounts (13 percent of proactively and 50 percent of reactively examined statements). In 9 percent of all cases, the ruling of the first tier was not accepted by the companies in question, resulting in proceedings of the BaFin (DPR 2007).

## 7.4 Financial regulation of listed firms: Europe vs the US

The previous two sections have described the enforcement regulation that evolved in Germany and the UK starting from the early 1990s. A common feature of the European systems is a focus on all firms in regulation rather than a limitation on the listed ones, the obvious reason being the absence of a limiting constitution. Yet additional rules may be necessary for listed firms, which has already become visible in the previous section and when discussing the regulation of stock markets in Chapter 5. This highlights that the US and European models are not likely to develop fully in parallel. In the following, we therefore contrast the regulation in the UK and in Germany for listed firms to that in the US.

The EU's intervention into the capital market oversight of the member states was a result of adopting IFRS, as the Regulation (EC) 1606/2002 also begged the question as to how to enforce compliance with IFRS. The role of the EU has been confined, though, to providing a consultative framework, which allows scope for individual arrangements within the Community.

The consultative framework can be briefly sketched as follows. The objective of the European Commission's Action Plan for Financial Services (IP/99/327) in 1999 was harmonizing the inconsistent systems of regulation within the EU in order to impede market abuse and financial fraud. Based on the Lamfalussy Report of 2001, the CESR was established (Decision 2001/527/EC), consisting of representatives from the member states' securities regulators. It consults the European Commission on questions of regulatory detail, and aims at increasing the consistency with which European acts are adopted within member states. The CESR has also the task to establish cooperation between the national capital market supervision and the enforcement authorities.

The CESR issued Standard No. 1 in 2003, aiming at harmonizing the enforcement of financial information within the EU. This standard, which has no binding powers, recommends to establish respective enforcement bodies with 'adequate independence from government, and market participants' (CESR 1.6) and endowed with sufficient competences to review any kind of disclosed 'harmonized documents' (CESR 1.7, 1.10). The Committee also suggests extending the procedures of enforcement bodies to a proactive selection method of financial statements based on risk-based rotation or sampling (CESR 1.13). Finally, a second standard concerning cooperation between enforcement authorities was issued in 2004. To assess the effects of Europeanization, a broad perspective on the institutions is involved.

*Exhibit 7.8*   Regulatory framework of enforcement in the UK

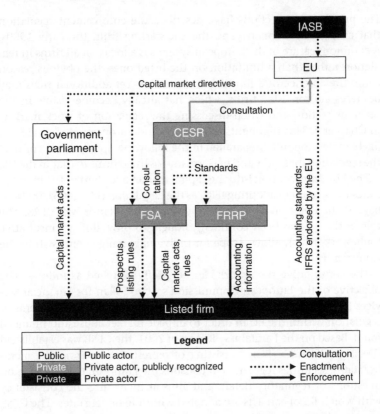

In a macroscopic assessment of the British capital market supervision, as seen in Exhibit 7.8, it becomes clear that endorsed IFRS are a basis for national enforcement bodies, in this case the FRRP. It may examine undisclosed documents if the firm in question cooperates. The Panel, in turn, agreed to comply with the CESR standards developed by the European securities regulators, as well as with the involvement of the FSA. Through this, the operating range of the FRRP, institutionalized under a private governance mode, is restricted by parameters set at the European level.

The FSA, for its part, is both a setter and an enforcer of listing rules at the same time. This setting is unique within our three-country sample, which might be caused by the specific and centralized structure of the British stock market, relying only on institutions of the City of London, where listing rules could easily be merged to a single authority. The FSA's review of prospectuses, however, is limited to formal aspects only.

Nevertheless, the FSA is a body run under a private governance mode, possessing the most comprehensive powers, even exceeding those of publicly governed authorities like the BaFin. The British FSA supervises all capital market sectors, including banks and insurance businesses, issues binding listing rules and is even allowed to impose criminal sanctions. The influence of the also privately governed SROs on enforcement has completely disappeared in turn. Instead, private bodies like the FRRP and the FSA serve all market participants and not only their members.

The German legal framework, as shown in Exhibit 7.9, is likewise subject to the influence of European bodies like CESR and the EU Commission. The setting and the enforcement of accounting standards are also – being part of the new European framework – separated here.

*Exhibit 7.9*  Regulatory framework of enforcement in Germany

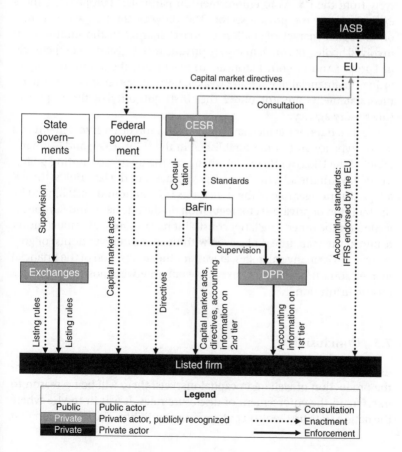

Enforcement is split into two tiers with hierarchic competences and supervision. The DPR is often considered as mimicking the British FRRP (Gros 2006), since it relies on cooperation and is an institution under a private governance mode. As to the enforcement of financial statements, both the German Panel and the BaFin are entitled to demand relevant documents from firms under review. Two aspects in the competences of the publicly incorporated BaFin stand out. First, its examination of prospectuses is restricted, as in the case of the FSA, to formal issues. Secondly, the German authority may issue directives concerning only detailed questions; most legislative authority remains with the federal government. Thus, both the SEC and the FSA have considerably more authoritative powers in contrast to the sparse legislative and executive competences of the German BaFin.

In sum, the relatively young European systems did not borrow extensively from the US. As to enforcement in particular, Europe relies more extensively on the private sector. The US with the SEC at the centre of all capital market regulation contrasts sharply to the multitude of involved bodies, of which many are private, with legislative competences in Europe. And in both European arrangements, the authorities supervising the financial markets are weaker: both prospectuses and regularly filed statements are not under the (first) authority of the respective supervisory agency.

The fact, but not the mechanism, of institutionalized enforcement was a prototype for authorities established in the UK in 1991; and Germany adopted the UK as a role model when drawing up its 'accounting police' in 2005. With the advent of a new government in the late 1990s, the UK adopted a stronger role of the state for its FSA, but found itself limited by the tradition of private-sector regulation on the one hand and Europeanization on the other. The latter constraint makes a full-SEC model, never really on the map, infeasible, even with the most interventionist of governments. Germany still relies, at least for the supervision of the financial markets, on the government executive but otherwise most strongly on a private institution.

## 7.5   Conclusion

As long as the nation state does not assume outcome responsibility for the production of welfare in capital markets, there will be no reason to interfere in the enforcement of disclosure rules. It was in the US where the nation state first took on outcome responsibility. The institution that the nation state created then – the SEC – extended its reach to enforcement in the mid-1960s. In the US, the state not only took on supervision responsibilities but also laid all operational tasks in the hands of the public agency. The UK, having acknowledged outcome responsibility of the state comparatively late, displays a bifurcated response to the challenge of enforcement. On the one hand, it created – in close cooperation with the private sector (see Chapter 3) – a review panel which has hardly any powers except those of adverse publicity, and places the operation and supervision responsibility with the private sector. For listed firms, however, comparatively recent regulation creates a body under private law with extensive regulatory, even penal powers. This body oscillates between the private and the public sector as its objectives are determined by the state and as it is answerable to the UK government. For listed firms, supervision responsibility has increasingly shifted to the state. For Germany, two new institutions, one private and one public, were created to enforce financial reports. For listed firms, the state has taken supervision responsibility, and in case of the financial market oversight also operational control. For general financial reporting matters, where there was no enforcement mechanism at all, the private sector exercises operation and supervision responsibility. However, the coercion and sanctioning powers of the German enforcement institutions are, taken together, somewhat limited compared to their UK and US counterparts.

Particularly in the two European countries, private actors now share competences with the state – but the level of overall regulation has also increased. The participation of non-governmental bodies is limited, though, as the public sector does not give away its responsibilities completely: all private actors involved in enforcement are instituted by law, recognized by the government; and it is possible to remove them in case of deficiencies.

It might appear at first glance that institutional arrangements in both European countries converged to the US model. However, the UK and Germany have only picked up some features of this model. The differences between the actualizations of the so-called 'Anglo Saxon model' regarding the institutional set-up stand out, and the two European countries have become more closely related to each other than any of them to the US. Overall, there is very little convergence in the institutions of enforcement, their powers and the cooperation of the respective actors. Internationalization in enforcement has not taken place, and even though Europe has provided only a consultative framework, this had some effect on the design of the authorities in Germany and the UK. This has only led to limited functional convergence, though; formal convergence is virtually absent. No country used the other's institutional set-up as a blueprint. No enforcement powers are transferred to supranational and transnational bodies. Enforcement agencies are still a stronghold of the nation state. The likely reason for this is the outcome responsibility of the nation state for welfare produced on capital markets.

# Part IV

# Forces of Transformation and Convergence: Potency and Impotence of the Nation State

The previous two parts have demonstrated that there have been substantial changes in accounting governance over the past decades. The role of the nation state has been redefined: some of its competences have been shifted to supranational, some to transnational bodies. The state now interacts more with private actors on the national level in certain regulatory domains, sharing or yielding its influence; in other domains it has clawed powers back from societal actors or augmented the role of the state, thus expanding its authority. Nation states seem to be both: powerful in some spheres and powerless in others. Part IV serves to examine reasons for this diagnosis in presenting a case of a strong and a case of a rather weakened nation state.

Part IV is structured into two chapters, covering aspects of both increased and decreased powers of the nation state. Chapter 8 deals with reasons why the nation state may have become weaker. Here, we provide evidence of how the financial markets have been globalized in recent decades and show that the nation state systematically yields to influence over the financial reporting process in phases of increasing internationalization. We also show how companies use partial opt-out opportunities such as cross-listings to put pressure on the nation state to adopt favourable legal arrangements, such as more harmonized disclosure rules. While we do not argue that the state is a 'helpless victim' of these pressures – as the opportunities from globalization arise only after the state has torn down barriers to trade – the possibility for turning back after deregulation is much reduced. This somewhat self-imposed restriction lets us speak of a weakened nation state.

Chapter 9 covers the most sweeping reforms of financial reporting regulation in the US since the 1930s: the Sarbanes–Oxley Act. The SOA is an example of one nation state flexing its muscles. After a series of accounting scandals, the US legislator has adopted stricter regulations, which bind not only US citizens and firms but also actors who are not domiciled in the US. This extraterritorial reach of US legislation could be taken as a demonstration of the increased regulatory power of a hegemon. However, we also provide evidence that reforms 'in the spirit of SOA' had already been enacted earlier in Europe. The idea of an empowered nation state thus needs to be taken with a pinch of salt.

# 8
# The Weakened Nation State: Economic Globalization and Regime Convergence

In this chapter, we will look more closely at the possible factors behind regulatory changes. After a short methodological note, we will focus particularly on the arguments and developments connected to economic globalization as the overarching driver of change. Although in reality globalization can be assumed to come to life through a mutual constitution of both markets and governments, there are clearly certain evolutionary traits independent of government or 'freed' from government through liberalization that form the constitutive force for institutional adjustment. We understand globalization as the growing interconnectedness of markets, which allows efficiency improvements in the allocation of resources mostly due to falling transaction costs.

Over the last two decades the structure of global equity markets has changed significantly. Technological progress and the liberalization of capital flows have lowered the barriers between national markets and allowed investors to access foreign capital markets more easily. Meanwhile, competition between stock exchanges around the world has increased. To assess the effects of this phenomenon, we also analyse cross-listings. Cross-listings can be understood as a means for companies within one jurisdiction to overcome local regulatory deficiencies or to opt for a capital market with higher liquidity. They have been made possible by globalization and can be regarded as an important economic outcome.

In defining 'globalization', management scientists tend to refer to Theodore Levitt's (1983) globalization hypothesis. Levitt outlines the causal cascade as follows: First, there is a lifestyle homogenization because of the increased flow of information due to innovations in transport and communication, which leads to harmonization in consumer taste. This, in turn, also leads to the standardization of products and services, as well as concentration of their production usually within few firms in order to utilize economies of scale. For cost and price reasons, these firms become multinationals in that they draw on capital from various countries. As a result, we observe further harmonization of lifestyles around the world through the availability of cheap uniform products.

This definition of globalization might be regarded as very narrow. More generally, globalization can be thought of as the 'widening, deepening and speeding up of worldwide interconnectedness in all aspects of contemporary social life' (Held 1999). This broader definition includes not only economic globalization understood as movement of goods, capital and labour across borders (Krugman and Obstfeld 2002), but also the creation and rising role of international governmental and non-governmental organizations, of technology and information flows, cultural influences, tourism and so forth. In order to arrive at a comprehensive definition, Beck (2000) identifies six dimensions of globalization: that of communication technology, ecology, economy, work organization, culture and civil society. Critical theorists, for instance Pierre Bourdieu, see globalization as 'a lethal status [of] economic forces unleashed from all control or constraint' (2002); in other words, the dominance of capital over politics. Zürn and Leibfried are similarly concerned about globalization, and view it as a threat to the concurrence of social and political 'spaces' (2005).

Even though the economic dimension of globalization is of particular interest for our investigation, questions of political order are necessarily interrelated. For example, globalization might require that market failures have to be dealt with at a global level. Additionally, globalization might put pressure on national regulators and lead to a regulatory situation that resembles a 'race to the bottom'. However, also a 'race to the top' might occur that leads to tightened regulation in all markets (Coffee 2002). In this chapter, we will describe how globalization affects regulation and thus might contribute to the convergence or the emergence of global governance structures. However, as globalization is a diffuse concept, we first try to measure the extent of globalization achieved.

## 8.1   Measuring the extent of globalization

International trade started to grow much faster than the overall world production, thus integrating the world economy in the current wave of globalization particularly since the early 1970s. Growth in investment and capital movements followed suit with a certain time lag. The fall of communism in 1989 resulted in the incorporation of the former socialist bloc into the system, with all its transforming and efficiency-boosting effects. Levels of migration peaked in the early 1990s.

Capital movements are an integral part of economic globalization. Increasing volumes of assets in the form of bonds or equity holdings, and also of foreign direct investment (FDI), keep flowing across borders particularly since the abandonment of the Bretton-Woods system of gold fixation and capital controls in the early 1970s. O'Brien (1992) cites the 1980s as the decade of the first true global securities market boom. The rapid development was spurred in part by capital market liberalization and partly by the spread of IT. With more use of electronic money and IT as its means of storage and transfer, capital became increasingly liquid on a worldwide scale. Although certain market access barriers still persist, capital can nowadays be considered to be able to move relatively freely around the world. Globalization of capital flows, in theory, leads to a more efficient pricing on the world market for funds, allowing for higher returns, efficient allocation of resources and higher living standards (Bernanke 2005).

Economic globalization is usually measured by tracking the cross-boundary dynamics of trade, migration and capital movements, either directly or indirectly. For instance, the OECD Handbook of Economic Globalization Indicators (OECD 2005) conceptualizes globalization in the mainstream manner as an 'increasing internationalization of markets for goods and services, the financial system, corporations and industries, technology and competition'. The globalization dimensions presented by the OECD include FDI, captured, for example, as FDI flows as a share of Gross Domestic Product (GDP), the activity of multinational firms, measured as their turnover, employment and value added, diffusion of technology, assessed in terms of internationalization of research and development activities (R&D), and trade, measured in terms of imports and exports as a share of GDP.

Focusing only on the capital movement part of the globalization definition, its direct measure is usually the capital mobility captured as a percentage of GDP, derived from the capital accounts of a country (published by the International Monetary Fund (IMF)). An often-used indicator is the amount of FDI relative to GDP, a subsection of all capital movements (OECD 2005). A growing ratio of FDI flows to GDP would suggest a growing economic interdependence (globalization) of a particular economy. Measuring FDIs is, however, not an easy task. Usually, an investment is classified as an FDI when at least 10 percent of the ordinary shares or voting rights are acquired by a foreign investor. According to the OECD benchmark definition, an FDI 'reflects the objective of obtaining a lasting interest by a resident entity in one economy ("direct investor") in an entity resident in an economy other than that of the investor ("direct investment enterprise")' (OECD 2005). In the following, we will use data provided by the IMF for 24 OECD countries[1] and the World Bank as well as the analyses in Werner (2008). For each country *i* and each year *t* from 1970 to 2005, we scale FDI outflows and inflows by the current GDP figure and compute first the years' means. Time-series data for this measure of overall globalization is shown in Exhibit 8.1.

Exhibit 8.1 indicates that globalization, measured as FDI inflows or outflows scaled by GDP was significantly higher ($\alpha<0.01$) in the 1990s compared to that in the 1970s. Nonetheless, according to these measures there was a decline in this trend in the beginning of the 2000s. In recent years, globalization seems to be increasing again. To gain further insights through data reduction, it is possible to compute five-year averages of the respective rates. Treating the data for all countries individually, it is possible to assess in which interval (compared to the previous period) globalization was on the rise. The decreases in globalization are not

*Exhibit 8.1*   Years' means for FDI inflows and outflows (relative to GDP) for 24 OECD countries

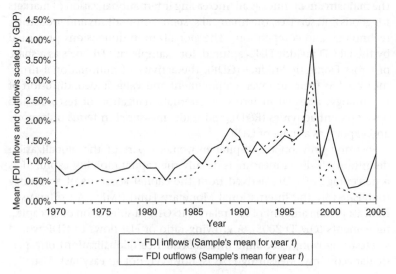

as important as the increases: it is reasonable to assume that increases in globalization trigger political and societal processes that will not be revised in cases of decrease in the globalization indicator.

According to Exhibit 8.2, globalization was consistently increasing in the US in the observed time period except for the beginning of the 1990s. In Germany and the UK, globalization was increasing in the end of the 1980s and 1990s, and in the UK additionally at the end of the 1970s. A further question is as to whether there is convergence in the country levels of capital interdependence. This can be analysed in terms of sigma-convergence (Heichel *et al.* 2005; Knill 2005), that is whether the variance (in our case, standard deviation) of the respective measure for the whole sample decreases over time.

*Exhibit 8.2*   Increases in globalization in 24 OECD countries

| Country | Increase in globalization at the ... | | | | |
|---|---|---|---|---|---|
| | end of the 1970s | beginning of the 1980s | end of the 1980s | beginning of the 1990s | end of the 1990s |
| Australia | | x | x | | x |
| Austria | x | | x | x | x |
| Belgium | | x | x | x | x |
| Canada | | x | x | | |
| Denmark | x | | x | x | x |
| Finland | x | | x | x | x |
| France | x | | x | x | x |
| Germany | | | x | | x |
| Greece | x | | x | x | |
| Ireland | | | x | | x |
| Island | x | x | x | | |
| Italy | x | x | | x | x |
| Japan | x | | | x | x |
| Korea | x | x | | x | |
| Mexico | x | | x | | x |
| Netherlands | | x | x | x | x |
| New Zealand | x | x | x | | x |
| Norway | x | x | x | x | |
| Portugal | x | x | x | x | |
| Spain | | x | x | | x |
| Sweden | x | x | x | x | |
| Switzerland | | x | x | x | x |
| UK | x | | x | | x |
| USA | x | x | x | | x |

aaa

*Note:* The 'x' in the table denotes an increase in average FDI inflows for a country in the respective five-year period compared to that five years before.

Exhibit 8.3 shows that a sigma-convergence process cannot be observed. Obviously, the level of globalization highly differs across the observed countries. This leads to the question as to which countries are the most globalized with respect to FDI flows. Here, we rank the countries according to their average FDI rate. For robustness, we also sum up the years in which one country has a higher FDI outflow rate than the average rate and rank the countries again according to this criterion. Results are shown in Exhibit 8.4.

Both criteria lead to similar results. Obviously, the UK is one of the most globalized countries within the OECD sample, whereas Germany and the US are ranked only in the middle. However, it should be kept in mind that the rankings accord with relative measures – that is, FDI outflows scaled by respective GDP. A ranking based on absolute FDI values would reveal that such a list would be led by the US, followed by Japan, Germany, the UK and France.

Similar statistics can be constructed for portfolio investments, defined as investments of less than the 10 percent criterion applying for FDIs (OECD 2005). Exhibit 8.5 shows the total foreign portfolio investments in the US, the UK and Germany in the period between 1980 and 2005, indicating an almost perfect exponential increase in the degree of capital market globalization for the respective countries. The volumes of equity investments have been growing in all three countries at an average

*Exhibit 8.3*   Standard deviation of FDI inflows and outflows (relative to GDP) for 24 OECD countries

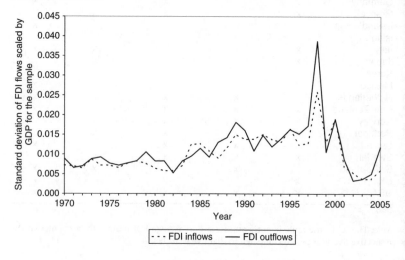

*Exhibit 8.4* OECD countries ranked according to the average level of globalization (FDI outflows relative to GDP) between 1970 and 2005

| Country | Rank | | Country | Rank | |
|---|---|---|---|---|---|
| Netherlands | 1 | (1) | USA | 13 | (12) |
| UK | 2 | (3) | New Zealand | 14 | (15) |
| Sweden | 3 | (2) | Ireland | 15 | (11) |
| Belgium | 4 | (5) | Australia | 16 | (18) |
| Switzerland | 5 | (6) | Spain | 17 | (17) |
| Finland | 6 | (7) | Portugal | 18 | (21) |
| Canada | 7 | (4) | Japan | 19 | (23) |
| Norway | 8 | (8) | Korea | 20 | (16) |
| Germany | 9 | (14) | Austria | 21 | (20) |
| Denmark | 10 | (13) | Island | 22 | (19) |
| France | 11 | (10) | Italy | 23 | (22) |
| Greece | 12 | (9) | Mexico | 24 | (24) |

*Note*: Figures in brackets are according to the number of years the respective country had a higher than average level of FDI flows.

*Exhibit 8.5* Total foreign portfolio investments in Germany, the UK and the US between 1980 and 2005

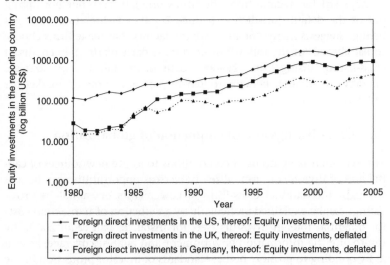

- Foreign direct investments in the US, thereof: Equity investments, deflated
- Foreign direct investments in the UK, thereof: Equity investments, deflated
- Foreign direct investments in Germany, thereof: Equity investments, deflated

*Note*: Figures in billion US $, deflated.

annual rate of about 12 percent, which is way above the growth of GDP or international trade.

It needs to be noted that there are several problems in interpreting the resulting numbers of almost any measure of globalization. Rajan and Zingales (2003) list both the strengths and the drawbacks of capital market globalization indicators. The problem of interpreting the share of equity investment, for instance, is that it does not represent corporate investments only, but all investments. In addition, it is susceptible to cyclicality: a disproportionate amount of equity issues is concentrated during the boom years (Choe *et al.* 1993). As we are looking at triggers for societal and political processes, this is not a serious problem: there are peaks at the end of the 1980s and 1990s. Especially in these years significant reforms took place in the respective jurisdictions.

In the following section, we discuss a specific outcome of capital market globalization: the occurrence of cross-listing. Cross-listings exist when companies domiciled in one country also use a stock market in at least one other country. In a cross-listing, a firm registers its shares for trading at no less than two stock exchanges located in different countries. Cross-listings can be a firm-specific policy to overcome domestic capital market deficiencies. They can be characterized as a limited type of jurisdictional choice that involves opting in to an alternative, perhaps stricter, regime from the firm's original base, but not opting out of the default jurisdiction (Coffee 2002). The literature on cross-listings suggests many potential driving factors that make firms choose to list abroad. In the following, we discuss particularly the benefits of cross-listing arising from (1) lower costs of capital, and (2) strategic operational or other benefits rooted in particular product markets or industries.

## 8.2   Cross-listings as a phenomenon of globalization

The ever-increasing needs of corporations to locate new sources of capital and of investors to capitalize on overseas opportunities can be met through international cross-listings. Lower costs of capital by cross-listings can be explained particularly by a reduction of transaction costs for potential foreign investors (see, for instance, Ball *et al.* 2000), by improving the information environment and analyst coverage, as well as by bonding to possibly higher standards of investor protection in the host country. They may also be explained by operational benefits. We will consider them in turn. Cross-listings may also have an impact on accounting regulation as firms may demand harmonization to reduce the related information production costs. Arguments and evidence for this will be discussed at the end of this section.

## Benefits from cross-listings

Companies wishing to enjoy the benefits of being subject to a stricter regulatory regime can do so by cross-listing their securities on an appropriate foreign market. In other words, cross-listing abroad can serve as a bonding mechanism for a company to commit to a better disclosure regime. This may also be helpful for the home market. Theory as well as empirical work suggests that committing to higher transparency and governance standards abroad reduces information and agency costs of controlling shareholders and, consequently, enhances the protection of the company's investors. As a result, lower monitoring costs reduce a firm's equity risk premium, since investors do no longer require the previous higher rate of return for their investment (Doidge *et al.* 2004; Pagano *et al.* 2002). Moreover, the ability and willingness to commit to higher and more costly standards is a signal for capital markets but only if the host country has a strict enforcement regime (Siegel 2005). Even though bonding is not the only determinant of a cross-listing decision (Licht 2004), it is noteworthy that particularly companies from European countries with poor investor protection cross-listed in the US while, at the same time, US companies did *not* cross-list their shares in those countries (Pagano *et al.* 2002).

Several authors argue that cross-listings reduce the cost of capital not only by making information of the listing firm more easily available but also by improving the overall information environment (Lang *et al.* 2003; Merton 1987). First, information provided by the firm through foreign disclosure requirements lower the cost of gathering information and enhance the comparability of investments, and as such may lead to greater incentives for demanding the firm's shares (Merton 1987). Second, depending on the foreign market's financial infrastructure, public scrutiny and media attention will increase when the company cross-lists (Baker *et al.* 2002). This also includes possibly higher analyst coverage, which can be an important motive for cross-listings. For instance, the US cross-listed foreign companies are to a large extent either big industrial or high-tech companies. They often aim at achieving additional coverage by specialized US analysts (Blass and Yafeh 2000; Das and Saudagaran 1998). When more analysts follow the firm and media attention increases, the information environment improves and can in turn influence the scope of the firm's investor base (Lang *et al.* 2003). Examples include software companies such as the German-based SAP AG that want to get visible among their US peers in the market.

Cross-listings aim at making shares more easily accessible to non-resident investors, who would otherwise find it less advantageous to hold the shares because of the barriers to international investment (Karolyi and Stulz 2002). Cross-listings reduce transaction costs by allowing investors to trade foreign shares in their home market. Diversification and a greater heterogeneity in the investor base will increase risk sharing and finally reduce the risk premium investors require to hold the shares (Howe and Madura 1990). Expansion and international diversification of the investor base could thus also increase the demand for a firm's shares and eventually lower the cost of capital.

Besides financial and disclosure aspects, cross-listings may also provide additional operational benefits of particular importance for multinational companies. The increased publicity and reputation that accompanies foreign listings could possibly increase the demand for the firm's products and services – that is, not only for its securities (Bancel and Mittoo 2001). In fact, this 'marketing motive' for a cross-listing applies not only to industries where product market reputation is important, such as in the market for consumer goods (Biddle and Saudagaran 1991). Cross-listings help to enhance the public relations between the firm and its customers, suppliers as well as the political authorities. These kinds of operational benefits are of crucial importance for infant and innovative high-growth companies in software or biotechnology, since those firms usually do not yet possess funds necessary for further expansion. The 'marketing motive' of cross-listings is supported by the empirical finding that companies are likely to cross-list in a country where they operated before (Saudagaran 1988).

Further operational benefits are associated with the quotation on a foreign market. Some companies might choose a cross-listing because they prepare for a merger or an acquisition; others choose to cross-list after such a transaction. For instance, Radebaugh *et al.* (1995) argue that Daimler–Benz's step into the US market was intended to implement its global business strategy including the merger with Chrysler. Additionally, a cross-listing may facilitate stock option plans for its employees abroad (Mittoo 1992; Radebaugh *et al.* 1995).

In sum, even when the bonding hypothesis does not apply, there are strong operational motives to cross-list. Whether a firm cross-lists out of operational or cost of capital considerations, the issues of complying with regulation remain the same. We will consider possible regulatory effects in the following.

## Arguments and evidence of accounting convergence through cross-listings

If companies start to act globally with nation states opening their borders to foreign investment, they are likely to be exposed to global competition. This relates not only to product markets but also to financing activities, because the globalized companies will be increasingly dependent on international investors – such as globally acting pension funds, of which the Californian pension fund CalPers, California Public Employees' Retirement System, is a prominent example – or other institutional investors. As institutional investors themselves operate under performance pressures, they are likely to demand a certain rate of return and thus push for a decrease in organizational and financing costs. Poor regulation in the area of disclosure and enforcement regulation – that is, poor investor protection – leads to higher financing costs as the risk of losses is higher. Firms have an incentive to reduce these costs.

One possibility to reduce such costs is opting out of a poorly regulated system by incorporating in another country. This would, however, also induce high adjustment costs and, in specific cases, might not even be legally possible. A less costly solution is to lobby for what is supposed to be an efficient regulatory solution or to cross-list in a more attractive jurisdiction. As securities regulation works on a territorial basis, cross-listed firms become, by tapping into foreign capital markets, additionally subject to the regulation abroad (Patel *et al.* 2003; Siegel 2005). Cross-listing firms also have to adapt to the listing countries' corporate governance if this is required by the relevant regulators, for instance the stock market. A flight of firms into foreign jurisdictions may eventually lead domestic exchanges to lose some of their business and thus result in their competitive disadvantage. In that case, either lobbying for higher standards in the home market or the emergence of privately set additional listing rules are likely effects. Moreover, cross-listed firms might demand changes in their home country legislation in order to be better aligned with the target jurisdiction's law. As a result, exchanges or countries have an incentive to improve their local securities laws in order to keep the trading of securities at home (Huddart *et al.* 1999). Obviously, such processes can lead to convergence of regulatory systems.

A necessary condition for regulatory consequences from cross-listings, particularly for a convergence of regulation, is that there are costs that can be decreased when regulation is harmonized. Cross-listings still tend to induce such types of information production costs. First, there are direct costs such as listing charges and fees for professional advice. Second, there are indirect costs connected to accounting and disclosure requirements (Saudagaran and Biddle 1992). Examples of the latter include reconciliations or additional reports that have to be prepared according to the foreign legal system. Additionally, by cross-listing, the company applying foreign regulations can bear higher risks of lawsuits in cases of misconduct (Pagano *et al.* 2002).

A cross-listing will take place only when benefits exceed the related costs. As many of the cross-listing costs are fixed, it does not surprise that mainly large companies choose a cross-listing (Saudagaran 1988). Due to bonding, it is relatively unlikely that costs of compliance with possibly higher disclosure standards or other enforcement mechanisms in the host country are regarded as a major obstacle. It is more likely that all costs arising from compliance with possibly lower home country standards will be regarded as avoidable. A cross-listing of a sufficient number of firms domiciled in a particular country might thus put pressure on the home country regulation. Here, Germany is a good example. The German firms with a cross-listing in the US traditionally had to prepare consolidated accounts following both German GAAP and US GAAP, while their US counterparts were allowed to cross-list in Germany without having to prepare German GAAP consolidated accounts. This dualism was one of the reasons to adopt the KapAEG in 1998, which allowed listed companies to publish consolidated accounts following international standards only (see Chapter 3 for a detailed description). This (de-)regulation can to some degree be traced back to the lobbying of firms cross-listed in the US.

Similar developments occurred in other stock markets as several European stock exchanges allowed foreign listed companies to prepare their financial statements according to internationally recognized standards such as US GAAP or IFRS. This option was later partly extended to domestic companies. This led to the situation that many European companies prepared their financial reports according to US GAAP. Even though the European Commission proposed, as early as in 1995, that member states should allow 'their' global players to prepare financial reports according to international standards (van Hulle 2000), the goal was not to make US GAAP the standards of choice. The shift towards US GAAP can be considered as unintended, but it was necessary due to the lack of alternatives: the quality of IAS was seen as low, and the national systems of financial reporting had not converged. With the institutional reforms in the setting of IFRS and no model of financial reporting arising from within the Community, the EU could at least regain some initiative. The overall situation resulted in the IAS directive (Schaub 2005).

Considering that many companies are cross-listed not only in the US but also in other jurisdictions (within the EU, and also in Japan or Switzerland), it can be supposed that there is a demand not only to harmonize national listing rules with the US standards, but also to harmonize them worldwide. Hence, cross-listings have been – and possibly still are – a driver of harmonization in the overall governance framework.

## 8.3 Influence of globalization on national legal systems

In the previous section, we argued that globalization puts firms under competitive pressure, which has an influence on a country's legal system. This argument can also be turned around by saying that globalization exercises efficiency stress on the economy as a whole, and political leaders choose competitive legislative frameworks for their countries.

In recent years, there is an intense debate in the literature on whether a functional or a formal convergence of legal systems has already occurred or can be expected in the near future. While there is a consensus that globalization can be supposed as the main driver of a possible convergence (see, for example, Busse von Colbe 2002; Haller 2002; Hopwood 1994; Thorell and Whittington 1994), the likely outcomes of such a process are under debate. Here, two positions can be separated (Khanna *et al.* 2006). The first position predicts a formal convergence of the investor protection systems.[2] Hansmann and Kraakman (2001) identify three arguments as to why such a convergence process will take place. The first driver of convergence is the 'force of logic' and stands for the economic logic of efficiency. The second is the 'force of example', focusing on the superior performance of jurisdictions based on the standard shareholder-oriented model. The 'force of competition', finally, is based on the competitive advantage of firms compared to their direct competitors – that is, lower costs of capital, more aggressive development of new product markets or access to institutional investors and international equity markets (Hansmann and Kraakman 2001). According to these arguments, companies domiciled in an inefficient legal system have to bear either the opportunity costs of better regulations or the costs of opting out, possibly through cross-listings. Given that better regulations in foreign jurisdictions can indeed be identified, it is likely that companies will lobby for a change of their home system. Hence, globalization at least indirectly puts regulation of nation states under pressure. This might also have a bearing on a country's disclosure and enforcement system: both are likely to affect capital costs at the firm level.

However, existing evidence for such a convergence process relies heavily on qualitative case studies. Empirical research with large samples in the area of convergence of regulatory regimes is rather rare. One of the few studies is by Khanna *et al.* (2006), who find that a regionalization of corporate governance in the sense of convergence among economically tied countries is taking place. Other authors doubt that there will be a formal convergence of legal systems – at least in the near future. The main obstacles for a convergence of legal systems are seen in path dependence and the complementarity of alternative models to local social structures or random mutations. The idea of path dependence is, for instance, discussed in Schmidt and Spindler (2002), who point to the fact that altering institutions induces adjustment costs. Their first argument is for stability: it is rational not to modify national institutions when adjustment costs outweigh possible welfare gains of changing arrangements which are inefficient only in a clean-slate design. Their second point is the complementary nature of institutions within (national) regulatory systems. This means that particular institutions are adapted to their local conditions, that is to other institutions within this system. Hence, national ownership and corporate structures, typical financing patterns, network externalities and rent-seeking motives can get in the way of convergence (Bebchuk and Roe 2004). Indeed, national peculiarities still exist, especially between the so-called 'insider and outsider economies' (see Chapter 1). While the latter are typically characterized by market transactions and thus a high relevance of capital markets, insider economies rely on network-like relationships. For companies domiciled in insider economies, bank and other debt financing have a high relevance. Hence, capital markets are typically less developed there. The differences between the three countries in our sample are still substantial. This can be illustrated by some statistics.

Exhibit 8.6 indicates that market capitalization of domestic listed firms (scaled by GDP) is significantly lower in Germany than in the US or the UK.[3] A further measure for the relevance of domestic capital markets is the number of listed domestic firms per one million inhabitants[4], a measure that indicates the relevance of the capital market for the financing of business. It is apparent from Exhibit 8.7 that capital markets play a relatively modest role for the financing of firms in Germany compared to the UK and the US.

Besides the number of foreign firms listed on national capital markets, the total value of foreign shares traded proxies for the international relevance of the respective national markets. Exhibit 8.8 indicates that also

*Exhibit 8.6* Market capitalization scaled by GDP in Germany, the UK and the US

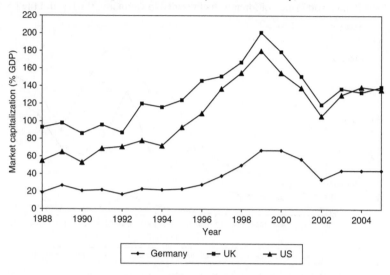

*Exhibit 8.7* Number of listed domestic companies per one million inhabitants

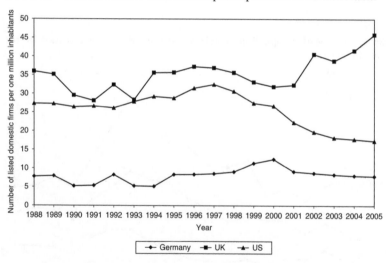

according to this measure the relevance of the German market is relatively low compared to the US or the UK. Exhibit 8.9 demonstrates that bank financing is indeed of higher relevance in Germany compared to outsider economies such as the UK and the US.

*Exhibit 8.8* Total value of foreign stocks traded in Germany, the UK and the US

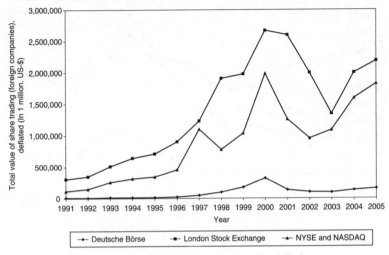

*Note*: Additional data obtained from the World Federation of Stock Exchanges.

*Exhibit 8.9* Market capitalization relative to domestic credit provided by the banking sector

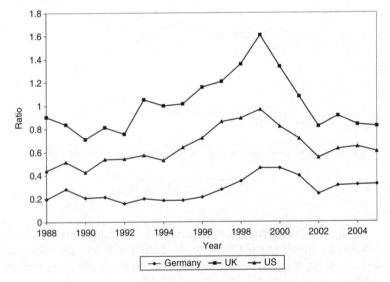

The presented data suggests that national institutional peculiarities still remain. If the fundamental national arrangements in the organization of the overall business activity have not yet sufficiently converged, then it is unlikely to observe substantial or complete convergence of the respective legal systems. For that reason, at the most a functional rather than a formal convergence of legal systems will take place in the short run (Gilson 2000). Even then, globalization puts non-standard national institutions increasingly under pressure. To the degree that such institutions will disappear, a harmonization of legal systems – and regulatory structures – can be expected in the future.

## 8.4 Conclusion

In this chapter we presented evidence that Germany, the UK and the US have been exposed to waves of globalization since the heyday of the golden-age nation state. Globalization allows companies and investors to act on an international scale and to use foreign capital markets. The emergence of cross-listings is an important outcome of this process.

This implies that globalization as such – in particular the use of foreign capital markets – can be regarded as a driver of the convergence of legal systems. We argued that globally acting companies domiciled in countries with poor investor protection would be able to incorporate within another ('better') jurisdiction. A simple and possibly cheaper solution is to cross-list shares in another country. Using foreign capital markets obliges a company to adopt foreign investor protection rules that are likely to be stricter than those of the home country.

The existence of a sufficient number of domestic firms being cross-listed on foreign stock exchanges can, as outlined, put pressure on national regulators. Due to bonding, a pressure towards higher standards of investor protection – in other words, a 'race to the top' – seems more likely than the contrary. This finding may explain why, in this book, we observed that the regulation protecting investors was increasing in the past few years in all the countries considered above. Global competition between stock exchanges promotes these developments because investors tend to invest where the best products and the lowest transaction costs are offered (Domowitz *et al.* 1998; Gehrke and Rapp 1994; Karolyi 1998). A larger number of listings also have advantages for stock exchanges as this allows achieving economies of scale. Attracting additional – even foreign – listings has therefore become a major objective of most stock exchanges (Macey and O'Hara 2002). Accordingly, several 'centres of finance' (big stock exchanges for example) have emerged in New York, London, Frankfurt and so on. These centres feature an extraordinary degree of permanent innovation and improvement of capital market products to satisfy the requirements of both companies and investors (Walgenbach 1990). Stock exchanges thus also play an important role in the emerging governance framework.

Taken together, a causal relationship between globalization on one hand and harmonization of disclosure and enforcement regimes on the other indeed seems to exist. Besides having advantages for economic actors by lowering the cost of capital, globalization also induces problems. An important observation is that political and economical 'spaces' are falling apart (Zürn and Leibfried 2005). Here, the globalization of capital markets is a good example of how nation states lost influence over the regulation of globally acting companies. Possible answers include organizing in supranational entities like the EU or aiming at implementing global governance structures. Another possibility is converging to the rules of a dominant country such as the US. This process is called 'delta-convergence' in political science (Heichel *et al.* 2005; Knill 2005). In the next chapter, we look at the SOA, which tightened US regulation and ask to what extent this induced delta-convergence. Finding German and British regulators mimicking US regulation would point to a dominance of the US model.

# 9
# The Powerful Nation State: Sarbanes–Oxley and the Global Reach of Regulation

This chapter looks at unilateral national legal reforms as well as if and how these reforms have spilt over into other countries. Our object is the Sarbanes–Oxley Act of 2002 (SOA), which may be seen as the biggest upheaval of accounting regulation in the US since the New Deal regulations, which established the SEC. The SOA is a reaction to the wave of accounting scandals in the US, which happened in the early 2000s. Share prices collapsed after aggressive or illegal accounting practices had come to light that either had slipped the auditors' attention or had even been accepted by them.

Corporate scandals which involve accounting matters are not peculiar to the US. Household names for corporate scandals in the UK are Maxwell and Polly Peck, both of which happened in the beginning of the 1990s. They do not stand so much for accounting scandals in the sense of wrongful reporting but for an absence of internal controls that made fraud by the owners impossible. This concerned corporate governance regulation rather than accounting rules. Maxwell and Polly Peck also differ in the sense that these scandals were clearly not systemic but Singular cases, driven by the personalities behind the respective corporations. Schneider, Balsam, Bremer Vulkan and Holzmann stand for similar corporate governance crises in Germany, with the difference that they were not so much personality-driven. As in the UK, they were perceived as singular cases, but they are a combination of poor corporate governance and fraudulent accounting that went undetected by the auditors.

Scandals have often been the reason for regulatory action. The SOA was the farthest-reaching unilateral regulatory response to the US scandals. In an attempt to cover most forms of possible misconduct, the legislation covered most business transactions that affected US business interests in one way or the other. Not only did it – for the first time in accounting and corporate governance – intervene in matters universally regarded as company law, it also established regulations with a deliberate extraterritorial reach, which rested in the belief of superior regulation. We analyse how this extension of powers affected other jurisdictions and we enquire whether the US managed to establish global rules unilaterally.

We first present the main provisions of the SOA. Their extraterritorial effects may have two consequences. First, affected foreign actors who come into conflict with their home country regulation might lobby for exemptions or for the enactment of similar rules in their country of domicile. Effects might therefore be driven by the demand side. Second, there may be a supply-side answer. Other countries could mimic the reforms undertaken somewhere else to prevent similar scandals from happening in their jurisdiction. While the first argument can be framed as one of transaction costs, the latter is a political one which can be traced to the crisis theory of regulation (Owen and Braeutigam 1978). To analyse such effects, we look at regulatory changes at the European and the national level (the UK and Germany). We show that reforms had been going on in these countries since the 1990s and that some of the SOA's later provisions had already been anticipated. We also find that the post-SOA reforms in Europe almost led to functional – but not formal – convergence with the regulation in the US.

## 9.1   The scope of the SOA

In the literature, there was a broad consensus that investor protection was high in the US (see, for example, La Porta *et al.* 1998). The large corporate scandals occurring in this system in the early 2000s therefore came as a great surprise to many. Among the most spectacular corporate scandals were those of Enron and WorldCom. Others include Adelphia, Qwest and Global Crossing. Enron is an outstanding case. In August 2000, Enron's stock price reached its peak at $90.56. By the end of November 2001, the stock had closed at 26 cents a share. Enron's share value came down because the (mostly legal, but aggressive) accounting practices, which allowed hiding liabilities and inflating the enterprise's income, were eventually detected (Stiglitz 2003). The company filed for bankruptcy protection in December 2001 (Thomas 2002). The occurrence of these scandals raised the question as to whether the current regulation of financial reporting, external audit and the internal governance structures of corporations in the US were appropriate.

Because of the public indignation in response to the failure of such a large enterprise and the repercussions on the stock markets by the general wave of scandals, politicians were seeking a renewed legitimacy in the eyes of their electorate. Two weeks after the public disclosure of Enron's bankruptcy filing, congressional hearings to the case began. Six months later, the Congress enacted H.R. 3763, the Sarbanes–Oxley Corporate Accountability Bill (Baker *et al.* 2006). The SOA has its main focus on the enhancement of the quality of corporate governance, accounting and the regulation of auditors (Delaney *et al.* 2004), and it possibly marks a fundamental transformation of the US legislation in regard to corporate disclosures and enforcement.

Corporate governance furnishes outside stakeholders with claims to disclosure, and corporate governance constitutes a control mechanism within the firm. This is why corporate governance was the first domain tackled by the SOA. Prior to its enactment, the regulation of corporate governance was considered to be in the jurisdiction of the states. As companies in the US can choose their state of incorporation, there is a certain level of competition between the states in offering an attractive company law climate. Critics point to the fact that this might impose a 'race for laxity'. Empirical evidence as to whether this sort of competition leads to problems in corporate governance is, however, mixed. One reason is that – at least for listed companies – federal securities laws apply, which provide for a high level of investor protection. The SEC, covered in detail in Chapter 7, has been the most important institution (Chandler and Strine 2003), and was further strengthened by the SOA (Crone and Roth 2003). Other institutions who act on behalf of the SEC, in particular the FASB, have also been affected.

However, the SOA (as federal regulation) also contains provisions that directly intervene into the internal corporate structures of listed companies, a matter traditionally regulated by the states and partly by the stock exchanges – but not by federal law (Cioffi 2006; Mäntysaari 2005). Examples of such new interventions include rules governing the composition and responsibilities of audit committees, the board of directors and the certification of the accuracy of the corporation's financial statements by the CEO and CFO (Fisch 2004). Altogether, the SOA is considered the most fundamental reform of the US capital market regulation since the enactment of the Securities Act of 1933 and the Securities Exchange Act of 1934 (Glaum *et al.* 2006).

The SOA is directed towards all SEC-registered companies, including foreign cross-listed companies ('foreign private issuers'). It also applies to affiliated companies domiciled in a foreign country. Moreover, the act affects all (including foreign) auditors who are appointed to conduct audits for SEC-registered issuers or their affiliates. This means SOA would apply to companies that have cross-listed only a minor part of their shares on any of the US stock markets, or it would regulate, for instance, UK auditors who vet a US firm's subsidiary in the UK. Hence, the act affects not only domestic but also a large number of foreign companies and auditors in a novel fashion.

Concerning the regulation of auditing, the act constitutes a shift from standards set by professionals and professional organizations to statutory duties and standards set by the PCAOB (Yakhou and Dorweiler 2004). The act does not itself predominantly contain detailed regulation; it places the responsibility to draft norms with the SEC (Hütten and Stromann 2003). In the following sections, we will describe the fundamental changes in the disclosure and enforcement system connected with the SOA, and will discuss the problems arising from this.

## 9.2    Institutional changes triggered in the US

### Corporate governance: The advent of audit committees

The US corporate governance is characterized by a one-tier board, which fulfils both executive and supervisory functions. In this model, outside (independent) directors have to oversee executive (managing) directors. Weak board control seemed to be a problem in the collapsed companies. The SOA thus requires every SEC-registered company to improve its corporate governance structure by setting up an audit committee composed of independent board members. Its main task is to ensure the transparency and integrity of financial reporting, intending to prop up investor confidence in US capital markets further. At least one member of the audit committee has to be a financial expert. The audit committee is directly responsible for the appointment, compensation and oversight of the issuer's audit firm. The auditor should report in a timely manner to the audit committee on all critical accounting practices used by the registrant. Additionally, the auditor has to inform the audit committee about other possible accounting treatments discussed with the management, as well as potential consequences that could arise from adopting these alternatives. Any allowable non-audit service has to be pre-approved by the audit committee. Furthermore, the audit committee has to act as a direct contact for employees' submissions concerning irregularities in accounting or auditing matters.

### Disclosure: Institutional changes and new types of rules

The SOA did not change the system of standard-setting in general, and the public–private mix stayed intact: standards are still set by the FASB, which is, still, supervised by the SEC. However, there are some alterations and extensions. The SOA now specifies the requirements that an (official) standard-setting body – this is the FASB – has to fulfil. First, it has to be organized as a private entity. Second, it must have a board of trustees and it must serve in the public interest. Beyond that, the standard-setter shall be able to react directly to changes in the business environment and keep the standards up to date. Enacted standards shall reflect the extent to which international convergence of high-quality accounting standards is necessary, in the public interest and beneficial for the protection of investors. The legislation additionally requires that accounting standards should be 'generally accepted' by the SEC. The SEC now officially states that the standards set by the FASB normally meet this and the other outlined requirements (SEC 2003a), which strengthens the role of the FASB, as it is now statutorily acknowledged. Hence, the FASB has – despite its organization as a private entity – moved closer to the status of a quasi-governmental agency (Williams 2004). However, most of the provisions in the SOA are only of declaratory character as the system already displayed these characteristics.

The SOA also regulates the funding of the FASB. Before the adoption of the SOA, the FASB was financed by voluntary contributions of accounting firms, the AICPA and other companies and interested organizations as well as by selling and subscribing documents (Cheney 2003). This was supposed to negatively affect FASB's independence. In fact, there were cases of corporations threatening to stop their donations if the FASB decided to adopt certain technical positions. With the enactment of the SOA, the SEC prohibits voluntary contributions to the FASB, which is now funded by annual accounting support fees and other receipts. The support fee is collected from all issuers and computed by a formula approved by the SEC. The amount of the fee shall suffice to finance the FASB's budget and provide for an independent and stable source of funding.

Besides these organizational reforms, there are also alterations regarding the content of accounting standards and requirements of further disclosure. To begin with the latter, the SOA requires companies to include an internal control report in their annual reports – that is, additional disclosures related to the management's assessment of the effectiveness of internal controls over financial reporting. This statement has also to be attested by the auditor. The evaluation of the effectiveness of the internal control system shall be based on an accredited framework (SEC 2006). There are also several further disclosures that the SEC require (Lunt 2006). Examples include the disclosure of off-balance-sheet transactions, the presentation of pro forma numbers and the report of whether a company has adopted a code of ethics for top managers.

Changes to the contents of accounting rules were also to be considered as firms had exploited loopholes, which arise by design in the FASB's standards. Traditionally, the US accounting system has been rules-based. Detailed prescriptions, rather than general treatment concepts, allow the structuring of transactions to arrive at the desired accounting outcome. If, for instance, a standard requires a certain percentage share of ownership for consolidation, the transaction can be structured in such a way that a smaller share of ownership is held and control is ascertained by other means. As a consequence, consolidation can be avoided even though it is 'against the spirit' of the regulation.

To address the question of whether a more principles-based system would be beneficial, the SOA required the SEC to conduct a study on the advantages of switching to a principles-based accounting system. The results of the report were presented in July 2003, showing that accounting standards should be in general principles-based but 'objectives-oriented' (SEC 2006). To meet this definition, standards shall

> (1) [b]e based on an improved and consistently applied conceptual framework; (2) [c]learly state the accounting objective of the standard; (3) [p]rovide sufficient detail and structure so that the standard can be operationalized and applied on a consistent basis; (4) [m]inimize the use of exceptions; (5) [a]void use of percentage tests ('bright-lines') that allow financial engineers to achieve technical compliance with the standard while evading the intent of the standard. (SEC 2006)

This brings the US standards closer to the concepts of IFRS. As a result, the FASB now has stronger incentives to cooperate with the IASB on new standards and a new common conceptual framework. This, however, has not yet led to fundamental changes in US GAAP.

### Enforcement: New rules for auditor independence and state-sector supervision

Auditing failures significantly contributed to the demise of Enron and the fall of several other corporations (Baker *et al.* 2006). Reacting to these failures involved, first, rules to ensure auditor independence and, second, the supervision of auditors by the PCAOB. To ensure independence of the auditor, the SEC had previously disallowed a variety of non-audit services in its 'auditor independence requirements', adopted in November 2000. As these broadly phrased requirements were not strictly followed, the

SOA introduced a detailed regulation to ensure auditor independence. For this reason, the SOA specifies a number of non-audit services that are prohibited from being provided by the issuers' CPAs. These include activities like bookkeeping, devising internal controls and the drawing up of financial reports. Furthermore, the auditor is allowed neither to design and implement an issuers' financial information system, nor to provide valuation and actuarial services. The CPA is not allowed to provide legal advice or any other service to the company's board. Tax consulting and allowable activities can be performed by the auditor only in conjunction with a pre-approval of the registrants' audit committee. Such services then have to be disclosed in the issuers' periodic reports required by the SEA of 1934.

Independence is also increased by physical distancing and the break-up of established relationships. The SOA does not demand a rotation of the audit firm; a complete break-up is therefore avoided. However, it establishes mandatory rotation of the lead and the review partners every five years to improve auditor independence. To steer clear of potential conflicts of interests, the Act prohibits members of an audit team to take up a responsible position (for example becoming CFO) in an audited company within one year after the audit.

Prior to the SOA, US auditors were overseen by the AICPA. The AICPA regulated the auditing profession through its ASB, Ethics Committee and the SEC Practice Section. Beyond that, auditors were also monitored by a peer-review system. The occurrence of accounting scandals also challenged the accounting profession's traditional self-regulation approach. In fact, it was substantially curtailed by the SOA via the establishment of the PCAOB. The PCAOB is a private non-profit corporation composed of five members, not more than two of which are allowed to work as CPAs. Its members are appointed by the SEC, after the Commission has consulted the Chairman of the Board of Governors of the Federal Reserve System and the Secretary of Treasury. The PCAOB is funded by an annual accounting support fee paid by each issuer. Through its wide remit, the PCAOB has effectively taken control of the regulation of accounting profession, which previously rested with the AICPA and the POB (Choi and Meek 2005).

Any domestic or foreign public accounting firm providing audit services for US-listed companies now has to register with the PCAOB. In the registration process, the public accounting firm has to disclose, for instance, the names of all SEC-registered companies for which audit reports are issued in the current year, or were issued during the last year. The auditing firm also has to list all accountants participating in the preparation of audit reports, and provide information about pending criminal or disciplinary proceedings against the firm with regard to any audit report. The information disclosed through the application has to be updated in an annual report to the PCAOB. Beyond registering public accounting firms, the PCAOB has several other rights and duties. It can set up or alter standards or procedures concerning auditing, corporate control, business ethics or independence of the involved parties. In addition, the PCAOB has to conduct annual inspections of public accounting firms for quality review purposes. When suspecting violations of the SOA by public accounting firms, the PCAOB can conduct investigations and disciplinary proceedings. It can also impose fines on accounting firms or withdraw their registration.

The PCAOB is not fully independent. It acts under the statutory oversight and enforcement authority of the SEC. Its rules become operative only after the SEC's approval. In addition, there is a possibility that the SEC will amend the existing PCAOB rules, or act as an appellate authority in cases of sanctions imposed on registrants by the PCAOB.

### Increasing litigation risk: Officers' certification duties and related mechanisms

The SOA requires several certifications from the CEO and CFO. These 'civil certifications' (Lunt 2006) require a company's CEO and CFO (or persons with similar functions) to certify in each annual or quarterly report that they personally reviewed the respective report and that the respective report does not, to the best of their knowledge, include untrue statements or omits reporting on material facts. The officers also have to state that financial statements and information included in the report lead, to the best of their knowledge, to a fair presentation. The certification further includes that the officers are aware of their responsibility to establish and maintain internal controls and a statement that such controls exist and are held for being effective; this even includes controls in subsidiaries recognized by the reporting entity. The officers need to certify that they reported to the auditors and the audit committee on problems with the design of the internal control system and that the report is informative on all significant changes that could subsequently affect the result of the evaluation undertaken, especially with regard to the internal control system's efficiency.

The SOA also deals with 'criminal certifications' (Lunt 2006) and requires each filing with the SEC to be accompanied by a written affirmation. Here, the CEO and CFO (or managers with similar functions) have to sign that 'the periodic report [...] fully complies with the

requirements of [...] the Securities Exchange Act [...] and that information contained in the periodic report fairly presents, in all material
respects, the financial condition and results of operations of the issuer'.
The Act specifies possible penalties for misconduct. Certifications made
in the knowledge that they are false or insufficient can be penalized with
a fine of up to $1 million and with an imprisonment of up to 10 years.
If wilfully wrong certifications are released by the managers, they can be
fined up to $5 million and imprisoned for up to 20 years.

**Other penalties imposed**

Additionally, criminal penalties for the destruction, alteration or falsi-
fication of records in federal investigations and bankruptcy documents
were toughened. For knowingly committing such acts, the penalty can
be up to 20 years of imprisonment and a fine. Further on, the company's
accountants can receive up to 10 years of jail and a fine if they knowingly
and wilfully violate the requirement to archive important documents for
five years. Another new rule is that fraud in connection with a security
registered under the SEC or obtained by means of fraudulent pretences
in connection with the sale or purchase of SEC-registered securities can
be fined or sentenced to imprisonment of up to 25 years. In the case that
financial reports have to be restated because of material non-compliance
due to misconduct, the CEO and CFO must '(1) reimburse the issuer for
any bonus or other incentive or equity based compensation they have
received [...] and (2) return any profits realized from the sale of securities of the issuer [...]'. Further, the SOA allows the SEC to 'prohibit
any person found guilty of violating certain provisions of the Securities
and Exchange Act of 1934 and the Securities Act 1933 from acting as an
officer or director of a public company [...]'.

## 9.3   The interference of SOA with extraterritorial regulation

The SOA was rushed through the legislative process in an impress-
ive speed. The financial community, still reeling from the corporate
scandals, did not have much lobbying power. The SOA thus imposed
a significant additional burden on listed companies. For example, it
necessitates the implementation of a number of new intra-corporate
processes, which in the meantime have been criticized to lead to an
intensified formalism. In particular, the SOA requirements concerning
the implementation of the internal control system have been extensively discussed. Companies in the US have complained that the costs of
compliance exceed the expected benefits of requiring an internal control

assessment. For instance, the Financial Executives International published a study of 217 companies with an average revenue of $5 billion and estimated the total compliance costs at an average of $4.4 million for the first year of application (Levinsohn 2005).

As the SOA applies to every company listed at US-American securities exchanges, Foreign Private Issuers (FPIs) and foreign-affiliated companies of US-listed companies are equally affected. Before the enactment of SOA, the SEC was satisfied with obtaining FPI data without bringing these firms into trouble with regulations of their countries of domicile (Rosen 1998). This approach is summarized in Hollister (2005). Characterizing the relationship between the SEC and the FPIs, the author outlines that '[...] the SEC has historically required *disclosure*, but has resisted regulating *governance*' as governance differs across nation states. Hence, prescribing SOA-like corporate governance rules for FPIs might lead to a conflict with their home-country regulation.

A considerable amount of provisions leading to possible conflicts can be identified (Kamann and Simpkins 2003). One important example is the certification required by the CEO and CFO, making them personally responsible for the accuracy of financial reports and internal controls. In the corporate governance systems of the UK and Germany, there is traditionally no special liability for such officers. Instead, the board has a collective responsibility (Lunt 2006). In Germany, the position of a CEO does not even formally exist, as the board is supposed to act collectively. Instead, the board elects a spokesman who acts as a *primus inter pares*. Thus, a cross-listing in the US introduces a higher litigation risk for senior managers who perform similar functions to that of a CEO or CFO rather than one stipulated by the domestic legal system. The same applies to the seizure of a manager's personal assets in cases of a restatement of financial reports. Given such rules, Lunt (2006) asks, 'With such burdensome provisions, [...] who will want to become a CEO or CFO of these companies?' As a consequence, cross-listings in the US have become less attractive due to high personal risks to the top managers.

Further examples of competing regulation are those of audit committees, which were non-existent in this form in European corporate law. Similar problems are related to the definition of the (one-tier) board system, which causes ambiguity in countries with a dualistic system such as Germany's (Schwarz and Holland 2002). For example, the question arises as to whether the audit committee should consist of members of the managerial or the supervisory body as there is no single board of directors. In Germany, the supervisory board consists, in addition, of employees because of mandatory co-determination, which means that the criterion of independence is generally not fulfilled. The SEC, however, grants an exception at this point and allows employees to be a member of the committee as long as they are not at the same time executive officers (SEC 2003b).

As outlined, costs and problems of compliance with the SOA are a concern especially for foreign cross-listed companies and foreign auditors. One option for these firms would thus be to leave the US capital market, which the new regulations have made rather burdensome, or, respectively for foreign auditors, not to accept mandates of SEC-registered companies. Another option would be to lobby for exemptions in the US or, alternatively, for a convergence of rules across the Atlantic. In the following, we will discuss whether such a move to convergence was observable in the years after the enactment of the SOA.

## 9.4 Pre-SOA developments in European countries

The traditional models of financial reporting and corporate governance in the European member states were changing even before the business scandals in the US occurred and the SOA was enacted. To a large extent, these regulatory changes were also a reaction to business scandals which occurred in the 1990s and early 2000s. The following sections take a particular look at the matter most unique to these countries: the corporate governance system.

### The United Kingdom

In the UK, corporate governance has not normally been a regulated matter (Dewing and Russell 2004). British company law does not yet, for instance, contain mandatory rules on the internal structure of the board (Davies 2002). In general, the constitution of a company is barely regulated and thus allows for flexibility and self-regulation of the economic actors. Business scandals, in particular the lack of control mechanisms in cases like Maxwell and Polly Peck, have challenged this traditional regulatory approach as early as the beginning of the 1990s. The regulatory answers to such crises in the UK followed an *ad hoc* approach (Dewing and Russell 2004): several times, commissions have been set up that had to evaluate reasons for the respective failures and propose improvements to the governance structure including suggestions for both law-makers as well as (further) self-regulation activities.

Reviewing corporate governance rules in the UK was the task of the Cadbury Committee, whose work began in 1991after the failures of

Maxwell, Polly Peck and some others. This committee was not established by the public sector as such, but by the FRC, the LSE and the accounting profession – that is three private institutions (Dewing and Russell 2004). One year later, the committee published its final report ('Report of the committee on the financial aspects of corporate governance') containing the first corporate governance code formalized in a written document (Conyon and Mallin 1997), but only applying to listed firms. It was recommended that listed companies should state whether they comply with the code, and disclose and justify any deviation ('comply or explain' approach). This code of best practice, effective until today, *inter alia* requires that any significant statements concerning the activities of the company shall be made public. It also contains sections on the role of the board, the auditors and shareholders. Among other things, it emphasizes that the board of directors plays an important role in monitoring and assessing the management. It also requires companies to establish an audit committee with a majority of non-executive directors to improve the auditing process (Cadbury 1993).

In 1995 the media turned its attention to large bonuses and salary increases at the top of privatized utilities. The following public indignation about high salaries when the country was still in a malaise – popularly dubbed as 'fat cats' eating the cream – led to the set up of the Greenbury Committee, concerned with the remuneration of directors. Its report tends to establish a linkage between management's salaries and their performance, and recommends timely and accurate disclosures (Solomon and Solomon 2005). In 1998, the Hampel Report followed. Unlike Cadbury and Greenbury, it tried to avoid the issues-based *ad hoc* nature of recommendations. Instead, the Hampel Report emphasizes the need for principles- rather than rules-based Corporate Governance (Short *et al.* 1999). This Report unites the issues of the two previous reports and thus has the intention to deal with the whole spectrum of Corporate Governance issues. With the Hampel Report as a basis, the Combined Code was created on 25 June 1998, which is the present Code of Corporate Governance for UK-listed companies. The Code is divided into two sections: one concerning companies and another institutional investors (FSA 1998). The section on companies deals with company directors in subsection A, while addressing directors' remuneration in subsection B, especially the details of the remuneration to be disclosed in the annual report. Subsection C covers the relations with shareholders and subsection D accountability and audit. The latter subsection deals with the establishment of an audit committee to keep an appropriate relationship with the company's auditors. Since 1998, a comply-or-explain statement according to the Combined Code was required by the UKLA. This was then the private stock exchange LSE, whose competence was later shifted in 2000 to the newly created FSA (see Chapter 5). Finally, in 1999, the Turnbull Committee was established to develop the Combined Code's section dealing with internal control mechanisms (Solomon and Solomon 2005).

Regarding the regulatory developments in the UK during the 1990s, at least four issues are noteworthy. First, compared to the US, the traditional model of regulation was less rigorous and is thus significantly different. In the US, there has been, since the advent of the SEC, a strong state intervention into securities law at the federal level while company law is regulated by the respective states of incorporation. In the UK, there was no strong state intervention into either securities law or company law. Second, the pre-SOA reforms can also be traced to business scandals. Third, reforms led to slightly increasing regulation since the 1980s but, fourth, the British pre-SOA model further relied strongly on self-regulation, which was transformed into an approach that can be labelled as 'regulated self-regulation'.

## Germany

The internal structure of German companies, as well as financial reporting, is generally regulated by law. Contrary to the US model and the usual practice in the UK, the German board has a two-tier structure and comprises an executive board of directors (*Vorstand*) and a supervisory board (*Aufsichtsrat*). The latter upholds the interests of stakeholders and therefore appoints, supervises and advises the members of the management board. The members of the supervisory board, which can be understood as non-managing external directors, are elected at the shareholders' meeting. However, special rules apply for the employees' representatives. They can make up to half of the representatives of the supervisory board in large corporations.

In 1998 the KonTraG was enacted, primarily as a reaction to German business scandals. With the KonTraG, corporate governance was strengthened especially to restructure investor protection (Cromme 2005), *inter alia*, by enhancing the control function of the management and supervisory board as well as the general assembly. For instance, differentiations of voting rights were abolished and the introduction of modern financing and compensation instruments was accelerated. The auditor was now intended to work in partnership with the supervisory board to keep a better check on management (Mattheus 1999). The KonTraG also required the board to implement an internal (risk) monitoring system and to report on risks in a special section in the annual accounts management report.

In 2000, the German federal government installed the Baums Commission to address further issues concerning corporate governance. Its final report contained several recommendations to enhance Germany's corporate governance system, such as the proposal to create a corporate governance code for listed companies comparable to that of the UK. Further examples include the improvement of corporate supervision, the strengthening of the supervisory board and the advancement of investor protection – among others through financial reporting and auditing of higher quality. Several of the Commission's recommendations were passed into legislation with the Transparency and Disclosure Act (TransPuG) of 2002. This amendment strengthened the position of the supervisory board, and management now has to inform the supervisory board about general aspects of financing, investment and employee matters. In addition, the reports to the supervisory board have to contain information on whether the aims stated in the past were achieved. Beyond that, the management has to transmit any information related to any affiliated company to the supervisory board of the parent company. Moreover, financial transactions, through which the company's earnings prospects are fundamentally altered, can be executed only with the supervisory board's approval. The TransPuG also obligated both the management and the supervisory board to publish an annual declaration of conformity with the German Corporate Governance Code (GCGC; Kübler and Assmann 2006). The Code was modelled on British legislation and developed and formulated by the Cromme Commission. Companies can either voluntarily follow its recommendations and suggestions or disclose any deviations in an annual declaration (see Goncharov *et al.* 2006 for evidence that such disclosures are value-relevant). The GCGC addresses several corporate governance issues – for example the cooperation between the management and the supervisory board, and the composition and compensation of the respective boards. Furthermore, it outlines the tasks and responsibilities of the supervisory board members, demands the formation of committees and gives guidance on several issues concerning financial reporting and auditing. For example, the GCGC recommends that the supervisory board or the audit committee has to obtain a declaration of independence from an auditor before the supervisory board or the audit committee proceeds with the engagement. In case there is a suspicion of management misconduct, the public accountant has to immediately inform the supervisory board.

Three features stand out in the case of Germany. First, the traditional model heavily relied on (federal) state intervention into the internal structure of the firm, that is on company law. Securities law and (minority) investor protection, in contrast, were rather underdeveloped until the 1990s. Second, as in the UK and the US, reforms can be traced back to the occurrence of business scandals. Third, with the GCGC, a new regulatory approach was introduced relying on soft (not binding) law and seeming to follow the model introduced in the UK.

## 9.5  Recent regulatory developments: Functional convergence to the US model

### The European level

To achieve the political goal of a single European (capital) market, numerous reforms were passed at the community level. Many recent reforms can be traced to the aforementioned FSAP (IP/99/327). This plan was implemeted between 1999 and 2005, and its intention was to strengthen the Community's financial market. A similar programme was proposed for the next five-year period and published by the European Commission in the 'White paper on financial services policy (2005-2010)'. In this paper, the Commission outlines its strategy to dismantle remaining ambiguity and inconsistence in national regulatory frameworks, and aims at achieving convergence in the national supervisory practices and standards.

A lot of reforms at the European level can be regarded as being 'in the spirit' of the rules laid down in the SOA. In this context, it is helpful to look at the guiding political criteria that were formulated in a communication by the European Commission in 2003, entitled 'Modernising company law and enhancing corporate governance in the European Union – A plan to move forward' (COM (2003) 284 final). Here, the Commission emphasizes on the one hand that, taking into account the member states' various traditions, a country-specific European approach to corporate governance has to be developed. On the other hand, the Commission also stresses that it has to be considered that corporate governance rules are increasingly set at an international level and that regulations in other countries, especially the US, might have significant impact on economic actors domiciled in the EU. With regard to the SOA, the Commission argues that it

[...] creates a series of problems due to its outreach effects on European companies and auditors, and the Commission is engaged in an intense regulatory dialogue with a view to negotiating acceptable solutions with the US authorities [ . . . ]. In many areas, the EU shares the same broad objectives and principles laid down in the Sarbanes–Oxley Act. In some areas, robust equivalent regulatory approaches already exist in the EU. In other areas, new initiatives are necessary. Earning the right to be recognized as at least 'equivalent' alongside other national and international rules is a legitimate and useful end in itself. (COM (2003) 284 final: 5)

These statements clarify that the SOA puts European regulators under pressure and also has some direct effects on both European companies listed on US stock exchanges and European auditors. As the EC has long tried to achieve full acceptance of EU rules by the SEC, there was an inevitable need to harmonize EU member state law and to adopt some of the SOA provisions (Mäntysaari 2005). Two recent examples of regulations that are clearly influenced by the SOA are the Transparency Directive of 2004 (2004/109/EC) and the new version of the Eighth Company Law Directive on statutory audit of 2006 (2006/43/EC). The Transparency Directive, among other matters, requires 'responsible persons' (that is top managers) of listed companies to affirm in the annual financial report that

to the best of their knowledge, the financial statements prepared in accordance with the applicable set of accounting standards give a true and fair view of the assets, liabilities, financial position and profit or loss [ . . . ] and that the management report includes a fair review of the development and performance of the business [ . . . ], together with a description of the principal risks and uncertainties that they face. (2006/43/EC Art. 4 (2c))

This regulation is quite similar to the respective requirement in the SOA. Eventually, Europe's efforts proved to be successful. From 2008, the SEC accepts annual reports based on IFRS from the EU member states. These European reports are now fulfilling the disclosure requirements on the regulated stock markets.

The new Eighth Directive is often supposed to be a regulatory answer to business scandals in Europe – especially that of the sinking of Parmalat in 2003/2004. Here, auditors did not discover that the conglomerate had not only overstated its profits, but also understated its debts by more than 50 percent. They also failed to detect that a substantial amount of financial assets, supposedly domiciled in the Caribbean, did not exist.

However, the new Eighth Directive is not independently designed as it contains numerous requirements similar to those outlined in the SOA. In fact, there are some direct links between the two pieces of legislation. For example, the SOA requires auditors of companies listed on SEC-controlled stock exchanges to register with the PCAOB. However, the PCAOB may accredit national oversight bodies to perform the task of supervision (Marten 2006). Such entities were traditionally not part of the regulatory framework in Europe and are now required by the modernized Eighth Directive.[1]

Even though EC directives are generally intended to harmonize the rules within the Community, they often leave scope that allows for particular national solutions. Hence, it is also necessary to look at the transposition of the respective directives into national law. Also, regulators in the member states may enact rules that are tougher than those prescribed by European legislation. We will therefore now take a closer look at the regulatory developments that took place in Germany and the UK after the enactment of the SOA.

### The United Kingdom

In the UK, there were a number of reforms concerning corporate governance, statutory audit and disclosure since the enactment of the SOA, which can partly be traced to developments started before the events in the US. In direct reaction to the collapse of Enron, the government initiated several reviews 'to examine whether changes were necessary to regimes for the regulation of UK audit and corporate governance' (Dewing and Russell 2004). One of the key concerns was that if business scandals of such scale could happen in the US with traditionally high level of investor protection and market liquidity, it is at least not unlikely that they might also happen elsewhere (Fearnley *et al.* 2002). The reports of the Higgs and Smith commission as well as those of the Co-ordinating Group on Audit and Accounting Issues (CGAA) and the DTI Review Team are considered as the most important analyses (Dewing and Russell 2004). These reviews led to several regulatory changes.

First, based on the recommendations in both the Higgs and the Smith report, the Combined Code of 1998 was redrafted to the Combined Code of 2003 (Solomon and Solomon 2005). With the Smith report, guidance on audit committees was added to the Code. For example, it was suggested that audit committee should consist of 'independent' non-executive directors, and that at least one of its members should have significant financial experience – a similar provision can be found in the SOA. The Higgs Report on the role and effectiveness of non-executive directors contained 55 recommendations (Dewing and Russell 2003; Higgs 2003) and also led to new Code provisions. Examples include the requirement that at least half of the members of the board should be independent non-executive directors and that a chief executive of the company should not become the chairman of the board.

Second, the DTI Review Team came to the conclusion that the FRC should take on the functions of the Accountancy Foundation and that there should be a professional oversight body within the structure of the FRC. Thus, the FRC now coordinates regulation of accounting and auditing standards to oversee regulatory activities of the professional accountancy bodies, to regulate the audit function, and to promote high standards of corporate governance (Mintz 2005). As outlined in Chapter 6, the Professional Oversight Board for Accountancy was established in 2005. In May 2006, its name was changed into Professional Oversight Board. It has, similarly to the PCAOB in the US, to supervise and recognize those accountancy bodies that are responsible for supervising auditors' work (Pinard-Byrne 2005). Another significant change led to the setting of auditor independence standards by the APB, which was formerly the responsibility of the professional bodies (Fearnley *et al.* 2005).

The outlined evidence suggests that the British system 'learnt' from the SOA provisions. Even though the sort of regulation differs from that in the US ('comply or explain' instead of mandatory legal rules), the outcomes are pretty similar. This suggests that a functional convergence has been achieved between the US and the UK.

### Germany

Hollister (2005) points to the fact that particularly German companies might have problems with following the SOA provisions. He argues that 'Germany's regulatory regime is less strict and its AGs, as a rule, are less appealing to small investors. As a result German AGs and markets are not competitive in the intensifying global battle for investment' (Hollister 2005). The SOA would thus be for German cross-listed companies a 'shock therapy' to achieve higher investor protection.

This view may be exaggerated as reforms intended to increase investor protection continued in Germany in the post-SOA years. In 2003, the German federal government announced a 10-point programme to enhance investor protection and corporate integrity (Menzies 2004; Pfitzer *et al.* 2006). Exhibit 9.1 summarizes the proposed reforms and gives an overview of important amendments according to the programme.[2] The programme and the connected legal reforms can partly be understood as a reaction to the SOA. However, they also continue to implement the recommendations of the Baums Commission of 2001 that were a reaction to corporate fraud in German companies. Some of the reforms are also connected with regulation at the European level.

*Exhibit 9.1*    The 10-point programme of the German federal government (2003)

| 10-point programme | Laws enacted according to the programme |
|---|---|
| 1. Management and supervisory board members shall be personally liable for the corporation, and the shareholders' rights to file an action shall be enhanced | → The Business Integrity and Modernization of Shareholder Actions Act (Gesetz zur Unternehmensintegrität und Modernisierung des Anfechtungsrechts of 2005, UMAG) reformed the law concerning the liability of the statutory organs |
| 2. Members of the management and supervisory board shall be personally liable for shareholders in cases of wilful or negligent misinformation of the capital market | → The Capital Investors Model Proceedings Act (Kapitalanleger-Musterverfahrensgesetz of 2005, KapMuG) improved procedural instruments for investors so that they may assert their claims before the court as a collective |
| 3. Further development of the German Corporate Governance Code, particularly concerning the transparency of management compensation based on stock options | → Since the Code is checked every year by the Code Commission, no reforms are needed<br>→ With the Director Remuneration Disclosure Act (Vorstandsvergütungs-Offenlegungsgesetz of 2005, VorstOG), it is now mandatory to disclose individualized executive compensation figures |
| 4. Further development of accounting rules and adjustment to international accounting principles | → Several changes in financial reporting were introduced with the Accounting Law Reform Act (Bilanzrechtsreformgesetz of 2004, BilReG) |
| 5. Enhancement of the role of the auditor | → Provisions to strengthen the statutory audit are contained in the BilReG |

*Exhibit 9.1* (Continued)

| | → The quality, integrity and independence of the annual audit were further enhanced with the Auditor Oversight Act (Abschlussprüferaufsichtsgesetz of 2005, APAG), which introduced a new oversight institution called APAK (comparable to the PCAOB and POB) |
|---|---|
| 6. An independent body shall be created that exerts oversight over true and fair presentation in financial reports ('Enforcement') | → The Financial Reporting Control Act (Bilanzkontrollgesetz of 2004, BilKoG) forms the legal basis for a new independent and private enforcement institution (Financial Reporting Enforcement Panel, FREP, or Deutsche Prüfstelle für Rechnungslegung, DPR)<br>→ The Federal Financial Supervisory Authority of Germany (Bundesanstalt für Finanzdienstleistungsaufsicht, BaFin) can intervene when companies refuse to cooperate with the DPR |
| 7. The reforms of stock exchanges shall proceed and oversight structures shall be enhanced | → First reforms are connected to the Securities Prospectus Act (Wertpapierprospektgesetz of 2005, WpPG) |
| 8. Improvement of investor protection in the unorganized market | → The Investor Protection Improvement Act (Anlegerschutzverbesserungsgesetz of 2004, AnSVG) implements the EC Directive 2003/6/EG concerning insider trading and market abuse. It enables inter alia a more effective oversight over financial analysts and enhances investor protection in the grey market |
| 9. Safeguarding the reliability of company valuation by financial analysts and rating agencies<br>10. Tightening of penal legislation in the field of capital markets | |

An important example of German regulation that seems to react to the requirements in the SOA and precedes European legislation is the enactment of the APAG in 2005. Chapter 6 showed that the new APAG requires that auditors are overseen by an independent APAK, which is a task transferred from the WPK. The APAK is constructed, however, as an oversight institution with ultimate responsibility, and it is independent from the profession (Böcking and Dutzi 2006). Its members are appointed by the authoritative Federal Ministry of Economic Affairs and Labour and shall not have been personal members of the WPK or have worked as public accountants in the last five years prior to their engagement. The APAK thus fulfils the SOA's requirement of an independent oversight over auditors commissioned by companies with a listing in the US.

In sum, the case of Germany is pretty similar to that of the UK in the sense that almost all major provisions of the SOA can now be found in German regulation as well. However, the type of regulation differs. Even though Germany introduced a soft law approach to corporate governance, requiring a declaration of conformity with the GCGC's recommendations, German corporate governance remains, especially compared to the UK, strongly legally regulated. Additionally, the traditional model partly lives on because of mandatory co-determination. This being said, functional convergence with the SOA provisions can also be identified in Germany.

## 9.6  Conclusion

In this chapter we showed that comparable reforms were introduced in auditing and corporate governance in the US, the UK and Germany, although the actual formal aspects of these provisions differ. Some of the reforms in the UK and Germany can be considered as having been implemented because of the SOA and because of 'local' business scandals. We find that the post-SOA reforms in Europe led to considerable convergence with the regulation in the US. However, the reforms only led to a functional, not a formal convergence. The latter may be desirable as it increases portability: after all, functional convergence relies also on systemic elements that are not easily transferred. The regulatory approach to corporate governance still varies significantly among the three countries: the British system (still) relies extensively on self-regulation, while the German system stays legalistic in its nature, even though elements of self-regulation have been incorporated here. It is an open question then as to which of the systems will be better capable to prevent or cope with possible new scandals. The price for more investor protection is an increase in the complexity of rules – binding or not – and the related costs of compliance, which have to be absorbed by the companies. This, in effect, means a greater burden for the investors and respectivef citizens.

The convergence that we find is not of the delta type. The enforcement systems are mimicking each other. Mutual learning seems to be the key feature of the process. Many provisions of the SOA had been enacted or at least discussed in Germany and the UK before they became law in the US. Conversely, prescriptions for the US which could not yet be found in the European systems were adopted. This means that all systems have changed, and consistently in one direction: to more state involvement and stricter regulation, thus all showing features of a 'race to the top'.

# Part V
# Analytical Summary and Conclusion

The academic literature commonly supposes that globalization narrows the scope of regulatory possibilities. As a consequence, the golden-age nation state with its wide powers to design its own rules and regulations is supposed to disappear. To enquire whether such narrowing takes place in accounting, we analysed three country cases in this book: Germany, the UK and the US. We contrasted the national models of these countries in the golden age with those in today's situation. In doing so, we restricted ourselves mostly to organizational changes in the national accounting regimes and did not investigate whether the accounting rules promulgated within the new structures also provided a new type of content. Our perspective can therefore be seen as actor-centred instead of object-centred, which is the more typical perspective in accounting research. Throughout our study, we separated accounting into the two constituent parts 'disclosure' and 'enforcement'. Changes in both fields were discussed qualitatively in Part II and Part III of this book.

In disclosure regulation, the golden-age nation state was characterized by an idiosyncratic interplay of a number of actors: the state, societal actors and individuals who used contractual and market arrangements. For the UK's disclosure regime, developments have been rather dynamic. In the golden age the system relied largely on self-regulation of the accounting profession and the state applied a *laissez-faire* approach. The EU regulation brought extensive codification of disclosure rules. It was relatively recent when a system of acknowledged private regulators under the umbrella of the FRC was established. The EU's IAS Regulation has installed the IASB as a single European standard-setter, superseding the national disclosure arrangements for listed companies. Where there is scope for national initiatives, standard-setters tend to follow the international precedent.

The IASB's standards are embedded in an endorsement process that involves private- and public-sector bodies. Here, the public sector – via the national governments – is mainly represented by the Accounting Regulatory Committee (ARC), which acts as a gatekeeper. The EFRAG is the most important private actor. Stock markets no longer play a decisive role in enhancing the disclosure environment. Their stipulations have also been widely superseded by public-sector initiatives.

Substantial changes can also be witnessed in Germany. The formerly predominant public sector – largely represented by the state and its laws – is now less influential than in the golden age. While jurisdiction has been of vital importance for interpreting the state's rules in the golden age, its relevance has diminished at least for group accounting. As in the UK, the EU-level institutions dominate today's regulatory system for listed firms. But changes in Germany are not only due to EU harmonization attempts. Shortly before the EU's strategy of endorsing IFRS was announced, the German legislator had initiated the establishment of a private standard-setter named the German Accounting Standards Board. Another attempt proving Germany's will of reforming the legalistic financial reporting system before the IAS regulation was the legal permission for listed groups to apply IFRS or US GAAP for their group accounts that was granted in 1998 and that represented a peak in private regulation, since the relevant standard-setters totally eluded from the regulator's influence. Unlike in the UK, stock markets still play a role in the German disclosure system. Augmented disclosure rules operate for firms that move into stock market segments of higher quality. The state holds its position in those areas where there is scope for national solution, and in this respect Germany also differs from the UK.

The US disclosure regulation experienced radical changes already in the New Deal years of the 1930s when the federal securities regulation created a comparatively stable configuration that has applied to listed firms and has persisted until today. This system is based on the cooperation of the powerful public sector SEC and a private-sector standard-setter. While the latter was still dominated by the accounting profession in the golden age, criticism led to the establishment of today's standard-setter, the FASB. Its promulgation procedures follow the due process of the US federal administration. The Board is now officially acknowledged by the SEC. At the same time, the FASB is crucially dependent on the Commission, which is responsible for disclosure regulation by statute. Overall, the public sector is very strong in the US, and it actively intervenes in disclosure regulation directly and indirectly, even though the direct interventions have become less substantial with the establishment and acceptance of the FASB. Stock market disclosure regulation has been all but crowded out by the interventions of the public sector, namely the SEC.

Enforcement in financial reporting has also seen massive changes, often in the same regulatory context that altered disclosure regulation. Here, the UK system has experienced a shift from professional self-regulation towards the establishment of publicly overseen bodies, analogous to the developments in disclosure regulation. Today's enforcement of financial reports is conducted both by the hybrid FSA and by an officially recognized body that operates under the Financial Reporting Council's umbrella, the FRRP. The profession is overseen by actors located with the FRC. Hence, the direction of change in governance was rather towards greater public-sector participation.

The German developments in enforcement prove to be rather revolutionary for the country. While the enforcement of the golden age relied only on auditing and cumbersome litigation procedures in courts, additional oversight institutions have appeared in all areas of enforcement in the meantime. Next to the introduction of a new branch of the government executive, the BaFin, litigation rights have been strengthened to foster the role of courts in matters concerning investor protection. The auditing profession is now supported and overseen by a new officially recognized body that is responsible for auditor oversight (APAK). Next to this, policing of financial reports has been introduced and conferred to an official private body, the DPR. Hence, both the public and the private sector gained in regulatory relevance, the former even more than the latter.

The US enforcement regulation did experience more change in enforcement than in disclosure regulation. Nevertheless, and contrary to the European systems, these changes did not alter the system's structural appearance. Due to the SEC's predominant role, the US enforcement remained stable over time. The most substantial change of the system is associated with the SOA: first of all, the law introduced the PCAOB supplementing (and partly curtailing) the accounting profession's self-regulation capabilities. Further changes are the increased importance of the SEC's enforcement activities and the tightened liability for managers and auditors. Outside the immediate regulatory scope of the state, the SOA strengthened audit committees in order to foster intra-firm governance. Overall, the US shows a stable configuration that moved in the same direction that we observed in Europe: an increased public-sector intervention.

The analysis of governance modes in disclosure and enforcement regulation demonstrates that the respective importance of various actors and their modes of interaction significantly changed over time. New actors entered the stage and supplemented or inherited the tasks of traditional institutions. Given that substantial changes took place in both disclosure and enforcement regulation, we examined reasons for these alterations and possible consequences for the golden-age nation state in Part IV. We provided evidence that globalization of financial markets increased in recent years and showed that the nation state systematically yields to influence in phases of increasing internationalization. We also showed that companies might partially opt out of regulatory systems by means of cross-listings. This outcome of globalization puts new pressures on nation states to adopt legal arrangements benefiting these firms. We also argued that pressures can arise due to foreign law-making. Referring to the SOA we provided evidence that national legislation can have serious extraterritorial effects. In sum, our previous findings suggest that the role of the nation state in financial reporting has been redefined. While some of its competences have been shifted to supranational or transnational bodies, interventions have been tightened in other spheres.

The final chapter attempts to quantify these developments using and expanding the analytical framework that was outlined in the first chapter of this book. A quantitative analysis will make shifts in statehood more visible and will answer more precisely questions as to which responsibilities were shifted from the public to the private sector (or *vice versa*) and to what extent transnational or supranational structures have emerged.

# 10
# Convergence Patterns in Public–Private Collaborations

In the first chapter of this book, we have introduced three bases of social order: market, community and state. Different actors playing a role in disclosure and enforcement regulation are rooted in these governance modes, and their importance for accountancy will now be considered in microscopic detail. We will use the microscopic analysis with its many data points to provide a quantitative analysis in the following.

A good starting point is parliamentary rule-making. Obviously, parliaments belong to the state sector. Parliaments enact basal rules concerning company and securities law that are important foundations of both disclosure and enforcement regulation. These foundations are, however, not sufficient for guiding companies as to how to prepare financial reports and they are neither sufficient in determining how enforcement shall work exactly (as, for example, routines for auditors or oversight agencies cannot be fully determined by means of law). Hence, further guidance beyond legal rules is necessary. Following an actor-centred research design, we first enquire into which actors are responsible for giving such guidance on how to prepare financial reports. Second, we will apply the same approach in enforcement. For both fields of regulation, the golden-age set-up is compared with today's situation. For analytical reasons, we relate the identified actors either to the state-, the community/society- or the market-based type of coordination.

In the state sector, relevant actors are – beyond parliaments – state agencies, courts and possibly bodies under public law. Societal coordination can not only substitute hierarchical coordination by the state but also support this type of governance. Hence, societal actors need not necessarily be free from state influence. Among societal actors, first, private institutions that are officially mandated or backed by the state come into question. Second, organizations not entrusted with such public power might also play a role in societal coordination. Third, acknowledged (individual) experts can also be rooted in the society and thus should be considered here. Finally, governance can be left to markets or, in other words, to individuals. Coordination will then be based on explicit or implicit contracts. Exhibit 10.1 summarizes the outlined actors and relates them again to the three archetypes of coordination.

The outlined framework allows us to compare the regulation of disclosure and enforcement in Germany, the UK and the US (Werner 2008). It also helps us to identify differences between the configurations in the

*Exhibit 10.1*   Type of coordination and the respective actors

| Type of coordination | Important actors | Example disclosure | Example enforcement |
| --- | --- | --- | --- |
| State (hierarchy) | Parliaments | Commercial Code (in Germany) | Legal sanctions for misconduct |
| | Agencies | SEC standard-setting (US) | SEC (US) |
| | Courts | Case law | Litigation risk (as according to legal practice) |
| | Organizations under public law (or similar) | Disclosure rules set by stock exchanges under public law in Germany | Chamber of Public Accountants (WPK, Germany) |
| Society (spontaneous solidarity) | Private actors (mandated) | Official standard-setter (for instance FASB, GASB) | Financial Reporting Enforcement Panel (DPR, Germany) |
| | Private actors (unmandated) | Institute of Auditors (IDW, Germany) | Supervisory boards, external directors, audit committee members |
| | Experts | Academics playing a role in standard-setting | Auditors |
| Market (dispersed competition) | (private) contracts | Disclosure rules in privately regulated stock market segments | Market control |

golden age and today. Overall, the analysis will show whether regulation has changed within each country during the observation period and whether convergence of the three country models has occurred over time.

## 10.1 Regulation in the golden age

### The disclosure regulation

In the golden age, the relevance of parliamentary rule-making differed significantly across the three countries. Germany followed a more legal-istic approach compared to the UK or the US. This became particularly visible in the codification of accounting rules in the Commercial Code and in specific company laws such as the AktG. In the US, legal founda-tions were outlined in the Federal Securities Act (1933) and the Securities Exchange Act (1934). These federal laws were passed by the Congress. However, the Congress seldom made use of its persisting right to inter-vene in disclosure regulation. Instead, operational competencies were delegated to an independently acting state agency, the SEC. With the Congress and the SEC having the formal right to intervene into disclos-ure regulation, the state has retained a key role (Choi and Meek 2005). In the UK, primarily the different Companies Acts are the legal foundations of accounting. The most significant legal amendments were related to the European Accounting Directives which were transposed into British law. Generally, the British legal requirements for financial reporting in the golden age can be described as the state requiring companies to prepare accounts following a true and fair view. Detailed rules or standards did not exist. The magnitude and relevance of legal regulation is thus low-est in the UK compared to the other two countries. This corroborates the common perception that the UK followed a *laissez-faire* approach in accountancy for a long time (Nobes and Parker 2004).

But even in Germany, where disclosure regulation is most detailed, legal sources were not sufficient in providing guidance on how to prepare financial reports. For all three countries, actors other than those of the state were integral parts of disclosure regulation in the golden age. In the US, the SEC has delegated the operational task of standard-setting to the private sector. Professional bodies were concerned with standard-setting from 1938, and since 1973 the standard-setting body is the FASB. Due to the statutory reference by the SEC, the FASB's pronouncements have a binding character. In other words, the FASB as a private actor is equipped with authority derived from the state. Such private bodies with a derived authority – or state agencies – did not exist in the UK or Germany. The role of courts in advancing disclosure rules was rather limited in the UK and the US. In contrast, courts played an important role in Germany as they were very active in defining some financial reporting rules (*Grundsätze ordnungsmäßiger Buchführung*). In all three countries, organizations established under public law were of minor relevance in the golden age. While such organizations did not play any role in the UK or the US, they were at least of marginal relevance in Germany in respect to the large number of mutual stock exchanges.

With the SEC delegating the creation of disclosure rules to the FASB, the US displays a higher relevance of officially mandated private actors in the golden age. This implies, in turn, that the relevance of private actors who are not officially mandated by the state was higher in Germany and the UK. In the latter, the ASC operated as an unofficial standard-setter that pronounced the SSAP. The ASC's standards were not legally binding due to a lack of legal acknowledgement. In Germany there was – and still is – only one relevant professional body: the IDW played an important role in disclosure regulation. Instead of directly putting forward disclosure standards, the IDW passed rules on proper auditing, which also contained important guidance for preparers of financial statements. Professional organizations like the British professions or the German IDW also existed in the US. Due to the existence of an officially mandated standard-setter, their regulatory relevance was, however, less pronounced.

In developing factually binding disclosure rules, individual experts such as influential academics and practitioners can also play a role in societal coordination. For instance, the German accounting literature was very active in advancing GAAP. This is confirmed by the practical relevance of the extant commentary literature (for example, the comment by Adler *et al.* (1938) has, in newer editions, high relevance until today). In the UK, experts were also important, while playing a minor role in the US due to the SEC's and FASB's high relevance (Power 2004). A pure market approach to disclosure regulation did not exist in any of the three countries. However, markets played a more important role in the Anglo-Saxon countries as disclosure rules were developed to support individual decision-making on markets – which was not the case in Germany.

Based on the outlined arguments, which are derived from the more narrative analyses of Part II and Part III, the relative importance of the respective actors in the three countries can now be quantified. We do this by assigning a numerical value to an actor, representing its importance in disclosure or enforcement regulation. We use a scale ranging from 0

*Exhibit 10.2* Relevance of different actors in disclosure regulation in the golden age

| Actors | Germany | US | UK |
|---|---|---|---|
| Parliaments (law) | 2 | 1 | 0 |
| State agencies | 0 | 2 | 0 |
| Courts | 3 | 1 | 1 |
| Public law institutions | 1 | 0 | 0 |
| Mandated private institutions | 0 | 2 | 0 |
| Non-mandated private institutions | 2 | 1 | 3 |
| Experts | 3 | 1 | 2 |
| Markets (contracting by individuals) | 0 | 2 | 2 |

to 3. If an actor does not play any role or if the role can be neglected, its respective importance is rated 0. A value of 1 indicates that the actor plays a marginal role. Medium and high importance of a particular actor are rated with a value of 2 and 3, respectively. Such quantifications cannot be regarded as an exact measurement, but they help to compare the regulatory solutions and to trace reconfigurations within the three systems. Exhibit 10.2 gives an overview of our estimates of the respective relevance of the different actors in the German, British and US-American disclosure systems.

Exhibit 10.3 visualizes the differences between the three country models. As can be seen from the exhibit, there were – from an actor-centred perspective – significant differences between the countries. It becomes clear that the state indeed did not play an important role in the UK, contrary to the US and particularly to Germany. While the state significantly intervened in both of the latter countries, means of intervention also differed. It is noteworthy that already in the golden age all three countries relied on societal actors in disclosure regulation. Their importance is particularly pronounced in the UK, where the public sector plays only a minor role in this policy field.

We now turn to measuring the differences between the countries. One common and straightforward approach is to measure the relative importance in 'distances' between the actor-variables. The difference, for instance, between a country where courts play a significant role and a country with only a marginal role of the courts would be 3 (= 3 − 0). We compute squared Euclidian distances between the three country models: let countries be denoted by $c_i$ ($i=1, 2, 3$) and the respective $n$ actor-variables by $a_{i,k}$ (value for actor-variable $k$ in

*Exhibit 10.3*   Visualization of different disclosure regulations in the golden age

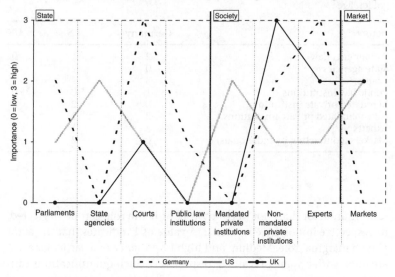

country *i*), then squared Euclidian distances between pairs of two countries ($c_{i=u}$ and $c_{i=v}$) are equal to

$$d_{u,v}^2 = \sum_{k=1}^{k=n}(a_{u,k} - a_{v,k})^2.$$

The pairwise distances between the three countries are reported in Exhibit 10.4. It is interesting to note that the UK's distance to both the German and the US model is almost equal. This fact is surprising as this contradicts the common understanding of an 'Anglo-Saxon' model of accounting. The high distance between the German and the US model in turn fits the common expectation that markets and private actors are of higher relevance in outsider economies while insider economies rely more strongly on state intervention.

*Exhibit 10.4*   Differences in disclosure regulation in the golden age

|  | **Germany** | **US** | **UK** |
|---|---|---|---|
| Germany | 0 | – | – |
| US | 23 | 0 | – |
| UK | 15 | 14 | 0 |

**The enforcement regime**

In the golden age, none of the three countries' enforcement regime was extensively regulated by means of law. Basal legal stipulations include the requirement of mandatory annual audits or regulate accession to the audit profession. In the golden age, state agencies played a role only in the US. The SEC is deemed of medium importance in enforcement as financial reports were checked rather infrequently. In Germany and the UK, enforcement agencies did not exist at all. Hence, the question arises whether other state-sector institutions were responsible for enforcement there. In Germany, courts theoretically played a role. However, there were no significant cases which would point to a high relevance for courts being an enforcement device. The factual relevance of courts was likewise low in the UK and thus probably highest in the US.

Public law institutions concerned with enforcement existed only in Germany. Here, the WPK had the general competence to govern the audit profession. This signals a medium importance of the Chamber in enforcement. This regulation is specific for Germany, and there are no comparable institutions in the other two countries. There were no private institutions officially mandated with enforcement in the golden age either in Germany, the UK or the US. Private organizations with factual relevance (but only for auditing, not for policing) existed in the three countries, notably the professional organizations such as the IDW in Germany, the ICAEW in the UK or the AICPA in the US.

According to our framework, auditors fall in the category of experts. The reason is that annual audits are, on the one hand, legally stipulated and partly regulated by law while they are, on the other hand, undertaken by private audit firms or individual auditors on a contractual basis. This implies a mixture of coordination patterns, making it appropriate to understand audits as a societal arrangement with roots both in the state and the private sector. Particularly in the UK, auditors played a significant role in enforcement. Due to the existence of the SEC or other relevant regulation, they were less important in the US and they were also less important in Germany. Further experts have to be considered in enforcement. In particular, the oversight systems within companies have to be addressed. In Germany, with its dual board structure, such experts can be found in supervisory boards. In the US and the UK, external directors have an equivalent function. Their position was, however, traditionally not very strong and probably even lower than the role of supervisory board members in Germany. Taken together, for all countries a medium relevance of experts in enforcement can be noted. Finally, the role of markets in enforcement has to be addressed. It was already pointed out that the role of takeover markets is an enforcement device and that such markets were, compared to Germany, of higher relevance in the two Anglo-Saxon countries.

Exhibit 10.5 gives an overview on our assessment of the importance of the different actors playing a role in enforcement in the UK, the US and Germany. Again, we attribute a value of 3 to actors being highly relevant and quantify a very low relevance with 0.

Exhibit 10.6 visualizes the differences in the configurations of enforcement in the three countries. The pairwise differences between two countries are reported in Exhibit 10.7.

*Exhibit 10.5*  Relevance of different actors in enforcement regulation in the golden age

| Actors | Germany | US | UK |
|---|---|---|---|
| Parliaments (law) | 0 | 0 | 0 |
| State agencies | 0 | 2 | 0 |
| Courts | 1 | 2 | 1 |
| Public law institutions | 2 | 0 | 0 |
| Mandated private institutions | 0 | 0 | 0 |
| Non-mandated private institutions | 2 | 2 | 2 |
| Experts | 2 | 2 | 3 |
| Markets (contracting by individuals) | 1 | 3 | 3 |

*Exhibit 10.6*  Visualization of enforcement regulation in the golden age

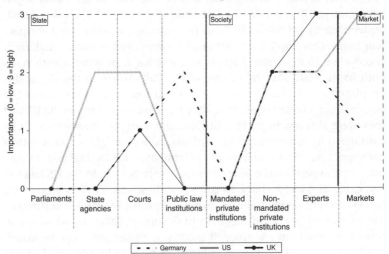

*Exhibit 10.7* Differences in enforcement regulation in the golden age

|         | Germany | US | UK |
|---------|---------|----|----|
| Germany | 0       | –  | –  |
| US      | 13      | 0  | –  |
| UK      | 9       | 6  | 0  |

A few observations are noteworthy. First, the overall coordination effort in enforcement is consistently lower compared to disclosure regulation in the three countries. Second, the role of the state in enforcement is again lowest in the UK. Third, comparing the US and the German model, one can note that the US system relies on both state intervention and private-sector coordination to a greater extent. Fourth, probably more than in disclosure, an Anglo-Saxon model becomes visible in which (takeover) markets play an important role.

## 10.2 Today's regulation

### The disclosure regulation

In the recent years, significant changes in the coordination efforts in disclosure regulation took place in all three countries. Partly, the basal legal foundations of disclosure regulation were considerably altered. Further, there is now binding European legislation, particularly the IAS Regulation of 2002. The most far-reaching legal reform in the US was the enactment of the SOA which not only altered the legal foundations of disclosure and enforcement in the US but also has had some extraterritorial effects. We will quantify in the following how these legal reforms translate into new governance structures of the three countries.

In the US, the SEC still dominates disclosure regulation. Similar state agencies responsible for disclosure regulation have neither emerged in Germany nor in the UK. With the FRC and the FSA, organizations with enforcement duties have been founded in the UK. Both are in fact not state agencies but, other than the SEC, entities under private law. Organizations under public law remain of minor importance in Germany. Still, such institutions do not play a role in the Anglo-Saxon countries. Officially mandated private institutions became more important in all countries. In the US, the relevance of the FASB as the official standard-setter increased with the enactment of the SOA. With the IAS regulation, the IASB became legally recognized as an official standard-setter, being important for all European member states. Besides the IASB, the German standard-setter (GASB) is of importance, having been created as an officially acknowledged body to develop national accounting rules further. It restricts itself, though, mostly on input to the international regulatory process. The FRC and in particular its subsidiary, the ASB, plays a role in the UK. However, since 2002, the ASB restricts itself mainly to harmonizing its own standards with that of the IASB (Parker 2004). Practically, the GASB and the ASB are therefore largely dependent on the IASB. Particularly due to the role of the IASB, officially mandated private actors gained a higher influence in all countries and these actors are, at least for the European countries, increasingly located at an international level. It follows that the relative importance of private organizations that are not officially mandated decreases. Factual standard-setters, for instance, play a lesser role. The same applies to courts and experts such as academics and practitioners. However, for the US, the IASB became a more important institution even though it is not officially mandated with standard-setting. The reason is that the FASB cooperates with the IASB to harmonize their respective standards. This, in fact, curtails the FASB's discretion in standard-setting at least partly and leads to a slight internationalization even of the US model.

Private solutions also play an increasing role for disclosure regulation. Private (demutualized) stock market operators occasionally became important private regulators. Their history is chequered: the crash and abolishment of the German *Neuer Markt* stands for a notorious failure, while the German Prime Standard or the UK AIM are success stories. Second, particularly in insider economies such as Germany, accounting rule-making for capital markets increased due to globalization and the cross-listing phenomenon. Exhibit 10.8 reports the importance of the respective actors in today's disclosure regulation in quantitative terms.

*Exhibit 10.8* Relevance of different actors in today's disclosure regulation

| Actors | Germany | US | UK |
|---|---|---|---|
| Parliaments (law) | 2 | 2 | 2 |
| State agencies | 0 | 2 | 0 |
| Courts | 1 | 1 | 1 |
| Public law institutions | 1 | 0 | 0 |
| Mandated private institutions | 3 | 3 | 3 |
| Non-mandated private institutions | 1 | 1 | 1 |
| Experts | 1 | 1 | 1 |
| Markets (contracting by individuals) | 3 | 3 | 3 |

*Exhibit 10.9* Visualization of today's disclosure regulation in three countries

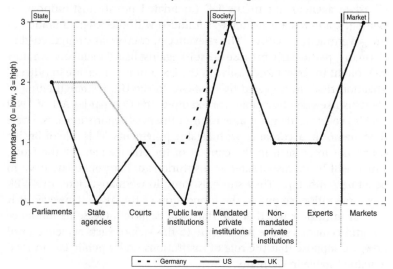

*Exhibit 10.10* Differences in today's disclosure regulation

|          | Germany  | US      | UK |
|----------|----------|---------|-----|
| Germany  | 0 (0)    | –       | –   |
| US       | 5 (23)   | 0       | –   |
| UK       | 1 (15)   | 4 (14)  | 0   |

*Note*: Numbers in brackets refer to the situation in the golden age.

The national configurations are visualized in Exhibit 10.9. They show that the national solutions indeed have converged. This finding is underlined when looking at the squared Euclidian distances reported in Exhibit 10.10. Interestingly, not only the distances between European countries decreased but also those in relation to the US.

**The enforcement regime**

The intensity of enforcement stipulation by law has consistently increased in all three countries. In Germany, this development can be traced to several legal amendments. Examples include the various Financial Market Promotion Acts or the APAG. In the UK, the most significant legal amendments are related to the FSMA, and in the US to the SOA.

The respective roles of state agencies were neither altered in the US (state agency) nor in the UK (mandated private institutions). In Germany, a new state agency was founded with the BaFin, a branch of the government executive. The relevance of courts was strengthened in Germany, particularly because lawsuits against board members can now be brought to court more easily. In the US, a similar increase in officers' litigation risk was triggered by the SOA. In the UK, a strengthening of courts is likewise observable. For example, the Companies Act of 1989 enables courts to demand a revision of financial reports in cases where they are not in accordance with legal requirements. This role of British courts has to be seen in the context of the enforcement by the FRRP, which will be discussed later as institutions under public law have to be addressed before. They still exist only in Germany. Here, the WPK lost some influence due to the foundation of the APAK. However, it is unclear until now whether the state will *de facto* increase its influence on enforcement via the APAK. Due to the lack of such evidence until now, we suppose that the role of institutions under public law in total remained stable in Germany.

Officially mandated enforcement organizations have gained importance in Germany, the UK and the US. The most remarkable organization among these actors is the British FSA, which was founded in 1997: even though its board members are assigned by state institutions, the FSA is an organization under private law and likewise privately financed, but it has ample sanctioning powers. With the FRRP, an additional privately organized professional enforcement organization exists. The emergence of these officially recognized institutions in the UK corroborates the view that the UK is turning away from a pure self-regulation approach in accountancy. The British FRRP was also a role model for the creation of the German Financial Reporting Enforcement Panel (DPR), being responsible for policing financial reporting. It is likely that the relevance of officially mandated private institutions will further increase for EU countries. With the new Eighth Company Law Directive (2006/43/EG), the Commission was mandated to put forward the adoption of International Auditing Standards in the Community. International Auditing Standards are developed by the IFAC, another (international) private organization. Hence, there will be another international private actor who is officially mandated at the European level. However, IFAC standards have not been endorsed at the EU level until now. Hence, a supranational sort of regulation not yet exists. Looking at officially mandated enforcement institutions in the US, the PCAOB has to be mentioned, which was founded under the rules of the SOA. It acts as a private organization mandated by the SEC and is – among other issues – responsible for developing audit standards and for overseeing the accounting profession. The PCAOB assumes several tasks that were formerly in the respective competences of private actors who traditionally did not have a comparable official mandate. This again points to an increase in state intervention in the US model.

We now address the role of private organizations without official mandate. In Germany, the IDW remains a relevant organization. However, since 1998, the Institute concentrates on incorporating IFAC's International Auditing Standards into its own pronouncements. In the future, the Institute's technical committee will primarily be concerned with filling possible loopholes and giving guidance on the application of International Auditing Standards (Schruff 2006). As far as the Institute has lost own discretion, within the private sector this loss seems to be compensated by the increasing relevance of the IFAC. This also applies to the UK. In both countries, ISA have already gained high practical relevance even though the application of these very standards is not yet prescribed by European legislation. The two European countries are in this respect again more internationalized than the US model.

Several legal amendments also led to a stronger role of experts in enforcement. In all countries, particularly the independence and role of auditors was strengthened. Additionally, audit committees were prescribed or recommended in the three countries advancing the relevance of external directors or supervisory board members, respectively. Finally, coordination through markets has to be addressed. The market's relevance remained at a high level for both Anglo-Saxon countries and increased in Germany. Still, markets play a more important role in the UK and the US.

According to the outlined observations, we now again estimate the relevance of the different actors in enforcement in the three countries. The results are shown in Exhibit 10.11. The respective national enforcement configurations are visualized in Exhibit 10.12.

Squared Euclidian distances are reported in Exhibit 10.13, revealing that the differences between the three country models are decreasing (US–Germany, UK–Germany) – or at least remain stable (US–UK).

202

*Exhibit 10.11*   Relevance of different actors in today's enforcement regulation

| Actors | Germany | US | UK |
|---|---|---|---|
| Parliaments (law) | 2 | 2 | 2 |
| State agencies | 1 | 2 | 0 |
| Courts | 2 | 3 | 2 |
| Public law institutions | 2 | 0 | 0 |
| Mandated private institutions | 3 | 3 | 3 |
| Non-mandated private institutions | 2 | 1 | 2 |
| Experts | 3 | 3 | 3 |
| Markets (contracting by individuals) | 2 | 3 | 3 |

*Exhibit 10.12*   Visualization of today's enforcement regulation in three countries

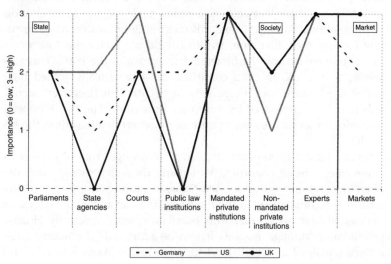

*Exhibit 10.13*   Differences in today's enforcement regulation

|  | Germany | US | UK |
|---|---|---|---|
| Germany | 0 | – | – |
| US | 8(13) | 0 | – |
| UK | 6(9) | 6(6) | 0 |

*Note*: Numbers in brackets refer to the situation in the golden age.

## 10.3   Conclusions

The evidence collected in this book supports the assumption that disclosure and enforcement governance in the three countries has converged over time. This becomes particularly visible when one considers the decrease of (squared) Euclidian distances in the pairwise comparisons of the three country models. This finding signals that a so-called 'sigma-convergence' has occurred: the variance between the systems is decreasing. It is often supposed that this process also implies that the German model has been adapted to the Anglo-Saxon model, which – according to common understanding – displays only minor tendencies of change. This can be rephrased as a so-called 'delta-convergence hypothesis', but such a hypothesis has to be rejected. Not only is there no clear evidence that an Anglo-Saxon model existed in the golden age in the first place. In addition, all three country models are subject to change.

From a governance perspective, the question is as to whether the relative importance of coordination by state and private actors has changed over time. To assess the relative importance of the coordination mechanisms, we have to first calculate the overall amplitude of coordination efforts in the respective policy fields for each country. Theoretically, it is possible to compute the areas in the respective graphs. However, there are some problems related to this approach. First, we only applied an ordinal measurement scale; second, the importance of different institutions is not weighted; and finally, the curve is not continuous. Following a simple approach, we multiply the respective importance of an actor by a standardized value of 1. We then sum up all the partial areas for the actors in one country adding up to a simple proxy for the overall coordination effort in the two policy fields. The resulting numbers are equal to the sums of the columns in Exhibits 10.2, 10.5, 10.8 and 10.11 and are reported in Exhibit 10.14.

Exhibit 10.14 shows that there is a slight increase in the coordination efforts in disclosure regulation and a large increase in coordination efforts

*Exhibit 10.14*   Overall coordination efforts: Golden age and today

|  | Disclosure | | Enforcement | |
|---|---|---|---|---|
|  | Golden age | Today | Golden age | Today |
| Germany | 11 | 12 | 8 | 17 |
| US | 10 | 13 | 11 | 17 |
| UK | 8 | 11 | 9 | 15 |

*Exhibit 10.15*　Relative importance of coordination by the state

|  | Disclosure | | Enforcement | |
|---|---|---|---|---|
|  | Golden age | Today | Golden age | Today |
| Germany | 1.20 | 0.50 | 0.60 | 0.70 |
| US | 0.67 | 0.63 | 0.57 | 0.70 |
| UK | 0.14 | 0.38 | 0.13 | 0.36 |

related to enforcement across all countries. In a further step, we can now sum up the partial areas belonging to the different modes of coordination in the three country models and compare their relative importance in the golden age and now. Exhibit 10.15 reports the relative importance of state-rooted actors compared to societal and markets actors (summarized to private-sector actors). Higher values point to a stronger role of the state compared to other actors.

In Germany, the state indeed played a stronger role in the golden age compared to the other countries. For the UK, the analysis shows that the role of the state in regulation was – and still is – relatively weak but increased in both fields over time. Some additional points are noticeable: first, the relative influence of the state on disclosure regulation decreased in Germany over time while it increased in case of enforcement. Second, US regulation witnessed a marginal decrease in state interventions in the field of disclosure regulation and a clear increase in state interventions in the field of enforcement. Taking the additional results reported in Exhibit 10.14 into account, the overall regulatory efforts have consistently increased for enforcement in all countries while they remained stable for disclosure. In the latter area there is hence just a shift in responsibility-sharing between the actors from the state sector and those from the private sector.

The emergence of 'cooperative statehood' is thus a two-sided phenomenon. On the one hand, it can, as seen in the case of Germany, imply that private actors are increasingly incorporated. On the other hand, it can also imply that the state takes over responsibilities that were formerly assumed by the private sector. The latter can particularly be observed in the UK. These findings accord, however, exactly with the hypotheses outlined in Chapter 1. We further conclude that the increase in the overall coordination efforts in enforcement is a necessary precondition for the state to hold on to supervisory responsibility in financial reporting. For Germany, it can be argued that the retreat of the state in disclosure regulation necessitated a stronger engagement with enforcement to obtain the means for fulfilling its supervisory responsibility. The UK, only taking on responsibility for outcomes in the golden age, also had to increase regulatory efforts in enforcement to assume supervisory responsibility, which became necessary with the advent of national disclosure regulation.

The preceding analysis did not explicitly address the spatial localization of the respective actors. To analyse these changes, we first concentrate on disclosure regulation. For the European countries, there is a tendency towards supranationalization as all international organizations incorporated in governance are mandated by the state sector. An important example is the endorsement of the IASB's pronouncements at the European level. Further, the state sector maintains its influence on supranational institutions like the ARC. A similar trend towards supranationalization cannot be observed in the US. The case of the US notably stays the most nationalized model among the three countries. However, even here, a tendency towards internationalization can be observed insofar as the FASB cooperates with the IASB. As the IASB is not officially mandated with developing accounting standards in the US, the move towards internationalization can be denoted as transnationalization. The findings are visualized in Exhibit 10.16.

Similar shifts can be observed in enforcement regulation. Here, several developments are remarkable. First, contrary to the field of disclosure regulation, overall regulatory efforts have increased in this policy

*Exhibit 10.16* Shifts in disclosure governance

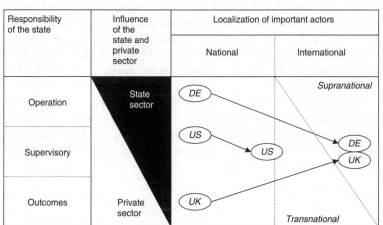

*Exhibit 10.17*  Shifts in enforcement governance

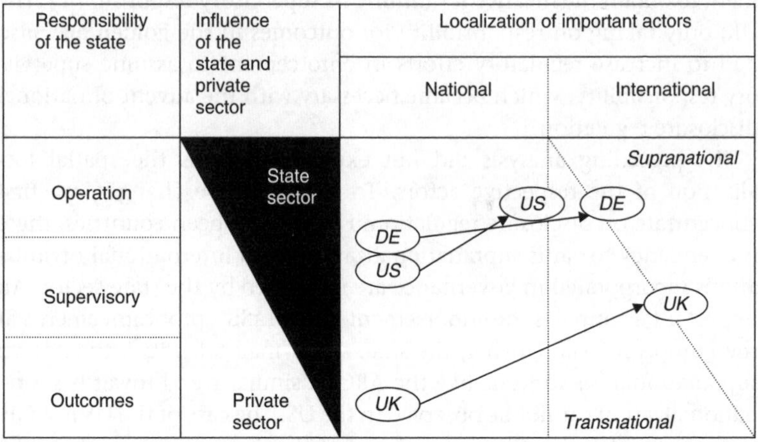

| Responsibility of the state | Influence of the state and private sector | Localization of important actors | |
|---|---|---|---|
| | | National | International |
| Operation | State sector | | Supranational / US DE / DE / US |
| Supervisory | | | UK |
| Outcomes | Private sector | UK | Transnational |

field compared to the golden age. That is, in enforcement, we observe not only a varying degree of sharing responsibilities between state and private actors but an increasing overall engagement of both groups of actors compared to the golden age. However, the degree of internationalization is, until now, much lesser than in the field of disclosure regulation. A possible explanation is that nation states try to compensate the loss of influence on disclosure regulation by expanding their efforts in enforcement. Moreover, for the European countries, supranational coordination in enforcement is less developed than in disclosure regulation. Even though the IFAC's pronouncements gained high practical relevance (transnationalization), their adoption is not yet prescribed by the nation states. Hence, as far supranationalization already exists, it is restricted to European harmonization efforts and takes place at the level of Community law. The changes in enforcement are summarized in Exhibit 10.17.

Both Exhibits 10.16 and 10.17 also point to the fact that statehood in accountancy has converged relatively consistently to a situation where the state has taken on supervisory responsibility in the fields under scrutiny in this study. Only the future will prove whether the achieved solution turns out to be stable.

# Epilogue

At the end of this investigation, some open questions remain, yet not so much about statehood but more so about the role and the use of accounting. In the structure of the book, we have concentrated on financial reporting with a perspective to capital markets, and we have designed the enquiry with the idea that accounting data is not only used but utilized on stock markets. This 'decision usefulness' perspective is most single-mindedly applied when the relationship between accounting information in financial reports and stock returns is analysed. An entire cottage industry of researchers is churning out papers on 'decision usefulness' of accounting for investors, mainly using the relationship between stock market returns and accounting information to build regression models, assuming a good use of accounting data on stock markets. After having written this book, after having looked at all that change in accounting governance, questions have emerged about whether this approach reflects well the actual uses of accounting and whether standards that try to make accounting more useful to investors are appropriate. All these are issues which we had excluded at the outset of our endeavour. An exhaustive discussion would warrant a new book, and in this epilogue we only want to raise some tentative questions.

The new gospel of accounting research is that accounting information is useful for investors in financial markets, and that it will help us understand accounting itself when we analyse how financial markets process accounting information. Previously, most German and a substantial body of international accounting research were rooted more in interpreting the law or in analysing practice and precedent. The perspective of financial markets and the economics of decision-making was novel. Beaver (1998) even called this new turn an Accounting

Revolution – leaving open the question as to whether this revolution is more of the French or the Russian style.

We show in this book that the capital markets perspective on standard-setting and disclosure, which has started in the US, is very likely the result of a historical accident: the New Deal. It must therefore be of little surprise that the capital markets perspective on accounting arose in the US, where it has gained some dominance in the academic community. It took a long time until this strand of research became even accepted in Europe, leave alone actively pursued. This is true not only for Continental Europe but also for the UK, where accounting was regulated, if at all, in the framework of company law. The organization of the economy and the importance of capital markets thus do not play a decisive role whether this capital markets research was initially accepted: after all, the UK has relied heavily on financial markets.

It may just be the case that the 'decision usefulness' approach teaches us little about accounting, how it is used in practice and how it can be improved. However, all standard-setters now follow the maxim of 'information usefulness' for capital markets. The standard-setters are currently dragging along the business community kicking and screaming. The recent exposure draft for business combinations, jointly released by the FASB and the IASB, is a case in point. Many of the suggested prescriptions were rejected by the community, and it is very rare that a draft standard receives overwhelming rejection. This list could easily be extended. What if the users of accounts actually have better insights into purposes and uses of accounting than the standard-setters and are not just fuddy-duddies resistant to change? The due process of standard-setting is now the only leverage left with the business community. The institutions are often self-selecting and tied to their constitutions, all of which stipulate a capital market focus, the US standard-setting organizations by legal design, the IFRS-setting one by choice. And the escape gates are barred. The convergence of standards in Europe and eventually also with the US will only lead to capital markets-based standards being applied.

The entire experiment of capital market-based informational standards may therefore turn sour. The dangers from a failed experiment are still limited. The governance changes that are the theme of this book also showed that the accounting community, sometimes with the helping hand of the state, has always found a way out of a difficult corner.

# Notes

## Part I Transformations of statehood in accounting: The framework

1. Technically, one also needs to distinguish between company accounts for the single legal entity and group accounts of the economic reporting unit. Changes for listed firms relate to the group accounts as they are the accounting signalling device to capital markets. It stands to reason that the developments in group accounting will not only spill over to small and medium sized firms (which tend not to be groups) but also to company accounts.

## 1 Accounting: A socio-economic view

1. In fact Streeck and Schmitter distinguish a fourth – 'associationist' – basis of social order as a qualitatively different mixture of the previous three. We, following Puxty (implicitly; 1987), consider these arrangements as part of the 'community' basis.
2. Economic analysis would tend to use the term 'public good' instead of 'normative good'. We prefer the latter term for two reasons: public goods can also be provided by private agents, and it requires a normative decision whether such a good is desirable at all.

## 2 Transformation of role models: Germany, the UK and the US

1. As Parker (1990) points out, some firms of high economic importance (such as railroad companies) were actually regulated rather intensively.
2. Today's accounting rules in HGB are mainly an outcome of the adoption of European directives.
3. In the process of restructuring banking and insurance oversight the BaFin was set up in 2002 as an integrated financial supervisory authority (Schüler 2004). One of its responsibilities is overseeing the trade in securities. It is not responsible for the oversight of stock exchanges.

## 3 Rise and fall of the golden-age nation state model

1. The AICPA was founded in 1887 as the American Association of Public Accountants, reorganized in 1916 and renamed as American Institute of Accountants in 1917. The present name was adopted in 1957.

2. During its tenure, the CAP issued 51 Accounting Research Bulletins on a variety of subjects. Accounting Research Bulletins are still recognized as GAAP except when they have been specifically superseded. SEC ASR No. 150 also acknowledges that ARB can be applied for filings.
3. The AAA was established in 1916 as the American Association of University Instructors in Accounting. The name was changed to the American Accounting Association in 1935.
4. A chronology of the developments, in particular the contents of the different Companies Acts, is provided in Nobes and Parker (1979).

# 4   The new accounting procedures in Europe: Combining transnational standard-setting and supranational rule-making

1. The 2000 Inter-Governmental Conference and the Treaty of Nice of 2001 led to a re-weighting of the number of votes allocated to each member state. After 1 January 2007, the Qualified Majority Voting (QMV) lies at 255 votes out of a total of 345. At the request of a member state, it must be demonstrated that at least 62 percent of the total population of the Union are represented by the vote for its becoming effective. From 1 November 2009 QMV requires a twofold majority, coming from at least 55 percent of the member states and at least 65 percent of the population. The blocking minority must at least comprise four member states.
2. Meijer (2003) mentions the positive effects of the use of information and communication technologies for accountability. Therefore, a well-designed and regularly updated website can play an important role in serving as a procedural control element ensuring accountability.

# 5   The struggle between private and public: The case of stock exchanges

1. The Paris Stock Exchange has shut down floor trading after the introduction of the electronic trading system CAC in 1989.
2. The Second Financial Market Promotion Act amended the German Capital Investment Companies Act (*Gesetz über Kapitalanlagegesellschaften,* KAGG) as well as the Law on Information Access (*Akteneinsichts- und Informationszugangsgesetz,* AIG).
3. According to the Stock Exchange Act, the admission requirements in the Regulated Market can be increased by the exchanges if this is necessary for due trade and investor protection. The FSE has not exercised this option yet.
4. In contrast to Germany, the requirements of *ad-hoc* reporting arise from the FSA's Listing Rules and not from law.
5. The competition among stock exchanges also relates to the respective commission rates and transaction costs.

## 6  Dawn and dusk of the nation state in auditing: From supervising private arrangements to transnational governance

1. A historical overview over the evolution of auditing in the US is given in Flesher *et al.* (2005). A similar description for the UK can be found in Matthews (2006) and for Germany in Quick (2005). An appealing comparison of the German and the UK model as of the 1990s can be found in Vieten (1995).
2. In this context, the terminology of Streeck (1995) is incomplete: the market exists and needs no 'market-making' interventions. It is rather in danger of collapsing and therefore is in need of 'backing' only.

## 8  The weakened nation state: Economic globalization and regime convergence

1. The countries are Australia, Austria, Belgium (together with Luxembourg), Canada, Denmark, Finland, France, Germany, Greece, Island, Ireland, Italy, Japan, Korea, Mexico, The Netherlands, New Zealand, Norway, Portugal, Spain, Sweden, Switzerland, the UK and the US.
2. The strand of literature cited here deals with the convergence of corporate governance systems. As financial reporting and auditing can be supposed to be part of a country's corporate governance system – or at least will be complementary to it – we use this literature as a natural starting point.
3. Market capitalization to GDP is relatively robust to cyclicality. However, the amount of equity listed, not the amount raised, is measured.
4. Number of companies listed relative to population in million is a non-fluctuating measure resistant to business cycles; it is, however, strongly influenced by the level of market concentration.

## 9  The powerful nation state: Sarbanes–Oxley and the global reach of regulation

1. To ensure effective coordination of the member states' oversight institutions and to assess third countries' public oversight systems, the Commission also set up a new entity which is called the European Group of Auditors' Oversight Bodies (EGAOB).
2. It must, however, be noted that there is often not an exact reference for an amendment to a particular point of the government programme. Additionally, some amendments are in the spirit of several programme points. Hence, mapping reform laws to one of the points in the '10-point programme' is a somewhat elusive task.

# References

Adler, H., Düring, W. and Schmaltz, K., Rechnungslegung und Prüfung der Aktiengesellschaft : Handkommentar für die Bilanzierungs- und Prüfungspraxis nach dem Aktiengesetz unter Berücksichtigung der sonstigen handelsrechtlichen Vorschriften (Stuttgart: Poeschel, 1938).

Aggarwal, R., 'Demutualization and corporate governance of stock exchanges', Journal of Applied Corporate Finance 15:1 (2002) 105–113.

Aggarwal, R. and Angel, J., 'The rise and fall of the Amex emerging company marketplace', Journal of Financial Economics 52:2 (1999) 257–289.

Alcock, A., The Financial Services and Markets Act 2000: A Guide to the New Law (Bristol: Jordans, 2000).

Alexander, D., 'A European true and fair view?' European Accounting Review 2:1 (1993) 59–80.

Alexander, D. and Archer, S., 'On the myth of "Anglo-Saxon" financial accounting: A response to nobes', The International Journal of Accounting 38:4 (2003) 503–504.

Altendorfer, C., Die US-amerikanische Kapitalmarktaufsicht (SEC): Ein Modell für Österreich? (Wien: Service Fachverlag, 1995).

Avenarius, H., Die Rechtsordnung der Bundesrepublik Deutschland: Eine Einführung (Bonn: Bundeszentrale für politische Bildung, 1997).

Baetge, J., 'Anmerkungen zum deutschen Enforcement-Modell', Zeitschrift für das gesamte Handelsrecht und Wirtschaftsrecht 23:4 (2004) 428–433.

Baetge, J. and Lutter, M., Abschlussprüfung und Corporate Governance (Köln: Otto Schmidt, 2003).

Baetge, J., Thiele, S. and Matena, S., 'Mittelbare Sicherung der Prüfungsqualität durch Enforcement geprüfter Jahres- und Konzernabschlüsse – Überlegungen aus ökonomischer Sicht', Betriebswirtschaftliche Forschung und Praxis 56:3 (2004) 201–218.

BaFin, Jahresbericht 2005 (Frankfurt/Main, 2005).

Baker, H. K., Nofsinger, J. R. and Weaver, D. G., 'International cross-listing and visibility', Journal of Financial and Quantitative Analysis 37:3 (2002) 495–521.

Baker, R. L., Bealing Jr., W. E., Nelson, D. and Staley, B. A., 'An institutional perspective of the Sarbanes-Oxley Act', Managerial Auditing Journal 21:1 (2006) 23–33.

Ball, R., 'Infrastructure requirements for an economically efficient system of public financial reporting and disclosure', in: R. E. Litan and R. Herring (eds.), Brooking-Wharton Papers on Financial Services (Washington D.C.: Brookings Institution Press, 2001).

Ball, R., Kothari, S. P. and Robin, A., 'The effect of international institutional factors on properties of accounting earnings', Journal of Accounting and Economics 29:1 (2000) 1–51.

Ball, R., Walker, R. G. and Whittred, G. P., 'Audit qualifications and share prices', Abacus 15:1 (1979) 23–34.

Ballmann, A., Epstein, D. and O'Halloran, S., 'Delegation, comitology, and the separation of powers in the European Union', International Organization 56:3 (2002) 551–574.

Ballwieser, W., 'Die Unabhängigkeit des Wirtschaftsprüfers – Eine analyse von Beratungsverbot und externer rotation', in: M. Lutter (ed.), Der Wirtschaftsprüfer als Element der Corporate Governance (Düsseldorf: IDW-Verlag, 2001).

Bancel, F. and Mittoo, U. R., 'European managerial perceptions of the net benefits of foreign stock listings', European Financial Management 7:2 (2001) 213–236.

Baumeister, A. and Werkmeister, C., 'Die Wirkung spezieller Börsenstandards am Beispiel des SMAX', Die Betriebswirtschaft 61:1 (2001) 121–141.

Bazerman, M. H., Morgan, K. P. and Loewenstein, G. F., 'The impossibility of auditor independence', Sloan Management Review 38:4 (1997) 89–94.

Beal, H. and Bennett, S., 'The companies act 2004: A bolt- on boost to market confidence?' Business Law Review 26:7 (2005) 166–170.

Beaver, W. H., Financial Reporting: An Accounting Revolution, 3rd ed. (London: Prentice-Hall, 1998).

Bebchuk, L. A. and Roe, M. J., 'A theory of path dependence in corporate ownership and governance', in: J. N. Gordon and M. J. Roe (eds.), Convergence and Persistence in Corporate Governance (Cambridge: Cambridge University Press, 2004).

Beck, U., What is Globalization? (Cambridge: Polity Press, 2000).

Bernanke, B., 'Monetary policy in a world of mobile capital', Cato Journal 25:1 (2005) 1–12.

Biddle, G. and Saudagaran, S., 'Foreign stock listings: Benefits, costs, and the accounting policy dilemma', Accounting Horizons 5:3 (1991) 69–80.

Birch, A. H., The Concepts and Theories of Modern Democracy (London Routledge, 1993).

Bishop, G., 'Die Regulierung oder Selbtregulierung der Finanzmärkte', in: C. Randzio-Plath (ed.), Zur Globalisierung der Finanzmärkte und Finanzmarktstabilität (Baden-Baden: Nomos, 2001).

Blair, M. and Walker, G., Financial Services Law (Oxford: Oxford University Press, 2006).

Blass, A. and Yafeh, Y., 'Vagabond shoes longing to stray: Why foreign firms list in the United States', Journal of Banking and Finance 25:3 (2000) 555–572.

Blume, M., Siegel, J. and Rottenberg, D., Revolution on Wall Street – The Rise and Decline of the New York Stock Exchange (New York: Norton, 1993).

Böcking, H.-J. and Dutzi, A., 'Neugestaltung der Berufsaufsicht für Wirtschaftsprüfer', Betriebswirtschaftliche Forschung und Praxis 58:1 (2006) 1–21.

Böcking, H.-J., Orth, C. and Brinkmann, R., 'Die Anwendung der International Standards on Auditing (ISA) im Rahmen der handelsrechtlichen Konzernabschlussprüfung und deren Berücksichtigung im Bestätigungsvermerk', Die Wirtschaftsprüfung 53:5 (2000) 216–233.

Borger, D., 'Der Sinn des Rechnungswesens: Finanzinstrumente und die Reproduktion von Unternehmensgrenzen', Soziale Systeme 5:1 (1999) 83–104.

Born, K., Rechnungslegung International, Einzel- und Konzernabschlüsse nach IAS, US-GAAP, HGB und EG-Richtlinien, 3rd ed. (Stuttgart: Schäffer-Poeschel, 2002).

Börsig, C. and Coenenberg, A. G., Controlling und Rechnungswesen im internationalen Wettbewerb (Stuttgart: Schäffer-Poeschel, 1998).

Bourdieu, P., 'The politics of globalisation', *Le Monde*, 24 January 2002.

Brackney, K. S. and Witmer, P. R., 'The European Union's role in international standards setting', The CPA Journal 25:11 (2005) 18–28.

Bratton, W., 'Private standards, public governance: A new look at the financial accounting standard board', Boston College Law Review 48:5 (2007) 5–53.

Brinkmann, R. and Spiess, A., 'Abschlussprüfung nach international standards on auditing : Überblick über aktuelle Entwicklungen durch die 8. EU-Richtlinie und das clarity-project des IASB sowie Auswirkungen auf die IDW-Prüfungsstandards', Kapitalmarktorientierte Rechnungslegung 6:6 (2006) 395–409.

Brown, P. and Tarca, A., 'Archieving high quality, comparable financial reporting: A comparison of independent enforcement bodies in Australia and the United Kingdom', Working Paper, University of Western Australia (2005).

Bushman, R. M. and Smith, A. J., 'Financial accounting information and corporate governance', Journal of Accounting and Economics 32:1–3 (2001) 237–333.

Busse von Colbe, W., 'Die deutsche Rechnungslegung vor einem Paradigmawechsel', Schmalenbachs Zeitschrift für betriebswirtschaftliche Forschung 54:2 (2002) 159–172.

Cadbury, A., 'Best practice the British way', Harvard Business Review 71:1 (1993) 80.

Chandler, R., 'IFAC: The consensus-seekers', Accountancy 106:1136 (1990) 84–85.

Chandler, W. B. I. and Strine, L. E., 'The new federalism of the American corporate governance system: Preliminary reflections of two residents in one small state', University of Pennsylvania Law Review 152:2 (2003) 953–1005.

Chaney, P. K. and Philipich, K. L., 'Shredded reputation: The cost of audit failure', Journal of Accounting Research 40:4 (2002) 1221–1245.

Cheney, G., 'No more donations: FASB readies for shift in funding', Accounting Today 17:12 (2003) 14.

Choe, H., Masulis, R. W. and Nanda, V., 'Common stock offerings across the business cycle: Theory and evidence', Journal of Empirical Finance 1:1 (1993) 3–31.

Choi, F. D. S. and Meek, G. K., International Accounting, 5th ed. (Upper Saddle River: Prentice Hall, 2005).

Cioffi, J. W., 'Corporate governance reform, regulatory politics, and the foundations of finance capitalism in the United States and Germany', German Law Journal 7:6 (2006) 533–562.

Coffee, J. C., 'Racing towards the Top? The impact of cross-listings and stock market competition on international corporate governance', Columbia Law Review 102:7 (2002) 1757–1831.

Conyon, M. J. and Mallin, C. A., 'A review of compliance with Cadbury', Journal of General Management 22:3 (1997) 24–37.

Craig, P. P., 'Democracy and rule-making within the EC: An empirical and normative assessment', European Law Journal 3:2 (1997) 105–130.

Cromme, G., 'Corporate governance in Germany and the German corporate governance code', Corporate Governance: An International Review 13:3 (2005) 362–367.

von der Crone, H. C. and Roth, K., 'Der Sarbanes-Oxley Act und seine extraterritoriale Bedeutung', Aktuelle Juristische Praxis 12:2 (2003) 131–140.

Cummins, J. G., Harris, T. S. and Hassett, K. A., 'Accounting standards, information flow, and firm investment behaviour', Working Paper, National Bureau of Economic Research (1994).

Dahl, R. A., Dilemmas of Pluralist Democracy: Autonomy vs. Control (New Haven Yale University Press, 1982).

Dahl, R. A., 'A democratic dilemma: System effectiveness versus citizen participation', Political Science Quarterly 109:1 (1994) 23–34.

Das, S. and Saudagaran, S. M., 'Accuracy, bias, and dispersion in analysts' earnings forecasts: The case of cross-listed foreign firms', Journal of International Financial Management and Accounting 9:1 (1998) 16–33.

Davies, P. L., 'Board structure in the UK and Germany: Convergence or continuing divergence?' Working Paper, London School of Economics (2002).

Deeg, R., 'Change from within – German and Italian Finance in the 1990s', in: W. Streek and K. Thelen (eds.), Change and Continuity in Institutional Analysis: Explorations in the Dynamics of Advanced Political Economies (Oxford: Oxford University Press, 2005).

Delaney, P. R., Epatein, B. J., Nach, R. and Weiss Budak, S., GAAP 2004: Interpretation and Application of Generally Accepted Accounting Principles (Hoboken, NJ: Wiley 2004).

Deutsche Börse A. G., History of the Exchange, http://deutsche-boerse.com (2006).

Deutsche Bundesbank 'Regulierung von Wertpapiermärkten: Internationale Ansätze', Deutsche Bundesbank Monatsbericht Januar 2006 (2006) 37–52.

Dewing, I. P. and Russell, P. O., 'Post-Enron developments in UK audit and corporate governance regulation', Journal of Financial Regulation and Compliance 11:4 (2003) 309–322.

Dewing, I. P. and Russell, P. O., 'Regulation of UK corporate governance: Lessons from accounting, audit and financial services', Corporate Governance: An International Review 12:1 (2004) 107–115.

Di Noia, C., 'Competition and integration among stock exchanges in Europe: Network effects, implicit mergers and remote access', European Financial Management 7:2 (2001) 39–72.

Dickey, J. C., Sturc, J. H., Collins, P. J. and Mack, S., 'SEC Investigations and enforcement actions: An overview and discussion of recent trends in accounting fraud investigations', Working Paper, Practising Law Institute (2001).

Doidge, C., Karolyi, A. and Stulz, R. M., 'Why are foreign firms listed in the U.S. worth more?' Journal of Financial Economics 71:2 (2004) 205–238.

Domowitz, I., Glen, J. and Madhaven, A., 'International Cross-listing and order flow migration: Evidence from an emerging market,' Journal of Finance 53:6 (1998) 2000–2027.

Downes, D., 'Progress on eighth law directive as council of the European Union reaches political agreement', Accountancy Ireland 37:6 (2005) 27–29.

DPR, Tätigkeitsbericht für den Zeitraum vom 1. January bis 31. Dezember 2006 (Berlin, 2007).

DRSC, 'Organisation und Ziele des DRSC', Working Paper, Deutsches Rechnungslegungs Standards Commitee (2007).

Dryzek, J., Deliberative democracy and beyond: Liberals, critics and contestations (Oxford: Oxford University Press, 2000).

Ebert, E., Private Normsetzung für die Rechnungslegung – Möglichkeiten und Grenzen (Sternfels: Verlag Wissenschaft und Praxis, 2002).

Eccles, T. and Holt, A., 'Financial statements and corporate accounts: The conceptual framework', Property Management 23:5 (2005) 374–387.

Edey, H. C., 'Company accounting in the nineteenth and twentieth centuries', in: T. A. Lee and R. H. Parker (eds.), The evolution of corporate financial reporting (Walton-on-Thames: Nelson, 1979).

Edwards, J. R., Anderson, M. and Matthews, D., 'Accountability in a free-market economy: The British company audit, 1886', Abacus 33:1 (1997) 1–25.

Ehrenberg, R., 'Makler, Hosteliers und Börse in Brügge vom 13. bis 16. Jahrhundert', Zeitschrift für das gesamte Handelsrecht und Wirtschaftsrecht 30:1885 (1885) 403–468.

European Commission, The EU Single Market, http://ec.europa.eu (2006).

Evans, L. and Nobes, C., 'Harmonization of the structure of audit firms: Incorporation in the UK and Germany', The European Accounting Review 7:1 (1998) 125–148.

Ewert, R. and Stefani, U., 'Wirtschaftsprüfung', in: P. J. Jost (ed.), Die Prinzipal-Agent-Theorie in der Betriebswirtschaftslehre (Stuttgart: Schaeffer-Poeschel Verlag, 2001).

FASB, Emerging Issues Task Force (EITF), General Information, http://www.fasb.org (2004a).

FASB, FASB Facts, An Open Decision-making Process, http://www.fasb.org (2004b).

FASB, Facts about FASB, http://fasb.org (2005).

Fearnley, S., Beattie, V. A. and Brandt, R., 'Auditor independence and audit risk: A reconceptualization', Journal of International Accounting Research 4:1 (2005) 39–71.

Fearnley, S., Brandt, R. and Beattie, V., 'Financial regulation of public limited companies in the UK: A way forward post-Enron', Journal of Financial Regulation and Compliance 10:3 (2002) 254–265.

Fearnley, S. and Hines, T., 'The regulatory framework for financial reporting and auditing in the United Kingdom: The present position and impending changes', The International Journal of Accounting 38:2 (2003) 215–233.

FEE, 'Enforcement mechanisms in Europe: A preliminary investigation of oversight systems', Working Paper, European Federation of Accountants (2001).

Firth, M., 'Qualified audit reports: Their impact on investment decisions', Accounting Review 53:3 (1978) 642–650.

Fisch, J., 'The new federal regulation of corporate governance', Harvard Journal of Law and Public Policy 28:1 (2004) 39–49.

Fishman, J. J., The Transformation of Threadneedle Street: The Deregulation and Reregulation of Britain's Financial Services (Durham: Carolina Academic Press, 1993).

Fleischer, H., 'Der financial services and markets act 2000: Neues Börsen- und Kapitalmarktrecht für das Vereinigte Königreich', Recht der Internationalen Wirtschaft 47:11 (2001) 817–825.

Flesher, D. L., Previts, G. J. and Samson, W. D., 'Auditing in the United States: A historical perspective', Abacus 41:1 (2005) 21–39.

Flower, J., European Financial Reporting, Adapting to a Changing World (London/New York: Palgrave MacMillan, 2004).

FRC, Annual Report 2006/07 (London, 2007a).

FRC, Organisation Chart, http://www.frc.org.uk (2007b).

FRRP, Activity Report (London, 2006).

FRRP and FSA, Memorandum of Understanding between the Financial Reporting Review Panel and the Financial Services Authority (London, 2005).

FSA, The Combined Code: Principles of Good Governance and Code of Best Practice (London: Committee on Corporate Governance, 1998).

FSA, Annual Report 2005/06 (London, 2006).

García Lara, J. M., García Osma, B. and Mora, A., 'The effect of earnings management on the asymmetric timeliness of earnings', Journal of Business Finance and Accounting 32:3–4 (2005) 691–726.

Gehrke, W. and Rapp, H.-W., 'Strukturveränderungen im internationalen Börsenwesen', Die Betriebswirtschaft 54 (1994) 5–23.

Geisst, C. R., Wall Street: A History (New York, 1997).

Gelter, M., 'Zur Ökonomischen Analyse der begrenzten Haftung des Abschlussprüfers', Die Wirtschaftsprüfung 58:9 (2005) 486–499.

Gilson, R. J., 'Globalizing corporate governance: Convergence of form or function', Working Paper, Columbia University Center for Law and Economics (2000).

Giner, B. and Arce, M., 'Lobbying on accounting standards: The due process of IFRS 2 on share-based payments', Working Paper, University of Valencia (2004).

Glaum, M., Thomaschewski, D. and Weber, S., 'Der Sarbanes-Oxley Act: Folgen für US-Börsennotierungen aus Sicht deutscher Unternehmen', Finanz-Betrieb 7:3 (2006) 182–194.

Goergen, M., Khurshed, A., McCahery, J. and Renneboog, L., 'The rise and fall of the European New Markets: On the short and long-term performance of high tech initial public offerings', in: J. McCahery and L. Renneboog (eds.), Venture Capital Contracting and the Valuation of High Technology Firms (Oxford: Oxford University Press, 2003).

Goncharov, I., Werner, J. R. and Zimmermann, J., 'Does compliance with the German corporate governance code have an impact on stock valuation? An empirical analysis', Corporate Governance: An International Review 14:5 (2006) 432–445.

Grimm, D., 'Der Wandel der Staatsaufgaben und die Krise des Rechtsstaats', in: D. Grimm (ed.), Wachsende Staatsaufgaben – sinkende Steuerungskraft des Rechts (Baden-Baden: Nomos, 1990).

Grofman, B., 'Models of voter turnout: A brief idiosyncratic review', Public Choice 41:1 (1983) 55–61.

Gros, S., 'Enforcement der Rechnungslegung – Die Deutsche Prüfstelle für Rechnungslegung aus Sicht des Chief Financial Officer', Deutsches Steuerrecht 44:6 (2006) 246–251.

Grundmann, S., Europäisches Gesellschaftsrecht (Heidelberg: C. F. Müller Verlag, 2004).

Hackethal, A., Schmidt, R. H. and Tyrell, M., 'Banks and German corporate governance: On the way to a capital market-based system?' Corporate Governance: An International Review 13:3 (2005) 397–407.

Hackethal, A., Schmidt, R. H. and Tyrell, M., 'The transformation of the German financial system', Revue d'économie Politique 116:4 (2006) 431–456.

Hall, P. A. and Soskice, D., Varieties of Capitalism (Oxford: Oxford University Press, 2001).

218   *References*

Haller, A., Die Grundlagen der externen Rechnungslegung in den USA – Unter besonderer Berücksichtigung der rechtlichen, institutionellen und theoretischen Rahmenbedingungen, 4th ed. (Stuttgart: Schäffer-Poeschel, 1994).

Haller, A., 'Financial accounting developments in the European Union: Past events and future prospects', European Accounting Review 11:1 (2002) 153–192.

Hansmann, H. and Kraakman, R., 'The end of history for corporate law', Georgetown Law Journal 89:2 (2001) 439–469.

Harding, N. and McKinnon, J., 'User involvement in the standard-setting process: A research note on the congruence of accountant and user perceptions of decision usefulness', Accounting, Organizations and Society 22:1 (1997) 55–67.

Hay, J. R. and Shleifer, A., 'Private enforcement of public laws: A theory of legal reform', American Economic Review 88:2 (1998) 398–403.

Hazen, T. L., The Law of Securities Regulation, 4th ed. (St. Paul, Minnessota: West Group, 2002).

Healy, P. and Palepu, K., 'Information asymmetry, corporate disclosure, and the capital markets: A review of the empirical disclosure literature', Journal of Accounting and Economics 31:2001 (2001) 405–440.

Heeren, K.-A. and Rieckers, O., 'Legislative responses in times of financial crisis – New deal securities legislation, Sarbanes-Oxley Act and their impact on future German and EU regulation', European Business Law Review 14:5 (2003) 595–628.

Heichel, S., Pape, J. and Sommerer, T., 'Is there convergence in convergence research? An overview of empirical studies on policy convergence', Journal of European Public Policy 12:5 (2005) 817–840.

Heintges, S., Bilanzkultur und Bilanzpolitik in den USA und in Deutschland: Einflüsse auf die Bilanzpolitik börsennotierter Unternehmen, 3. Aufl. ed (Sternenfels: Verlag Wissen und Praxis, 2005).

Held, D., Global Transformations (Palo Alto, CA: Stanford University Press, 1999).

Hendriksen, E. S., Accounting theory, 3rd ed. (Homewood: Irwin, 1977).

Herzig, N. and Watrin, C., 'Obligatorische Rotation des Wirtschaftsprüfers – ein Weg zur Verbesserung der externen Unternehmenskontrolle?' Zeitschrift für betriebswirtschaftliche Forschung 47:9 (1995) 775–804.

Heuser, P. J., Theile, C., Pawelzik, K. U. and Heuser, T., IAS/IFRS-Handbuch: Einzel- und Konzernabschluss, 2., neu bearb. Aufl. ed (Köln: Otto Schmidt Verlag, 2005).

Hicks, E. L., 'APB: The first 3600 days', Journal of Accountancy 128:3 (1969) 56–60.

Higgs, D., Review of the Role and Effectiveness of Non-Executive Directors (London: The Department of Trade and Industry, 2003).

Hilke, J., 'Early mandatory disclosure regulations', International Review of Law and Economics 6:2 (1986) 229–239.

Hines, R. D., 'Financial accounting: In communicating, we construct reality', Accounting, Organizations and Society 13:3 (1988) 251–261.

Hix, S., The Political System of the European Union (Basingstoke: Palgrave MacMillan 2005).

Hobsbawm, E., The Age of Extremes: A History of the World 1914–1991 (New York: Pantheon Books, 1995).

Hollister, H. T., 'Shock therapy for Aktiengesellschaften: Can the Sarbanes-Oxley certification requirements transform German corporate culture, practice and prospects?' Northwestern Journal of International Law and Business 25:2 (2005) 453–484.

Hopt, K., 'Europäisches und deutsches Insiderrecht', Zeitschrift für Unternehmens- und Gesellschaftsrecht 20:1 (1991) 17–73.

Hopwood, A., 'Some reflections on 'The harmonizing of accounting withing the EU', European Accounting Review 3:2 (1994) 241–253.

Hopwood, A. and Vieten, H., 'The United Kingdom', in: S. McLeay (ed.), Accounting Regulation in Europe (Houndsmills, Basingstoke: Macmillan, 1999).

Howe, J. and Madura, J., 'The impact of international listings on risk: Implications for capital market integration', Journal of Banking and Finance 14:6 (1990) 1133–1142.

Howells, P. and Bain, K., Financial Markets and Institutions (Harlow: Prentice Hall, 2004).

Huddart, S. J., Hughes, J. S. and Brunnermeier, M. K., 'Disclosure requirements and stock exchange listing choice in an international context', Journal of Accounting and Economics 26:1–3 (1999) 237–269.

Hurrelmann, A., Leibfried, S., Martens, K. and Mayer, P., Hg., Transforming the Golden-Age Nation State (Houndmills, Basingstoke: Palgrave, 2007).

Hütten, C. and Stromann, H., 'Umsetzung des Sarbanes-Oxley Act in der Unternehmenspraxis', Betriebsberater 58:42 (2003) 2223–2227.

IASB, About Us, http://www.iasb.org (2007).

IASC, 'IASC Constitution', Working Paper, IASC (1992).

IASCF (2006) Due Process Handbook for the IASB Hg., London: International Accounting Standards Committee Foundation.

Jennings, A. R., 'Accounting Research', Accounting Review 33:4 (1958) 347–355.

Joerges, C. and Neyer, J., 'From intergovernmental bargaining to deliberative polit-ical processes: The constitutionalisation of comitology', European Law Journal 3:3 (1997) 273–299.

Johnson, S. B. and Solomons, D., 'Institutional Legitimacy and the FASB', Journal of Accounting and Public Policy 3:3 (1984) 165–183.

Kamann, H.-G. and Simpkins, M., 'Sarbanes-Oxley Act – Anlass zu verstärkter internationaler Kooperation im Bereich der corporate governance?' Recht der internationalen Wirtschaft 49:3 (2003) 183–189.

Kaplan, D. and Fender, E. A., 'The development of comment letters on FASB pro-posals by the AICPA accounting standards executive committee', Accounting Horizons 12:2 (1998) 184–187.

Karolyi, G. A., 'Why do companies list abroad? A survey of the evidence and its managerial implications', Financial Markets, Institutions, and Instruments 7:1 (1998) 1–60.

Karolyi, G. A. and Stulz, R. M., 'Are financial assets priced locally or globally?' in: R. E. Litan and R. Herring (eds.), Brookings-Wharton papers on financial services (Washington D.C.: Brooking Institution Press, 2002).

Kersting, M. O., 'Der Neue Markt der Deutsche Börse AG', Die Aktiengesellschaft 42:5 (1997) 222–228.

Keßler, J., 'Länderbericht Vereinigtes Königreich', in: J. Keßler and H.-W. Micklitz (eds.), Anlegerschutz in Deutschland, Schweiz, Großbritannien, USA und der Europäischen Gemeinschaft (Baden-Baden: Nomos, 2004).

Khanna, T., Kogan, J. and Palepu, K. G., 'Globalization and similarities in corporate governance: A cross-country analysis', The Review of Economics and Statistics 88:1 (2006) 69–90.

Kiefer, M., Kritische Analyse der Kapitalmarktregulierung der U.S. Securities and Exchange Commission: Lösungsansatz für eine deutsche und europäische Enforcement-Instanz als Bestandteil der Corporate Governance (Wiesbaden: Deutscher Universitäts-Verlag, 2003).

Kirchhof, P., 'Gesetzgebung und private Regelsetzung als Geltungsgrund fuer Rechnungslegungspflichten?' Zeitschrift fuer Unternehmens- und Gesellschaftsrecht 29:4–5 (2000) 681–692.

Kirsch, G., Neue Politische Ökonomie, 5th ed. (Stuttgart: Lucius and Lucius, 2004).

Knill, C., 'Introduction: Cross-national policy convergence: Concepts, approaches and explanatory factors', Journal of European Public Policy 12:5 (2005) 764–774.

Krugman, P. R. and Obstfeld, M., International Economics: Theory and Policy, 6th ed. (Boston, MA: Addison Wesley, 2002).

Kübler, F. and Assmann, H.-D., Gesellschaftsrecht – Die privatrechtlichen Ordnungsstrukturen und Regelungsprobleme von Verbänden und Unternehmen (Heidelberg: C.F. Müller, 2006).

Kümpel, S., Kapitalmarktrecht: Eine Einführung (Berlin: Erich Schmidt Verlag, 2004).

Küting, K. and Hayn, S., 'Börseneinführungsmodalitäten in den USA', Die Wirtschaftsprüfung 46:13 (1993) 401–411.

Kwok, W. C. C. and Sharp, D., 'Power and international accounting standard setting: Evidence from segment reporting and intangible assets projects', Accounting, Auditing and Accountability Journal 18:1 (2005) 74–99.

La Porta, R., Lopes-de-Silanes, F. and Vishny, R. W., 'Agency problems and dividend policies around the world', The Journal of Finance 55:1 (2000) 1–33.

La Porta, R., Lopez-de-Silanes, F., Shleifer, A. and Vishny, R., 'Legal determinants of external finance', Journal of finance 52:3 (1997) 1131–1150.

La Porta, R., Lopez-de-Silanes, F., Shleifer, A. and Vishny, R. W., 'Law and Finance', Journal of Political Economy 106:6 (1998) 1113–1155.

Lamb, M. and Whittington, G., 'United Kingdom', in: D. Alexander and S. Archer (eds.), Miller European Accounting Guide, 4 (New York: Aspen Law and Business, 2001).

Lambert, R. A., 'Contracting Theory and Accounting', Journal of Accounting and Economics 32:1–3 (2001) 3–87.

Lanfermann, G., 'Modernisierte EU-Richtlinie zur gesetzlichen Abschlussprüfung', Der Betrieb 58:49 (2005) 2645–2650.

Lang, M., Lins, K. and Miller, D., 'ADRs, analysts, and accuracy: Does cross listing in the United States improve a firm's information environment and increase market value?' Journal of Accounting Research 41:2 (2003) 317–345.

Larson, K. D. and Holstrum, G. L., 'Financial accounting in the United States: 1973?' Abacus 9:1 (1973) 3–16.

Larson, R. K., 'Corporate lobbying of the international accounting standards committee', Journal of International Financial Management and Accounting 8:3 (1997) 175–203.

Larson, R. K., 'The IASC's search for legitimacy: An analysis of the IASC's standing interpretations committee', in: J. T. Sale (ed.), Advances in International Accounting (Greenwich, Connecticut: JAI, 2002).

Leach, R., 'The birth of British accounting standards', in: R. Leach and E. Stamp (eds.), British accounting standards: The first 10 years (Cambridge: Woodhead – Faulkner, 1981).

Lee, G. A., 'Accounting in the United Kingdom', in: H. P. Holzer and D. T. Bailey (eds.), International accounting (New York: Harper and Row, 1984a).

Lee, R., What is an Exchange? The Automation, Management and Regulation of Financial Markets (Oxford: Oxford University Press, 1998).

Lee, T. A., The evolution of corporate financial reporting, Reprinted. ed (New York: Garland, 1984b).

Leffson, U., 'Gläubigerschutz', in: H. Sauermann and E.-J. Mestmäcker (eds.), Wirtschaftsordnung und Staatsverfassung (Tübingen: J.C.B. Mohr, 1975).

Leibfried, S. and Zürn, M., Hg., Transformations of the State? (Cambridge: Cambridge University Press, 2005).

Leuz, C. and Wüstemann, J., 'The role of accounting in the German financial system', in: J. P. Krahnen and R. H. Schmidt (eds.), The German Financial System (Oxford: Oxford University Press, 2004).

Levinsohn, A., 'First-year verdict of SOX 404: Burdensome, costly, and confusing.' Strategic Finance 86:12 (2005) 67–68.

Levitt, T., 'The globalization of markets', Harvard Business Review 61:3 (1983) 92–102.

Licht, A., 'Cross-listing and corporate governance: Bonding or avoiding?' Corporate Ownership and Control 1:4 (2004) 36–48.

Livne, G. and McNichols, M., 'An empirical investigation of the true ands fair override', Working Paper, London Business School (2003).

Loft, A., Humphrey, C. and Turley, S., 'In pursuit of global regulation: Changing governance and accountability structures at the International Federation of Accountants (IFAC)', Accounting, Auditing and Accountability Journal 19:3 (2006) 428–451.

Löhr, A., Börsengang: Kapitalmarktchancen prüfen und umsetzen (Stuttgart: Schäffer-Poeschel, 2006).

London Stock Exchange, Our history, http://www.londonstockexchange.com (2006).

Lunt, M. G., 'The extraterritorial effects of the Sarbanes-Oxley Act 2002', Journal of Business Law 50:3 (2006) 249–266.

Lütz, S., 'The revival of the nation-state? Stock exchange regulation in an era of globalized financial markets', Journal of European Public Policy 5:1 (1998) 153–168.

Lütz, S., Der Staat und die Globalisierung von Finanzmärkten: Regulative Politik in Deutschland, Großbritannien und den USA (Frankfurt: Campus-Verlag, 2002).

Macey, J. R. and O'Hara, M., 'The economics of stock exchange listing fees and listing requirements', Journal of Financial Intermediation 11:3 (2002) 297–319.

Mäntysaari, P., Comparative corporate governance: Shareholders as a rule-maker (Berlin: Springer, 2005).

Marten, K.-U., 'Die Bedeutung einer international anerkannten Abschlussprüferaufsicht für deutsche Unternehmen', Der Betrieb 59:21 (2006) 1121–1125.

Marten, K.-U., Quick, R. and Ruhnke, K., Wirtschaftsprüfung: Grundlagen des betriebswirtschaftlichen Prüfungswesens nach nationalen und internationalen Normen, 2nd ed. (Stuttgart: Schäffer-Poeschel, 2003).

Martin, K. and Turkington, S., 'Comparison of the financial systems in England and Germany', Working Paper, Libera Università Internazionale degli Studi Sociali Guido Carli (2004).

Mattheus, D., 'Die gewandelte Rolle des Wirtschaftsprüfers als Partner des Aufsichtsrats nach dem KonTraG', Zeitschrift für Unternehmens- und Gesellschaftsrecht 28:5 (1999) 682–714.

Matthews, D., A History of Auditing : The Changing Audit Process in Britain from the Nineteenth Century to the Present Day (London et al.: Routledge, 2006).

McCormick, E., 'Reporting to stockholders', Accounting Review 35:2 (1960) 223–227.

McCraw, T., Creating Modern Capitalism: How Entrepreneurs, Companies, and Countries Triumphed in Three Industrial Revolutions (Cambridge: Harvard University. Press, 2000).

Meijer, A. J., 'Transparent government: Parliamentary and legal accountability in an information age', Information Polity: The International Journal of Government and Democracy in the Information Age 8:1/2 (2003) 67–78.

Meitner, M., Hüfner, F., Kleff, V., Lehmann, E. and Lüders, E., 'Bilanzskandale und Börsencrash: Neue Herausforderungen an die Aktienanalyse', Finanz Betrieb 4:9 (2002) 537–540.

Menzies, C., Sarbanes-Oxley Act: Professionelles Management interner Kontrollen (Stuttgart: Schäffer-Poeschel, 2004).

Merkt, H., Unternehmenspublizität: Offenlegung von Unternehmensdaten als Korrelat der Marktteilnahme (Tübingen: Mohr-Siebeck, 2001).

Merton, R. C., 'A simple model of capital market equilibrium with incomplete information', The Journal of Finance 42:3 (1987) 483–510.

Michie, R. C., 'Development of stock markets', in: P. Newman, M. Milgate and J. Eatwell (eds.), The New Palgrave Dictionary of Money and Finance (London: Macmillan Press, 1992).

Michie, R. C., The London Stock Exchange: A History (Oxford: Oxford University Press 1999).

Miller, P. B. W., 'Viewing the 1996 FAF Restructuring as Policy Making without a Formal Due Process', Accounting Horizons 16:3 (2002) 199–214.

Miller, P. B. W. and Bahnson, P. R., 'Audit revolution: From compliance to adding value', Accounting Today 18:13 (2004) 14–17.

Miller, P. B. W., Redding, R. J. and Bahnson, P. R., The FASB: The people, the process and the politics, 4th ed. (Boston, Mass.: Irwin/McGraw-Hill, 1998).

Mintz, S. M., 'Corporate governance in an international context: Legal systems, financing patterns and cultural variables', Corporate Governance: An International Review 13:5 (2005) 582–597.

Mittoo, U. R., 'Additional evidence on integration in the Canadian stock market', Journal of Finance 47:5 (1992) 2035–2054.

Möller, A., Kapitalmarktaufsicht: Wandel und Neubestimmung der nationalen und europäischen Kapitalmarktaufsicht anhand des Beispiels der Aufsicht über die Börsen und den Börsenhandel (Berlin: Duncker and Humbold, 2006).

Moran, M., The Politics of the Financial Services Revolution: The USA, UK and Japan (New York: St. Martin's Press, 1991).

Morgan, M. and Previts, G. J., 'The SEC and the profession, 1934–84: The realities of self-regulation', Journal of Accountancy 158:1 (1984) 68–80.

Mues, J., Die Börse als Unternehmen: Modell einer privatrechtlichen Börsenorganisation (Baden-Baden: Nomos, 1999).

Mutchler, J. F. and Smith, C. H., 'The development of financial accounting standards in the United States: Past and present', in: H. P. Holzer and D. T. Bailey (eds.), International Accounting (New York: Harper and Row, 1984).

Nakayama, M., Lilien, S. and Benis, M., 'Due Process and FAS No. 13', Management Accounting 62:10 (1981) 49–53.

New York Stock Exchange, Fact Book Online, http://www.nyse.com/ (2006).

Newman, D. P., 'The SEC's influence on accounting standards: The power of the veto', Journal of Accounting Research 19 (1981) 134–156.

Nichols, C. and Wahlen, J., 'How do earning numbers relate to stock returns? A review of classic accounting research with updated evidence', Accounting Horizons 18:4 (2004) 263–286.

Nobes, C. W., 'A judgemental international classification of financial reporting practices', Journal of Business Finance and Accounting 10:1 (1983) 1–19.

Nobes, C. W., 'The true and fair view requirement: Impact on and of the fourth directive', Accounting and Business Research 24:93 (1993) 35–48.

Nobes, C. W., 'On the myth of "Anglo-Saxon" financial accounting: A comment', The International Journal of Accounting 38:1 (2003) 95–104.

Nobes, C. W. and Parker, R. H., 'The development of company financial reporting in Great Britain 1844–1977', in: T. A. Lee and R. H. Parker (eds.), The Evolution of Corporate Financial Reporting (Walton-on-Thames: Nelson, 1979).

Nobes, C. W. and Parker, R. H., Comparative International Accounting, 8th ed. (Harlow: Prentice Hall, 2004).

Nugent, N., The government and politics of the European Union, 5th ed. (Basingstoke, Hampshire: Palgrave Macmillan, 2003).

O'Brien, R., 'Securities markets: Big bang across the globe', in: R. O'Brien (ed.), Global Financial Integration: The End of Geography (London: Pinter for Royal Institute of International Affairs, 1992).

OECD, OECD Handbook of Economic Globalization Indicators (Paris: OECD Publishing, 2005).

Olson, W. E., The Accounting Profession, Years of Trial: 1969–1980 (New York: AICPA, 1982).

Ordelheide, D., 'A European and a German perspective', European Accounting Review 2:1 (1993) 81–90.

Ordelheide, D., 'True and fair view. A European and a German perspective II', European Accounting Review 5:3 (1996) 495–506.

Ordelheide, D., 'Germany', in: S. McLeay (ed.), Accounting Regulation in Europe (Houndsmills, Basingstoke: MacMillan, 1999).

Ouchi, W. G., 'A conceptual framework for the design of organizational control mechanisms', Management Science 25:9 (1979) 833–848.

Owen, B. M. and Braeutigam, R., The Regulation Game: Strategic Use of the Administrative Process (Cambridge: Addison-Wesley, 1978).

Pagano, M., Röell, A. and Zechner, J., 'The geography of equity listing: Why do companies list abroad?' Journal of Finance 57:6 (2002) 2651–2694.

Parker, R., 'Financial reporting in the United Kingdom', in: C. u. P. Nobes, Robert (ed.), Comparative International Accounting (Harlow et al: FT Prentice Hall, 2004).

224    *References*

Parker, R. H., 'Regulating British corporate financial reporting in the late nineteenth century', Accounting Business and Financial History 1:1 (1990) 51–71.

Patel, S., Balic, A., Bwakira, L., Bradley, N. and Dallas, G., Transparency and Disclosure Study: Europe (London: Standard and Poor's, 2003).

Pellens, B., Internationale Rechnungslegung, 4th ed. (Stuttgart: Schäffer-Poeschel, 2001).

Pellens, B., Fülbier, R. U. and Gassen, J., Internationale Rechnungslegung: IFRS 1 bis 7, IAS 1 bis 41, IFRIC-Interpretationen, Standardentwürfe: Mit Beispielen, Aufgaben und Fallstudie (Stuttgart: Schaeffer-Poeschel Verlag, 2006).

Pfitzer, N., Oser, P. and Orth, C., Reforem des Aktien-, Bilanz- und Aufsichtsrechts (Stuttgart: Schäffer-Poeschel, 2006).

Pinard-Byrne, K., 'Audit frustration – A cautionary tale', Accountancy Ireland 37:5 (2005) 23.

Pong, C. K. M. and Whittington, G., 'The withdrawal of current cost accounting in the United Kingdom: A study of the accounting standards committee', Abacus 32:1 (1996) 30.

Porter, M. E., 'Capital disadvantage: America's failing capital investment system', Harvard Business Review 70:5 (1992) 65–82.

Power, M., 'Academics in the accounting policy process: England and Germany compared', in: C. Leuz, D. Pfaff and A. Hopwood (eds.), The Economics and Politics of Accounting – International Perspectives on Trends, Policy, and Practice (Oxford: Oxford University Press, 2004).

Puxty, A. G., Willmott, H. C., Cooper, D. J. and Lowe, T., 'Modes of regulation in advanced capitalism: Locating accountancy in four countries', Accounting, Organizations and Society 12:3 (1987) 273–291.

Quick, R., 'The formation and early development of German audit firms', Accounting, Business and Financial History 15:3 (2005) 317–343.

Radebaugh, L. H., Gebhardt, G. and Gray, S. J., 'Foreign stock exchange listings: A case study of Daimler-Benz', Journal of International Financial Management and Accounting 6:2 (1995) 158–192.

Rajan, R. G. and Zingales, L., 'The great reversals: The politics of financial development in the twentieth century', Journal of Financial Economics 69:1 (2003) 5–50.

Ritter, E.-H., 'Das Recht als Steuerungsmedium im kooperativen Staat', in: D. Grimm (ed.), Wachsende Staatsaufgaben – sinkende Steuerungsfähigkeit des Rechts (Baden-Baden: Nomos, 1990).

Roberts, C., Weetman, P. and Gordon, P., International Financial Accounting: A Comparative Approach, 3rd ed. (Harlow: Prentice Hall, 2005).

Rockness, H. O. and Nikolai, L. A., 'An assessment of APB voting patterns', Journal of Accounting Research 15:1 (1977) 154–167.

Rodda, A. K. and Volkert, L. A., 'Financial accounting', Journal of Accountancy 175:2 (1993) 67–70.

Rosen, R. V., Zugang zum US-Kapitalmarkt für deutsche Aktiengesellschaften (Frankfurt am Main: Deutsches Aktieninstitut, 1998).

Ryder, N., 'Financial services and markets act 2000', Business Law Review 21:11 (2000) 253–256.

Sanders, T. H., 'Influence of the securities and exchange commission upon accounting principles', Accounting Review 11:1 (1936) 66.

Saudagaran, S. M., 'An empirical study of selected factors influencing the decision to list on foreign stock exchanges', Journal of International Business Studies 19:1 (1988) 101–127.

Saudagaran, S. M. and Biddle, G. C., 'Financial disclosure levels and foreign stock exchange listing decisions', Journal of International Financial Management and Accounting 26:2 (1992) 106–148.

Schaub, A., 'The use of international accounting standards in the European Union', Northwestern Journal of International Law and Business 25:3 (2005) 609–629.

Scheffler, E., 'Der europäische Endorsement-Prozess: Europäischer Einfluss auf die Fortentwicklung der international financial reporting standards', in: T. A. Lange and E. Loew (eds.), Rechnungslegung, Steuerung und Aufsicht von Banken (Wiesbaden: Gabler Verlag, 2004).

Scheffler, E., 'Corporate Governance – Auswirkungen auf den Wirtschaftsprüfer', Die Wirtschaftsprüfung 58:9 (2005) 477–486.

Schildbach, T., US-GAAP, Amerikanische Rechnungslegung und ihre Grundlagen, 2nd ed. (München: Vahlen, 2002).

Schildbach, T., 'Rechnungslegung im Spannungsfeld zweier Kulturen der Regulierung – Gute Gründe für die Kombination privater mit obrigkeitlicher Regulierung', Der Schweizer Treuhaender 78:3 (2004) 159–172.

Schmidt, M., 'On the legitimacy of accounting standard setting by privately organised institutions in Germany and Europe', Schmalenbach Business Review 54:2 (2002) 171–193.

Schmidt, R. H., 'Corporate governance in Germany: An economic perspective', Working Paper, Johann Wolfgang Goethe-Universität Frankfurt (2003).

Schmidt, R. H. and Spindler, G., 'Path dependence, corporate governance and complementarity', International Finance 5:3 (2002) 311–333.

Schruff, W., 'Die Rolle des Hauptfachausschusses (HFA) des IDW', Die Wirtschaftsprüfung 59 1–2 (2006) 1–8.

Schüler, M., 'Integrated financial supervision in Germany', Working Paper, Zentrum für Europäische Wirtschaftsforschung (2004).

Schuppert, G. F., 'Grenzen und alternativen von Steuerung durch Recht', in: D. Grimm (ed.), Wachsende Staatsaufgaben – sinkende Steuerungskraft des Rechts (Baden-Baden: Nomos, 1990).

Schuppert, G. F. and Bumke, C., 'Verfassungsrechtliche Grenzen privater Standardsetzung – Vorüberlegungen zu einer Theorie der Wahl rechtlicher Regelungsformen (Regulatory Choice)', in: D. Kleindiek, and O. Wolfgang (eds.), Die Zukunft des deutschen Bilanzrechts im Zeichen internationaler Rechnungslegung und privater Standardsetzung (Köln: O.Schmidt Verlag, 2000).

Schwarz, G. C. and Holland, B., 'Enron, worldcom... und die corporate governance-diskussion', Zeitschrift für Wirtschaftsrecht 23:37 (2002) 1661–1672.

Scott, W. R., Financial Accounting Theory, 4th ed. (Toronto: Prentice Hall, 2006).

SEC, Securities and Exchange Commission Reaffirms Status of Pronouncements of the Financial Accounting Standards Board, http://www.sec.gov (2003a).

SEC, Standards Relating to Listed Company Audit Committees, http://www.sec.gov (2003b).

SEC, 2006 Performance and Accountability Report (Washington D.C.: Securities Exchange Commission, 2006).

Seligman, J., The Transformation of Wall Street, A History of the Securities and Exchange Commission and Modern Corporate Finance (Boston: Northeastern University Press, 1995).

Shapiro, J., 'The New York stock exchange: The market and its listing requirements', in: R. V. Rosen and W. Seifert (eds.), Zugang zum US-Kapitalmarkt für deutsche Aktiengesellschaften (Frankfurt a. M.: Deutsches Aktieninstitut, 1998).

Sharpe, W. F., Alexander, G. and Bailey, J., Investments (London: Prentice Hall, 1995).

Short, H., Keasey, K., Wright, M. and Hull, A., 'Corporate governance: From accountability to enterprise', Accounting and Business Research 29:4 (1999) 337–352.

Siegel, J., 'Can foreign firms bond themselves effectively by renting U.S. securities laws?' Journal of Financial Economics 75:2 (2005) 319–359.

Sikka, P., 'The politics of restructuring the standard setting bodies: The case of the UK's auditing practices board', Accounting Forum 26:2 (2002) 97–125.

Skousen, F., An introduction to the SEC (Cincinnati: South Western Publishing, 1991).

Sloan, R. G., 'Financial accounting and corporate governance: A discussion', Journal of Accounting and Economics 32:1–3 (2001) 335–347.

Smith, C. F., 'The early history of the London stock exchange', American Economic Review 19:2 (1929) 206–216.

Smith, F., 'Accounting requirements of stock exchanges', Accounting Review 12:2 (1933) 145–153.

Smith, F., 'Stock exchange listing requirements and publicity', Accounting Review 11:1 (1936) 35–43.

Sobel, R., Amex: A History of the American Stock Exchange 1921–1971 (New York: Weybright and Talley, 1972).

Solomon, J. and Solomon, A., Corporate Governance and Accountability (Chichester: John Wiley and Sons Ltd., 2005).

Spindler, G., 'Prime standard und general standard – Die Börse als Ersatzgesetzgeber für Quartalsberichte', Wertpapier Mitteilungen 57:43 (2003) 2073–2120.

Sprouse, R. T., 'Commentary on The SEC-FASB partnership', Accounting Horizons 1:4 (1987) 92–95.

Steffek, J., 'The legitimation of international governance: A discourse approach', European Journal of International Relations 9:2 (2003) 249–275.

Steil, B., 'Changes in the ownership and governance of securities exchanges: Causes and consequences', Working Paper, Financial Institutions Center at The Wharton School (2002).

Steunenberg, B., Koboldt, C. and Schmidtchen, D., 'Policymaking, comitology, and the balance of power in The European Union', International Review of Law and Economics 16:3 (1996) 329–344.

Stiglitz, J. E., The Roaring Nineties (London: Penguin Books, 2003).

Strange, S., The retreat of the state: The diffusion of power in the world economy (Cambridge: Cambridge University Press, 1996).

Streeck, W., 'From market-making to state-building? Reflections on the political economy of European social policy', in: S. Leibfried and P. Pierson (eds.), European Social Policy: Between Fragmentation and Integration (Washington, D.C.: The Brookings Institution, 1995).

Streeck, W. and Schmitter, P. C., 'Community, market, state – and associations? The prospective contribution of interest governance to social order', in: W. Streeck and P. C. Schmitter (eds.), Private Interest Government: Beyond Market and State (London: Sage, 1985).

Tandy, P. R. and Wilburn, N. L., 'Constituent participation in standard-setting: The FASB's first 100 statements', Accounting Horizons 6:2 (1992) 47–58.

Taylor, M., 'Accountability and objectives of the FSA', in: M. Blair (ed.), Blackstone's Guide to the Financial Services and Markets Act 2000 (London: Oxford University Press, 2000).

The Economist, 'No quarter given', in: The Economist, 13 November 2004.

Théodore, J.-F., 'The Paris Bourse's experience: Building a fully electronic national market and facing the challenge of a European unified market', in: W. Gerke (ed.), Die Börse der Zukunft: Märkte, Plätze, Netze (Stuttgart: Schäffer-Poeschel, 1997).

Thiele, S. and Tschesche, F., 'Zur Bilanzierungspraxis der DAX-Unternehmen im Geschäftsjahr 1996 – Mehr "Einblick" durch internationale Rechnungslegungsnormen?' Der Betrieb 50:50 (1997) 2497–2502.

Thomas, C. W., 'The rise and fall of Enron', Journal of Accountancy 193:4 (2002) 41–48.

Thompson, J. W. and Lange, G., 'The Sarbanes-Oxley Act and the changing responsibilities of auditors', Review of Business 24:2 (2003) 8–12.

Thorell, P. and Whittington, G., 'The harmonizing of accounting within the EU', European Accounting Review 3:2 (1994) 215–239.

Tiedeken, R., Die Entwicklung der staatlichen Regulierung des Wertpapiermarktes in den USA (Regensburg: Roderer, 1999).

Tiedje, J., 'Die neue EU-Richtlinie zur Abschlussprüfung', Die Wirtschaftsprüfung 59:9 (2006) 593–605.

Turkington, S., Financial Services Regulation – The Reform of the English System, http://www.archivioceradi.luiss.it (2004).

van Hulle, K., 'Die Reform des europäischen Bilanzrechts: Stand, Ziele, Perspektiven', Zeitschrift für Unternehmens- und Gesellschaftsrecht 29:4–5 (2000) 537–549.

Vieten, H. R., 'Auditing in Britain and Germany compared: Professions, knowledge and the state', European Accounting Review 4:3 (1995) 485–511.

Vitols, S., 'Changes in Germany's bank-based financial system: Implications for corporate governance', Corporate Governance: An International Review 13:3 (2005) 386–396.

Vogel, S., 'International games with national rules: Competition for comparative regulatory advantage in telecommunications and financial services', Working Paper, University of California at Berkeley (1996).

Vos, E., 'The rise of the committees', European Law Journal 3:3 (1997) 210–229.

Walgenbach, B., 'Börsen im internationalen Wettbewerb', Wirtschaftsdienst 70:7 (1990) 427–432.

Walter, R., 'Geld- und Wechselbörsen vom Spätmittelalter bis zur Mitte des 17. Jahrhunderts', in: H. Pohl (ed.), Deutsche Börsengeschichte (Frankfurt a. M.: Knapp, 1992).

Walton, P., 'Introduction: The true and fair view in British accounting', European Accounting Review 2:1 (1993) 49–58.

Weetman, P., Davie, E. and Collins, W., 'Lobbying on accounting issues Preparer/user imbalance in the case of the operating and financial review', Accounting, Auditing and Accountability Journal 9:1 (1996) 59.

Werner, J. R., Unternehmenspublizität und Corporate Governance im Wandel: Staatliche Steuerungsmodelle im internationalen Vergleich (Frankfurt, New York: Campus, 2008).

Werner, W. and Smith, S., Wall Street (New York: Columbia University Press, 1991).

Wever, K. S. and Allen, C. S., 'Is Germany a model for managers?' Harvard Business Review 70:5 (1992) 36–43.

Whittington, G., 'Accounting standard setting in the UK after 20 years: A critique of the dearing and solomons reports', Accounting and Business Research 19:75 (1989) 195–205.

Williams, J. R., 'Funding FASB: Public money, public domain', The CPA Journal 74:5 (2004) 9.

Williamson, C., 'Structural changes in exchange-traded markets', Bank of England Quarterly Bulletin 39:2 (1999) 202–206.

Wolk, H. I. and Tearney, M. G., Accounting theory : A conceptual and institutional approach, 4th ed. (Cincinnati, Ohio: South-Western College Publication, 1997).

Wüstemann, J., 'Disclosure regimes and corporate governance', Journal of Institutional and Theoretical Economics 159:4 (2003) 717–726.

Yakhou, M. and Dorweiler, V. P., 'Dual reforms: Accounting and corporate governance', Managerial Auditing Journal 19:3 (2004) 361–377.

Zänsdorf, K., Verfassung und Organisation der deutschen Börsen im Lichte der rechtsgeschichtlichen Entwicklung (Würzburg: Triltsch, 1937).

Zeff, S. A., 'The evolution of the conceptual framework for business in the United States', Accounting Historians Journal 26:2 (1999) 89–132.

Zeff, S. A., 'How the U.S. accounting profession got where it is today: Part I', Accounting Horizons 17:3 (2003) 189–205.

Zimmermann, J., 'Beurteilungskriterien für enforcement-Modelle: Eine Analyse und Darstellung anhand des britischen financial reporting review panels', Steuern und Bilanzen 5:8 (2003) 353–360.

Zimmermann, J. and Abeé, S., 'Börsenregulierung als Wettbewerbsfaktor', Wirtschaftsdienst 87:9 (2007) 607–612.

Zülch, H., 'Die Deutsche Prüfstelle für Rechnungslegung DPR e. V. – Organisation und Prüfverfahren', Steuern und Bilanzen 7:13 (2005) 565–570.

Zürn, M. and Leibfried, S., 'Reconfiguring the national constellation', European Review 13:S1 (2005) 1–36.

# Index

In this index exhibits and notes are indicated in italics, enclosed in parenthesis, following the page number. E.g. governance, 118*(Ex.6.1)*. Exhibits are indicated by Ex. Notes are indicated by *n*.